THE ANTHROPOLOGY OF THE FUTURE

Study of the future is an important new field in anthropology. Building on a philosophical tradition running from Aristotle through Heidegger to Schatzki, this book presents the concept of "orientations" as a way to study everyday life. It analyzes six main orientations – anticipation, expectation, speculation, potentiality, hope, and destiny – which represent different ways in which the future may affect our present. While orientations entail planning towards and imagining the future, they also often involve the collapse or exhaustion of those efforts; moments where hope may turn to apathy, frustrated planning to disillusion, and imagination to fatigue. By examining these orientations at different points, the authors argue for an anthropology that takes a fuller account of the teleologies of action.

REBECCA BRYANT is Professor of Cultural Anthropology at Utrecht University.

DANIEL M. KNIGHT is a Lecturer in Social Anthropology and Director of the Centre for Cosmopolitan Studies at the University of St Andrews.

NEW DEPARTURES IN ANTHROPOLOGY

New Departures in Anthropology is a book series that focuses on emerging themes in social and cultural anthropology. With original perspectives and syntheses, authors introduce new areas of inquiry in anthropology, explore developments that cross disciplinary boundaries, and weigh in on current debates. Every book illustrates theoretical issues with ethnographic material drawn from current research or classic studies, as well as from literature, memoirs, and other genres of reportage. The aim of the series is to produce books that are accessible enough to be used by college students and instructors, but will also stimulate, provoke, and inform anthropologists at all stages of their careers. Written clearly and concisely, books in the series are designed equally for advanced students and a broader range of readers, inside and outside academic anthropology, who want to be brought up to date on the most exciting developments in the discipline.

Series Editorial Board

The Anthropology of the Future

REBECCA BRYANT
Utrecht University, The Netherlands

DANIEL M. KNIGHT
University of St Andrews, Scotland

CAMBRIDGE
UNIVERSITY PRESS

University Printing House, Cambridge CB2 8BS, United Kingdom

One Liberty Plaza, 20th Floor, New York, NY 10006, USA

477 Williamstown Road, Port Melbourne, VIC 3207, Australia

314–321, 3rd Floor, Plot 3, Splendor Forum, Jasola District Centre,
New Delhi – 110025, India

79 Anson Road, #06–04/06, Singapore 079906

Cambridge University Press is part of the University of Cambridge.

It furthers the University's mission by disseminating knowledge in the pursuit of
education, learning, and research at the highest international levels of excellence.

www.cambridge.org
Information on this title: www.cambridge.org/9781108421850
DOI: 10.1017/9781108378277

First published 2019

Printed in the United Kingdom by TJ International Ltd. Padstow Cornwall

A catalogue record for this publication is available from the British Library.

Library of Congress Cataloging-in-Publication Data
NAMES: Bryant, Rebecca (Professor of anthropology), author. | Knight, Daniel M.,
author.
TITLE: The anthropology of the future / Rebecca Bryant, Universiteit Utrecht, The
Netherlands; Daniel M. Knight, University of St Andrews, Scotland.
DESCRIPTION: Cambridge, United Kingdom ; New York, NY, USA : Cambridge
University Press, 2019. | Includes bibliographical references and index.
IDENTIFIERS: LCCN 2018046533 | ISBN 9781108421850 (hardback) | ISBN 9781108434379
(paperback)
SUBJECTS: LCSH: Future, The – Social aspects. | Time – Social aspects. | Expectation
(Philosophy) | Hope. | Opportunity. | Fortune.
CLASSIFICATION: LCC HM656 .B78 2019 | DDC 304.2/3–dc23
LC record available at https://lccn.loc.gov/2018046533

ISBN 978-1-108-42185-0 Hardback
ISBN 978-1-108-43437-9 Paperback

RB: For Mete, as ever.

DK: For Bella Eugenia. The Future.

Contents

Preface

This book has its origins in Rebecca's childhood in the American South, when she developed an early interest in time. Or rather, she saw in the racial divides and material deprivations all around her the way that the past was chained to the present and had to be dragged along into the future. All the Southern writers that she admired also had a tormented relationship to the temporal. When she went to university, she wrote in her college application that she wanted to study philosophies of time and history. Although US philosophy departments at that time insisted on teaching logical formulas instead, she still managed to write a thesis on amnesia as a recurring theme in one of her favorite Southern writers. Wiping out the past; making room for the future. She wasn't satisfied with her conclusions and sensed then that there was much more to be said about the temporal and its affects, but it took a couple more decades of thinking and reading and studying other people's temporalities even for the questions that she wanted to ask to become clear.

The theoretical framework of this book is the result of those several decades of thinking. That thinking took place in relation to her ongoing ethnographic research on long-term displacement and conflict and post-conflict temporalities in the Eastern Mediterranean. Although she began thinking about these questions – as many researchers have – from the perspective of memory and the past, she slowly began to understand that she needed to turn her perspective around and that the phenomena she was studying, such as conflict materialities and crisis, needed to be viewed through the lens of the future.

The future has been of growing interest in the discipline, as anthropologists have acknowledged the ways that studies of temporality had been for so long primarily focused on the past–present relationship. The anthropology of the future, however, has developed primarily in relation to emerging studies of energy futures, biomedicine and biotechnology, and risk and finance, less so in relation to Rebecca's subjects of displacement, conflict, and transitional justice. When she began to write this book, then, it seemed appropriate to bring on board someone whose body of work has made important contributions to the study of energy, austerity, and financial crisis. Moreover, Daniel's work in Greece intersected in thought-provoking ways with Rebecca's research in Cyprus and Turkey. A collaboration was born that enriched Rebecca's several decades of thinking about temporality with the new ethnographic contexts and subjects that Daniel contributed.

Daniel's interest in temporality has its roots in his pre-university studies of archaeology, with its focus on reconstructing the past, and the philosophy of religion, more interested in pondering the beginnings and ends of the universe. He fondly remembers lunchtimes spent aptly integrating soccer with theorizing the trajectories of life beyond the limits of our planet. Whereas Rebecca's childhood in the American South shaped her passion for better understanding pasts and futures, for Daniel it was the trappings of the British class system that seemed to direct those around him toward preordained ends.

His doctoral studies produced a thesis on the everyday experience of nonlinear time in austerity Greece, introducing a theory of disparate "culturally proximate" pasts that provide direction to people in the clutches of severe socioeconomic crisis. Like Rebecca, Daniel's initial focus was on history and memory, and it was only after high-tech photovoltaic panels started appearing on land previously belonging to large Ottoman estates that he realized that his research participants' future lay with the future. Needless to say, Daniel is immensely grateful to Rebecca for the opportunity to collaborate on this book and share in her long-term intellectual project.

Because this work builds on numerous projects over many years, it would be impossible to thank all the many persons who contributed to Rebecca's thinking – and often entirely rethinking – on the subject. Both

Charles Stewart and Nicolas Argenti contributed through their own work and through stimulating conversations. Two persons who are no longer with us had significant influence: Peter Loizos, who always encouraged historical thinking that was firmly rooted in a future-oriented present; and Paul Friedrich, who always challenged his students to think "otherwise." Rebecca also wishes to express her gratitude to Mete Hatay, not only for putting up with an intense period of writing and many irritable outbursts, but also for allowing this project to take precedence over their own joint work.

While so many people have helped Daniel think through the orientations presented in this book – and a list of acknowledgements would be extensive – here he would simply like to express special gratitude to three friends and major influencers: Debbora Battaglia, Charles Stewart, and David Valentine. In March 2018 Daniel organized an international conference hosted at the University of St Andrews on the theme "Orientations: The Anthropology of the Future." Funded by the Ladislav Holy Memorial Trust and Centre for Cosmopolitan Studies, the event was designed to take further conversations on time, temporality, and futural orientations. Thanks go to all the contributors for three days of stimulating debate. Above all, and as always, Daniel is grateful for the support and encouragement of Stavroula Pipyrou, his inspiration for life.

In the chapters that follow, Rebecca is the sole author of Chapters 1 ("Anticipation"), 2 ("Expectation"), and 6 ("Destiny"). The Introduction and Chapters 3 ("Speculation") and 4 ("Potentiality") are coauthored, while Daniel is the sole author of Chapter 5 ("Hope") and the Conclusion.

Introduction
The Future of the Future in Anthropology

A reader opening this book already has expectations. You, the reader, may have prepared yourself, based on other literature that you have read, to sit down with a book about time and temporality. As you begin reading this page, you may have already anticipated how such a book will fit into a course that you are studying or research that you are planning. You may see the potential for such a book to help you with a particular problem, and you may already be speculating, based on the chapter titles, about what such a book would include or leave out.

We ask you to look up from the page. Turn your head. You may be sitting in your own home, a space of familiarity, as we are while writing. In front of us is a desk that needs to be cleaned of the remnants of another project, and a bookshelf that needs to be packed in anticipation of a move. In another room is the low hum of a washing machine spinning clothes from a recent trip and reminding us not to leave the house until the cycle has finished and the clothes have gone in the dryer. Outside the window, at something of a distance, is the buzzing and hammering of a seemingly never-ending construction project a block away. At a closer distance, not far from the window, ravens caw to each other and take us, for a flitting moment, on a flight outside the trajectory of the human.

The desk, the bookshelf, the mechanical spinning, the birdcall, and the flicker of this screen as we write are all materialities that engage and embed us in layered and entangled but separable temporalities. The temporality of the washing machine is not the same as that of the birdcall, which in turn is not the same as the desk that needs to be cleaned. Each engages us in temporal orientations of differing depth and urgency. Sometimes these are orientations that require us to act, while at other times – such as the never-ending construction project – they are orientations that simply enter our awareness, at least for now.

This book traces ways in which anthropology may examine such orientations. The orientations that we have chosen – anticipation, expectation, speculation, potentiality, hope, and destiny – all represent differing depths of time and different, though often related, ways in which the future may orient our present. Obviously, our list of such temporal trajectories is far from complete, but we believe it is sufficient to help orient anthropology toward futural orientations, or a way of thinking about the indeterminate and open-ended teleologies of everyday life. Teleology has gotten something of a bad rap in the social sciences ever since it was harnessed to the temporality of modernity and progress. Teleology also often carries a whiff of the eschatological. However, in consonance with a recent neo-Aristotelian turn in philosophy, we see a revived understanding of teleology as the only way to make sense of the future's role in orienting quotidian action.

This introduction, in turn, is intended to orient you, the reader, toward our understanding of the future's role in the study of society and culture. After all, not all of the orientations that we experience as we sit writing or reading help us to understand the temporalities of collectives. The hum of the washing machine constraining me from leaving the house is not the same as a whole neighborhood speculating together about when they will get relief from the noisy, never-ending construction project. Our focus in this book is on what the former may tell us about the latter, or what philosophical conjecture about the role of the future in shaping temporality may tell us about the ways that we act together in our orientations toward the future.

In order to do this, we first trace a brief history of the future in anthropology. Our main question in this introduction is why the study of the future in the discipline has not achieved the centrality or complexity of studies of the past, and why that is changing today. We show how this shortchanging of the future reveals to us the temporality of anthropology, as it has changed over the course of the twentieth century. If anthropology's temporality is changing today, how is the discipline being reoriented? We then discuss futural orientations as a theoretical tool to help anthropology move beyond an overweening emphasis on the past. In particular, we discuss how teleologies may be indeterminate and open-ended, and how an approach to timespace rooted in the materialities of everyday life may help us to understand the role of the future in collectivities.

Anthropology's History of the Future

Historically, as they say, the future has gotten short shrift in anthropology. In her landmark 1992 essay on the anthropology of time, Nancy Munn observed that in the discipline, "the future tends to be a displaced temporal topic, absent from its homeland in the past-present-future relation" (p. 116). She speculates that the reason for this is anthropology's focus on "long-term historical-mythic time," which lends itself to a concentration on the past. Congruently, Joel Robbins (2007) has argued that anthropology is fundamentally concerned with the continuity of tradition and culture and cannot take account of the sorts of ruptured pasts and messianic futures represented, say, by the Protestant faith as reflected in postcolonial regions. What Munn and Robbins share is a conviction that the absence of an anthropology of the future reveals to us certain central tenets of the discipline.

Indeed, the future has been a literal dead-end for the discipline. In contrast to the sociological emphasis on modernity, progress, and the new social forms wrought by it, early anthropologists understood their subject as tradition or custom and their task as documentation, salvage, and rescue. Despite the emphasis of a Durkheimian-inspired sociology on defining the social structure of modernity and the modern, the early sociological encounter with time primarily broke down into a dualist periodicity ("the premodern" and "the modern") and interrogation of modernity's – as opposed to premodernity's – temporality. As Ron Eyerman (1991: 37–38) notes, modernity in the work of sociology's "founding fathers," Marx, Weber, and Durkheim,

referred to a world constructed anew through the active and conscious intervention of actors and the new sense of self that such active intervention and responsibility entailed. In modern society the world is experienced as a human construction, an experience that gives rise both to an exhilarating sense of freedom and possibility and to a basic anxiety about the openness of the future.

This openness to the future, moreover, was related to the way in which time is "emptied" in modernity, based no longer on seasons and rituals but instead on clocks and calendars (esp. Giddens 1990). What is notable for our purposes is that the emphasis on progress as definitional of modernity, and of anxiety regarding it, did not go along with a concomitant interest in the future as a dimension of temporality.[1]

In the USA and UK, anthropology emerged from its evolutionary roots with either a synchronic interest in the functional or a historical interest in the particular. In US anthropology, Boas and his students – who, from the perspective of the UK, appeared unnecessarily concerned with historical ephemera – saw the pursuit of a historical particularism as the key to breaking apart social evolutionism, or the ranking of human groups on an evolutionary scale. "First of all," remarked Boas in a 1920 article, "the whole problem of cultural history appears to us as a historical problem. In order to understand history it is necessary to

---

[1] The sociological literature on utopia may count as an important exception to this, although we should note that, following Karl Mannheim, there has been a tendency in sociological theory to interrogate utopian thinking as part of the historical trajectory of ideologies.

know not only how things are, but how they have come to be" (Boas 1920: 314). In contrast not only to the evolutionists but also to the synchronism of the functionalists and structural functionalists, Boas notes that while the influence of society on the individual is certainly important, it has to be complemented by study of the ways in which individuals may influence society and produce social change. He remarks that this problem:

is also beginning to attract the attention of students who are no longer satisfied with the systematic enumeration of standardized beliefs and customs of a tribe, but who begin to be interested in the question of the way in which the individual reacts to his whole social environment, and to the differences of opinion and of mode of action that occur in primitive society and which are the causes of far-reaching changes.

In short then, the method which we try to develop is based on a study of the dynamic changes in society that may be observed at the present time.

(ibid., 316)

In staking his ground against both the evolutionists and the functionalists, then, Boas describes the distinctive territory of "American scholars" as being "primarily interested in the dynamic phenomena of cultural change" (ibid., 314) and the particulars of cultural history.

Only two years later, Bronislaw Malinowski would articulate the rules of method that would become a guide not only for his own students in the UK, but for other students elsewhere who recognized in his description of the heroic ethnographer a way of methodologically cataloguing what fieldworkers in the USA, at least, were already beginning to accomplish: "The Ethnographer has in the field ... the duty before him of drawing up all the rules and regularities of tribal life; all that is permanent and fixed; of giving an anatomy of their culture, of depicting the constitution of their society" (1922: 9).

Malinowski observes that, unlike in "our society," most of the rules of social institutions in the societies anthropologists study are not written down and are not recorded by the society's "intelligent members, its historians, and its archives and documents." In such societies, he remarks, "There is no written or explicitly expressed code of laws, and their whole tribal tradition, the whole structure of their society, are embodied in the most elusive of all materials; the human being." He explains the method that he has discovered to overcome this problem: "This expedient for an Ethnographer consists in collecting concrete data of evidence, and drawing the general inferences for himself" (ibid.).

We see, then, the emergence of two temporalized approaches to society, usually described in anthropology textbooks as diachronic and synchronic: on the one hand, Boas's insistence on examining "the dynamic changes in society that may be observed at the present time," and on the other hand, Malinowski's description of the anthropologist's task as recording the rules of its institutions.[2] While both are focused on the artifacts of the past in the present, Malinowski stresses the regularities that create social harmony and Boas the irregularities that produce social change.

This focus on the past in the present and the mythical-historical time of custom and tradition has meant that, when anthropology has addressed something that we might be able to call temporality, "futurity is poorly tended as a specifically temporal problem" (Munn 1992: 115). Indeed, anthropology has had a difficult time overcoming its rootedness in the tradition/modernity dichotomy that has founded its distinction from sociology. Although today few anthropologists would claim to be researching "tradition" except as a cultural construct, we find the lingering effects of that dichotomy in, for example, what Carol Greenhouse (1996) has argued is a naturalization of European clock time within the discipline. As Munn also noted, much anthropological thinking about time has centered on other peoples' time-reckoning or other temporalities – a way, we might add, of ontologizing difference, where what

---

[2] Although Malinowski would, of course, later become much more concerned with social change, he remained very much a presentist insofar as he preferred his "tradition live and active," in contrast to those "who prefer their past dead and buried" (1946: 6).

remains of concern is to document how time can be reckoned, felt, and understood in ways that are different from "our own." As Kevin Birth remarks, "In thinking about the human understanding of time through the human past and across cultural differences, we have adopted a unique and artifactually mediated set of ideas as the ideal type against which all other ideas are understood and evaluated" (2012: 169). In the background, argues Birth, is a uniform, homogeneous conception of (modern) time against which other, "traditional" times are measured.

Our concern in this book is not with a metaphysics of time, as important as this may be to the past-present-future relationship. Instead, we are interested in how the discipline of anthropology has periodically and sporadically concerned itself with time and temporality while almost always shortchanging the future. We see this not only in the early synchronic emphasis on documentation and diachronic attempts to historicize the present, but also in more recent work that claims to address time and temporality while focusing almost entirely on the past-present relationship.

Over the past three decades, social anthropologists have developed a robust literature that studies history, historicity, memory, nostalgia, and the past, particularly in relation to the state and social change. Although these themes were not new for anthropology, this literature acquired momentum with the rise of nationalism studies in the 1980s and a renewed focus on collective memory, national histories, and post-socialist nostalgia. While this produced an interest in the "homogeneous time" of the nation (Anderson 1983) and in the ways that national pasts are created or nations "remember" (e.g., Connerton 1989; Gillis 1994; Nora 1989; and the classic Halbwachs 1992), there was surprisingly little interest in national futures, despite the obvious fact that founding a new state is future-oriented, however much it may be justified by the past. Hence, while many of these studies claimed to focus on time and temporality, they rarely addressed the relationship between collective pasts and their anticipated futures. Temporality was truncated at the relation between past and present, where the future often represented an unknown against which persons struggling to maintain stability clung to particular histories.

The 1990s saw the publication of two important works that attempted to unravel anthropology's engagement with temporality and simultaneous hesitation fully to engage with the philosophy of time. Alfred Gell's *The Anthropology of Time: Cultural Construction of Temporal Maps and Images* (1992) and Carol Greenhouse's *A Moment's Notice: Time Politics across Cultures* (1996) both begin with assertions of the inadequate ways in which anthropology has dealt with time as an idea, as opposed to time as a social construct. For Gell, the proper scope of anthropological inquiry is a Husserlian-inspired interrogation of internal time-consciousness, or temporal cognition:

In general terms, temporal cognition can therefore be conceptualized as a triangular relationship between perception (input), memory (schema, recall), and anticipation (foresight, projection). Perception appertains to the present, memory to the past, anticipation to the future. The basic cycle runs from perception (present) to memory (past) to anticipation (future), and so on, in an endless round. It is the continuous activity which we ourselves engage in, generating images, matching them with perceptual input and locating them at co-ordinates on our internalized maps of the world, which persuades us that future, present, and past are rushing by with an uncontrollable dynamism of their own.

(Gell 1992: 237)

For Gell, then, as for Husserl, the present is primary in the temporal triangle, because it is in the present that we imagine the future and map the past.

Greenhouse, in turn, makes a subtle argument about the embeddedness of time in social practice. Time is, for her, "what makes things happen, and what makes acts relevant in relation to social experience, however conceived" (1996: 1). As a result,

Time, whatever its "shape," calls forth loyalties of various kinds: to God, land, descent group, king, nation, employer, one's children, and so on. Concepts of time might be dominated by one "shape" or another (e.g., a circle, line, or pendulum motion) or by no shape at all . . . but all concepts of time are flexible, permeable, and capable of proliferation.

(1989: 1632–1633)

In Chapter 1, we will develop a conception of timespace that, as the reader will see, has resonance with Greenhouse's argument, particularly its foundation in practice. It is noteworthy, however, that despite – or perhaps because of – her critique of linear time as anthropology's de facto point of reference, Greenhouse does not fully address temporality – our relationship to time – or the future as part of Gell's temporal triangle.

The future emerged as a developing field for anthropology in the 2000s, when the "war on terror" and global financial crisis and its aftershocks left many people around the world unable to anticipate the following day. Combined with growing literatures on risk and finance, as well as climate change and alternative energies, it became clear that any return of the past was directly related to the uncertain future. Moreover, the past itself seemed foreshortened by social media, which effectively telescoped the immediate future as an anticipated present. Probability, anticipation, and expectation all acquired new subjects and methods as anthropologists began to examine the frenzy of trading floors and the future of the anthropocene.

Anthropological interest in the future has rapidly expanded since the turn of the millennium, with the future being encountered in the realm of macroeconomics and finance (Guyer 2007; Ouroussoff 2010); in processes of modernity and globalization (Appadurai 2013; S. G. Collins 2008; Ssorin-Chaikov 2006, 2017); urban and state planning (Abram 2014, 2017); biotechnology (Fortun 2009); in considering the Anthropocene (Zee 2017); and through theories of temporal succession and duration (Crapanzano 2003; Hodges 2008, 2014; Knight 2012, 2015a;

Moroşanu and Ringel 2016; Nielsen 2011). Further interventions maintain focus on the past-present relationship, citing the ethical weight of anthropology's unfinished project of reflecting on its colonial past (Pels 2015) and need for continued engagement with the discipline of history (Baca *et al.* 2009; Palmié and Stewart 2016; Shryock and Smail 2011). While we have built on some of these works in the development of this book's argument, we have pushed against others in our own conceptualizations of what is essential for a dynamic anthropology of the future.

One area in which anthropology has long shown an interest is in the occult or predictive elements of time-management, and this interest acquired new direction as more recent ethnographic accounts have focused on, for instance, prediction (Malaby 2003; Puri 2015), divination (Stein Frankle and Stein 2005), and dreaming (Edgar and Henig 2010; Stewart 2012). During eras of dramatic social change on the Greek island of Naxos, Charles Stewart shows how dreaming – prophetic, apocalyptic, rational historicist – is a means to predict the future. In a Heideggerian-inspired approach to multitemporality, Stewart demonstrates that dreams violate the dictates of historicism, bringing past, present, and future into coexistence (2012: 10–11). For Naxiots, dreams work through the constraints of village futurity by harnessing histories to activate the future and make life in the present tolerable. Like us, Stewart focuses on collective experiences of temporality, placing individual imaginative processes within society and in relation to ongoing historical processes (2012: 210).

Yet, in a theme that has often repeated itself throughout the ethnographic literature, Stewart maintains that while imaginary temporal excursions are vital to uncovering new possibilities for being, the future is faced using knowledge of the past. Although he notes that his study could be reoriented toward futurity, he instead builds on earlier work on historicity (Hirsch and Stewart 2005) to keep his focus on "the point where, in addressing the past, temporalizing tips over into historicization" (Stewart 2012: 212). A similar point could be made for numerous recent works that fall into the bracket of "historicity" (summarized by Stewart in a 2016 *Annual Review of Anthropology* piece) – for instance, collections on the presence of the past in shaping the future of the nation-state (Argenti 2017) and the construction of future archives (Zeitlyn 2015).

The future plays a more decisive role – as it perhaps inevitably must – in studies of the ecological limits of our own planet and beyond. In an era when climate change is a topic of political contention, sustainability is a catchword across academic disciplines, and Western governments are generally investing in long-term energy transition, the polemics of debate on ecological futures position the creative emergent possibilities (Kirksey 2015; Zee 2017) against apocalyptic scenarios of social break-down in the postcarbon future (Schneider-Mayerson 2015). Either way, scholars traversing the outer edges of planetary capacity are reaching into the future and pulling figures and scenarios into the present through a combination of anticipation, hope, and fantastical speculation.

Scaling up planetary futures still further, science fiction, space travel, and alien encounters have long fueled imaginings of the future, with "outer space" becoming a significant field of anthropological interest since the turn of the millennium. Much literature has dealt with the technological and ethical limits of the human, asking us to reorient our spatial and temporal horizons from Earth to consider futures beyond planetary and species boundaries. In Debbora Battaglia's seminal volume *E.T. Culture* (2005a), we are invited to explore topics as diverse as ufology (Roth 2005), alien languages (Samuels 2005), and close encounters (Doyle 2005), as well as revisit previous musings on cyborgs and cloning (Battaglia 2005c; Haraway 1991). The field has rapidly expanded over the past fifteen years to include studies of atmosphere, gravity, and scale (Valentine 2016); how agencies such as NASA map other worlds (Messeri 2016); meditation on the uncanny and unseen (Lepselter 2005, 2016); and the ethics of off-world food production and space-farming (Battaglia 2014, 2017).

Introduction

The body of literature on outer space most certainly foregrounds the future, both pulling it into present cross-disciplinary debates on global ecological and multispecies futures and projecting from the present into an unknown of indeterminate distance and immediacy. For instance, Lisa Messeri (2016, 2017) provides an innovative look at how scientists imagine what it might be like to inhabit exoplanets, arguing that astronomers, geologists, and computer scientists transform the vast darkness of space into a place of opportunity and abundance, making the "extreme" familiar (also Battaglia, Valentine, and Olson 2012). The reproduction of Martian environments in the US desert; mapping worlds in our own galactic neighborhood; and modelling environs on distant planets are all speculations about the not-yet that change how we perceive the future of Earth, as well as universal distinctions of nature and culture (Messeri 2016, 2017; Valentine 2016, 2017b).

The challenge that studies of outer space present to anthropology is the possibility of inhabiting the future and gazing back toward Earth in deliberation over what humanness might look like from elsewhere in the cosmos. Using gravity as both metaphor and physical quality, David Valentine (2017a) examines how both those who advocate settlement in outer space and their critics use fixed imaginations of humans and their histories in thinking about what "the human" will become in nonterrestrial sites. Displacing the human from its natural earthly environment offers new anthropological insights into questions of difference, specificity, and universality, and – a topic inherent to much of our theorization of orientations – scale.

We find, however, that while there is a growing interest in futurism and the futuristic, especially in realms of science fiction and millennialism (Rosenberg and Harding 2005), such futur*istic* imaginations take us too far beyond the futur*alism* of everyday life. Back on terra firma we find that anthropologists concerned with documenting the influence of globalization on local communities have shown the most interest in the future (Bear 2014; Pandian 2012; Wallman 1992). Studies from sites as diverse as India (Appadurai 2013), Fiji (Miyazaki 2004), and Mozambique (Nielsen 2014) have all emphasized the urgency of addressing the future for those people with whom we work. Nevertheless, we find that Arjun Appadurai's work, for instance, represents a continuing tendency in the discipline to, on the one hand, call for a revitalized anthropology of the future, while, on the other hand, continuing to understand that future primarily through the histories of inequality that shape the present from which the future is imagined. Appadurai highlights the need for anthropology to move beyond its "double burden" of studying "societies of the past" and peoples immune to modernity toward accounts of humans as "future-makers." But while he calls for investigation into human preoccupations with imagination, aspiration, and anticipation (2013: 285–286), he does not go so far as to sketch methods and particular ways of understanding the future that may help the discipline move in the direction to which he points.

In attempting to break away from the future of culture as being a return to the past, Samuel Gerald Collins argues for open, uncertain futures. Employing the useful term "tempocentrism" (2008: 11) for anthropology's approach to time, Collins suggests that in overarching categories of modernity and globalization, cultures are often placed on different temporal paths, inevitably heading toward designated futures of repetition disguised as perpetual change (2008: 5). Similar to the argument that we develop in this book, Collins proposes that we not look to the future for the legitimation of the present, but rather look to the future to radically shake our understandings of the past and to remake identity in the present (2008: 125). However, while Collins engages with the role of the future in anthropology, his primary concern is still with anthropology's ability to predict and speculate about the future on the basis of present versions of globalization and modernity.

At the heart of modern time is the time-reckoning of capitalism and its conflict with everyday experiences of time, as well as the clash between secular and religious temporalities. Once again, the trajectory is toward siting the past in the present through historical time and a reassessment of the universality of the neoliberal condition – or of modern time as contingent historical product. Modern time, Laura Bear (2014: 6) argues, is characterized by doubt, conflict, and mediation channeled through the layered rhythms and forms of political, economic, and bureaucratic institutions. In the management of time in modern institutions, time thickens with ethical problems and practical dilemmas. The thickening and thinning of temporal horizons is a theme we engage with at length in this book. Introducing more layers of scale to how modern time is experienced, Moroşanu and Ringel (2016) provide the concept of "time-tricking" – the "different ways in which people individually and collectively attempt to modify, mangle, bend, distort, speed up or slow down or structure the times they are living in" (ibid., 17). In their collection of essays authors insist that the future can be tricked, manipulated, and molded into, amongst other things, self-fulfilling prophecy (Ringel 2016: 25–26).

Although the politics and bureaucracy associated with modern time are features of a number of the ethnographic cases in this book, we do not focus on the time of modernity or capitalism per se – projects that invite suspicion about "the future" owing to their distinctly universalizing teleologies (Valentine 2012: 1064). Our attention to the temporal rhythms of politics and economy has more to do with the affects of time within different shared timespaces through which we move in life. Further, we are concerned with how the future resides in or draws in the present. Like Morten Nielsen's Mozambiquan informant who starts to build his house before gaining consent, thus collapsing the future into the present in order to materialize his claim, it may be possible for the future to "wedge itself" within the present (Nielsen 2014: 170). Such ways of futuralizing the present constitute the orientations that we discuss in this book.

Nonlinear chronology has been a feature of anthropological writing on time throughout the past fifteen years, with authors from Marilyn

Strathern (2005) to Hirokazu Miyazaki (2006) offering cases where people's actions in time are informed by imaginations of the future – what Miyazaki calls reimagining "the present from the perspective of the end" (2006: 157). One of the most provocative explorations of interconnecting temporalities is Nikolai Ssorin-Chaikov's (2006, 2017) work on heterochrony and temporal disjunctures in the Soviet Union and post-socialist Russia. His anthropological interrogation of where multiple temporalities coexist or cross over – in both human relations and material artifacts – and his engagement with utopias of imagination speak to our own project – described in more detail below – of multi-temporal timespaces, teleoaffects, and orientations to the future.

In his earlier work on heterochrony, Ssorin-Chaikov examines the meanings of time in global modernity, temporal fragility, timelessness, and the teleology of socialism, reading the present from the point of view of the future (2006: 358). His most recent publication, *Two Lenins* (2017), takes things further by investigating the composition and structure of multiple temporalities, and, importantly for us, how temporalities are relational rather than relativist across space and time. Ssorin-Chaikov opens up challenging questions about shared time and relatedness, distinctions between temporalizing and temporalization (p. 127), and multitemporality as method.

On the methodological front, recent volumes have admirably covered the temporal rhythms of conducting fieldwork and methodologies for accounting for local imaginaries of time (Baca *et al.* 2009; Crapanzano 2003; Dalsgaard and Nielsen 2015; Salazar *et al.* 2017). In these studies, emphasis is placed on exploring the field as temporal phenomenon, allowing local temporal imaginaries to condition analytical frameworks (Dalsgaard and Nielsen 2015: 10). Despite attention to the temporality of our own methods, however, these contributions still invite us to think about the future as a means to understand the present rather than starting *from* the future, and from that point contemplating the multi-temporality of the present, or the temporal dynamism of our actions.

Introduction

While these works all in some way call for increased attention to the role of the future in anthropological investigation, the majority offer no tools for thinking cross-culturally about the study of futural temporalities. In outlining the study of the future as a newly emerging field for anthropology, we employ our own ethnographic research on the precarious futures of the Eastern Mediterranean, where financial crisis, large-scale displacement, climate change, and state collapse are reshaping historical and temporal consciousness. We use examples from the region to reinterpret certain existing studies of history, historicity, tradition, and the past through a future-oriented lens. In doing so, throughout the book we both ask what assumptions have previously led to a blindness to the future in the discipline and also ask what changes about anthropology's method and scope when we incorporate the future more centrally into the past-present-future relation.

Futural Orientations

In one sense, ours is a story focused on time and temporality. Yet, we argue in the first chapters that neither the measurement of passing time nor the relationship of past-present-future fully encapsulates the effects of the future on everyday action. The concept of "orientations" is intended to help us gain an ethnographic hold on the relationship between the future and action, including the act of imagining the future. Our claim throughout the book is that our concept of the present *as present* derives from the future; that without a concept of futurity the present ceases to exist as such. This is not a radical claim, and indeed similar claims have been made by other thinkers. However, our concern is to translate this claim into a more programmatic method for thinking about the future within anthropology. As social scientists, how do we examine something that does not yet exist? How do we understand its relationship to the action of everyday life?

We find it useful to think of this effect of the future as a way of orienting us. By "orientation" we intend to break from the notion of linear time while still retaining an aspect of teleology that we find to be important for thinking about everyday lives. Teleology concerns "ends" in the plural – multiple ways of navigating the course of the quotidian. If we return to the moment of looking up from this book with which we began the introduction, ravens cawing and washing machines spinning orient us in different, often coexisting but occasionally mutually contradictory, trajectories toward the future. We build our argument from a particular philosophical tradition – running from Aristotle through Martin Heidegger to Theodore Schatzki and speculative materialism – that has understood temporality as inherently teleological. As we remarked earlier, this is not the teleology of evolutionism and progress that has made anthropologists shy of being concerned with ends. Rather it is an open-ended, indeterminate teleology concerned with the practices and orders of everyday life.

To understand this, we begin in the first chapter to build on Theodore Schatzki's important work, particularly articulated in *The Site of the Social* (2002) and *The Timespace of Human Activity* (2010), in which he incorporates futurity into practice theory. Schatzki defines what he calls "the site of the social" as an order or mesh, as human activity that is "caught up in orders of people, artifacts, organisms, and things" (2002: 123). Social worlds emerge, he claims, through the dense interweaving of such practices, practices that are also bound up with the material world. Moreover, whether it is human beings speaking or making, "social practices make and have spaces," while the practices that define those spaces are inherently temporal, having rhythm, duration, and longevity. Time and space, then, are interwoven in what Schatzki calls "practice-arrangement bundles."

In making this argument, Schatzki also directly responds to Deleuze and Guattari's *A Thousand Plateaus* and its concept of rhizomatic assemblages, a strand of contemporary philosophy that has been actively appropriated in anthropology. While elsewhere in this book we employ Deleuze and Guattari's observations, we agree with Schatzki that the former are unable to account for teleology, or the way in which what Husserl called our "retentions" and "protentions" shape our relationship with objects and imbed us in temporal trajectories. Instead, we find it useful to think with Schatzki's notion of "practice-arrangement bundles" that create their own timespace – what he calls a "teleoaffective structure," i.e., a structure that is affective but also teleological, oriented toward ends. For Schatzki, this structure is "a range of normativized and hierarchically ordered ends, projects, and tasks, to varying degrees allied with normativized emotions and even moods" (2002: 80).

Put another way, the impatience that I feel waiting for the washing machine to finish on a sunny day, or the annoyance that I feel at the never-ending construction project, or the sense of time both compressing and stretching that comes from working toward a writing deadline are all the teleoaffects produced by our orientation toward particular ends within "practice-arrangement bundles." If Schatzki's abstractions seem far removed from ethnography, we might return to Nancy Munn, who had expressed a similar understanding of what she called "the co-constitution of time and space in activity" in her critique of Evans-Pritchard. Building on an image in a song of the Nilotic Atuot ("the ashes of the dung fire in my [cattle] camps are so very deep"), she observes,

The image of the deepening ash suggests the experience of temporal increment from the originating past (an "ancient ancestor"). Such images do not simply represent time in spatial metaphors. They are built on the spatio-temporal constitution of the world (the increasing ash in the hearth; the sense of a continuous or recurrent spatial occupation) emerging in and from daily activities, which conveys the connection of people with their ancestors.

(Munn 1992: 98)

While Munn's concern is with "the spatiotemporal constitution of the world" through the accretion of the past, Schatzki's work helps us to understand the indefinite teleological constitution of all such timespaces.

Of course, one of the facets of the future as a specific mode of temporality is its relationship to knowledge: our lack of knowledge of the future is understood to be different from our lack of knowledge of the past. Reinhard Koselleck (1985) expressed this difference in terms of the "space of experience" that is the past living in the present, as opposed to the "horizon of expectation" that opens before us at a point that is barely visible, present but unknown. That horizon may sometimes appear closer – indeed, right on our threshold – or at other times may seem to be imperceptibly blended with the sky.

We argue throughout this book that the limit of knowledge defined by the future shapes perception of the familiarity of everyday life. It shapes, in other words, how we find our temporal orientations. As we discuss in Chapter 1 on anticipation, in situations of social and political turmoil, the unknown may come right to one's door, may threaten to cross one's threshold. In situations of social and political calm, that unknown may be pushed farther away, onto what Reinhart Koselleck calls the "horizon of expectation." Or at times of more distant threat, such as looming ecological disaster, the present may appear stretched to the horizon and hence take on elements of the surreal. The thickness of the present, as Husserl called it, is always related to the unknowable, to something that we cannot see.

In outlining the study of the future as a newly emerging field in anthropology, we offer the concept of orientations as a way continuously to orient ourselves to the indefinite teleologies of everyday life. While orientations entail planning, hoping for, and imagining the future, they also often entail the collapse or exhaustion of those efforts: moments in which hope may turn to apathy, frustrated planning to disillusion, and imagination to fatigue. By examining both the temporal dynamism and potential temporal stasis of such orientations, we argue for an anthropology that takes fuller account of the teleologies of action. In so doing, we introduce a robust understanding of the "quotidian" into anthropology's grappling with the everyday, and thereby chart a new future for future in the discipline.

In this book, then, we outline how presents and pasts are always and inevitably shaped by the ends for which we strive. If the book surprises you, it will be because it goes beyond your expectations; if it disappoints, it will be because it cannot meet them. Whenever we open the pages of a book, curiosity mingles with possible boredom, and any book's potential destiny is to gather dust. Whatever this book's *telos*, we maintain hope that our conception of orientations opens up new possibilities for anthropology's future.

ONE

Anticipation

To think the disaster . . . is to have no longer any future in which to think it. . . . The disaster is its imminence.

Blanchot 1995: 1

Several months before intercommunal fighting began in Cyprus in 1963, an incident between two families in a village in the foothills of the Troodos Mountains caused tension. Ayhan was a boy of twelve at the time, and he was one of the small Turkish Cypriot minority in a settlement of more than 3,000. He says that after that incident, they began sleeping in a neighbor's home, which they considered safer, and his older brothers kept guard over the house at night. At first, he did not understand why his brothers were keeping guard until one night he saw a group of Greek Cypriots wandering the neighborhood with guns and sticks. Then one evening his mother told him that the following day they would move to his sister's house in another village, and that they should get ready.

I asked my mother why we were going there when we had our own home, and she told us that this was what was necessary. So, we got ready, and in those days, we didn't have a lot of belongings, we just took a table and chairs and two beds. I remember that there was a woodcased bus, and we tied my wardrobe to it.

The experience of guarding one's home all night in expectation of violence mirrors that of many Turkish Cypriots of the period. One large landowner told Bryant that although he has visited his properties since the division that displaced him in 1974, he would never return to his home in the island's south. "In any case," he remarks, "we weren't able to live there, all night we would stand by the windows waiting to see if they were going to kill us." Many others, as in Ayhan's case, fled their homes in search of neighborhoods and villages where they would feel safer. As another woman who was also displaced to the north in 1974 explained, "We came of our own will, but because we were afraid for our lives."

These examples from a period of conflict place in stark relief the concepts of anticipation and expectation that we wish to develop in these first two chapters. Ayhan's older brothers expected violence, and they guarded their homes in anticipation of it. Similarly, Ayhan's mother felt tension in the air and acted anticipatorily by getting her five children out of the village. These were future-oriented actions: ones that projected the present into the future and attempted to shape the future in the present.

While expectation and anticipation are closely related, we draw a heuristic distinction between them here in order to think about the different thicknesses of the present, and therefore relationships to the past, that are contained in each. These differing thicknesses, we suggest, give us insights into distinct teleologies of action. One may, for instance, expect rain and take an umbrella when going out "just in case." The expectation of rain is, in this instance, still on the horizon and is tempered by, for example, weather reports that have failed in the past. As we explore in the following chapter, expectation may be viewed as a conservative teleology, one that gives thickness to the present through its reliance on the past. To anticipate rain, however, is to feel and smell it in the air, to close one's windows and cover lawn furniture while imagining the future in the present. Anticipation slims the present, often breaking entirely with the past as it draws present and future into the same activity timespace.

This chapter will first examine philosophical and anthropological approaches to anticipation before turning to anticipation as an ethnographic teleology. The middle section will ask what we gain, as anthropologists, by distinguishing anticipation as an orientation. In particular, we explore there the idea of *vernacular timespace* to help us think through futural orientations. In the final section, we will illustrate the ethnographic gains by asking what happens when we are unable to anticipate. There, we develop an argument that Bryant began elsewhere (Bryant 2014), regarding the failure to anticipate as an important way of defining what creates crisis.

Theorizing Anticipation

In what is often cited as the first philosophical reflection on our subjective experience of time, Augustine observes,

Suppose I am about to recite a psalm which I know. Before I begin, my expectation (or "looking forward") is extended over the whole psalm. But once I have begun, whatever I pluck off from it and let fall into the past enters the province of my memory (or "looking back at"). So the life of this action of mine is extended in two directions – toward my memory, as regards what I have recited, and toward my expectation, as regards what I am about to recite. But all the time my attention (my "looking at") is present and through it what was future passes on its way to become past.

(Augustine 1998: 282)

This first summation of what is sometimes called "A-series" time focuses on the tenseness of temporality, the sense of past flowing into future and future becoming past. While Augustine describes how it is that we perceive time's flow, thereby referring to time as something objective, we consider it important that he focuses on time as an element of doing, something that we perceive within human practice or activity.

Phenomenology, of course, is less interested in time itself than in our consciousness of it, but we may see the beginnings of a phenomenology of time-consciousness in Augustine's observations of the present as a moment not only of "looking at" but also simultaneously of "looking back at" and "looking forward." It is the latter that Husserl called retention and protention to refer to specific intentionalities related to past and future. As with Augustine's "looking back at," Husserl understands retention as the immediate awareness of what is no longer now. Retention "transcends itself and posits something as being – namely, as being past – that does not really inhere in it" (Husserl 1991: 356). Protention, on the other hand, "is the impressional openness of consciousness to the future," "a moment of the actual phase of the ongoing perception that immediately opens me up to further experience" (Brough and Blattner 2006: 129).

For Husserl, the phenomenology of time-consciousness is consciousness of an "extended present," "an epochal moment that endows experience with its seemingly 'flowing' quality" (Hodges 2010: 117). Husserl's student, Martin Heidegger, however, found it more fruitful to focus his own phenomenology on the primacy of the future. This is because "for Heidegger the life of Dasein is not primarily the life of consciousness, but rather, the life of a concrete social agent" (Brough and Blattner 2006: 132). He views existence as one in which we are at work in the world being who we are. Moreover, being who we are, or understanding ourselves, "is not to grasp, imagine, or know ourselves cognitively or reflectively. Rather, to understand ourselves is to be capable of being who we are" (ibid.). Dasein, or this "who we are," remarks Heidegger, "is not something present-at-hand which possesses its competence for something by way of an extra; it is primarily Being-possible. Dasein is in every case what it can be, and in the way in which it is its possibility" (Heidegger 1962: 183). It is in this sense that Dasein is always pressing forward, indeed understands itself through what Heidegger calls "projection":

Projecting has nothing to do with comporting oneself towards a plan that has been thought out, and in accordance with which Dasein arranges its

Being. On the contrary, any Dasein has, as Dasein, already projected itself; and as long as it is, it is projecting. As long as it is, Dasein always has understood itself and always will understand itself in terms of possibilities.

(ibid., 185)

In other words, who I am is a matter of what I strive for, what or who I am trying to be, or what Heidegger calls "anticipatory resoluteness" (ibid., 370). It is only through such resoluteness aimed at the future that I become self-constant, and it is only in this way that I can understand the past: "Only so far as it is futural can Dasein *be* authentically as having been. The character of 'having been' arises, in a certain way, from the future" (ibid., 373). This self-constancy or self-understanding, then, is a "being-towards," or "a future in which I press, a future for the sake of which I act as I do" (Brough and Blattner 2006: 132). In the indeterminate teleological terms that Schatzki employs, this may be summarized by saying that "the temporality of activity is . . . acting toward an end from what motivates" (2010: loc. 1053).

Our particular concern here is with this futural "pressing ahead" that Heidegger viewed as primordial to Dasein. We take this to be fundamental to anticipation, even when it does not contain the existential element of resolve so important to Heidegger's definition. For Heidegger, "authentic" temporality was one determined by self-understanding:

For example, I may understand myself as a musician by projecting myself forward into a musician's way of life. Such projection, moreover, is not a cognitive or intellectual achievement, nor even an imaginative one, but rather a concrete form of conduct.

(Blattner 2005: 312)

While the individualizing focus on self-constancy may be of less use to anthropology, we find it helpful to think with the last part of *Being and Time*, where Heidegger makes clear that he saw this future-orientedness as something constituting "who we are" at a primordial level. Indeed, he calls this "primordial temporality," a temporality that in every instant recalibrates the relationship of future, present, and past. This is what he calls temporality temporalizing itself:

Primordial and authentic temporality temporalizes itself in terms of the authentic future and in such a way that in having been futurally it first of all awakens the Present. *The primary phenomenon of primordial and authentic temporality is the future.*

(1962: 378; emphasis in original)

Indeed, Heidegger is explicit that "temporality 'is' not an entity at all. It is not, but it *temporalizes* itself" (p. 377). It does this through the relationship that it creates between time's three *ecstases* of past, present, and future.

Temporality temporalizing itself seems at first paradoxical until we consider Heidegger's insistence throughout that it is only by being futurally that we "awaken" the present. As we will argue further below, Heidegger here suggests that we have no sense of the present or the now, in much the same way that we have no sense of "here." The present is "awakened," in Heidegger's terms, through what we have called its *orientations* toward the future. Heidegger's primary form of temporalizing – the orientation around which his discussion mainly revolves – is anticipation. This becomes clear in his description of the moods of fear and anxiety that he uses as examples of temporal states of mind and which, as we discuss below, we associate firstly with the orientation of anticipation.

It should be no surprise that Heidegger's focus appears to be primarily on anticipation, since as an orientation it permeates everyday life. At the mundane level, this includes, e.g., anticipating what other drivers will do while driving a car, or how someone will react when we give them a piece of bad news. This allows us to take precautions, to prepare ourselves for our friend to be upset, or to decide that neither is worth the risk and to stay at home. Husserl's discussion of protentions, and its focus on the immediate future of action, had opened up the space for considering the pervasiveness of anticipatory action:

> In every action we know the goal in advance in the form of an anticipation that is "empty," in the sense of vague ... and [we] seek by our action to bring it step by step to concrete realization.
>
> (quoted in Schutz 1997: 58)

The "emptiness" of anticipation we understand to indicate both its pervasiveness and its indeterminateness. While we may, as Schatzki suggests, act toward ends, those ends may be vague, "empty," unrelated to larger ends. For instance, I may act toward the end of avoiding an accident by not driving in front of an oncoming truck, but this is a finite and empty end – unless, for instance, I have been considering suicide, and the moment at which I refuse to pull in front of the truck becomes a moment of existential crisis. Even in that moment of existential crisis, however, the actual moment of anticipation – the anticipation of the speed of the oncoming vehicle and my own car's capacity to make it into the other lane without an accident – is one that remains, in itself, empty.

One of Husserl's examples to explain protention comes from the visceral feelings of anticipation that we experience when listening to music, and this example also gives us further insight into the effects of anticipation. Both psychology and musicology have used music as an example of pressing toward the future, though seemingly with less concern to distinguish between anticipation and expectation (esp. Huron 2006). In an early work, for instance, musicologist Leonard Meyer (1956) argues that music is able to evoke emotion because composers choreograph expectations – what we argue are in fact anticipations. While ethnomusicologists have noted that the ability to do this is culturally specific (see Huron 2006: 2–3), within the constraints of culture we see that music has a visceral effect that pulls us forward. This happens because when I listen to a piece of music in a form that I know, I not only expect but anticipate the resolution of a particular passage. In my anticipation, my body prepares itself for a resolution of a particular kind, and much musical surprise comes from foiling that anticipation.

Anticipation, then, is more than simply expecting something to happen; it is the act of looking forward that also pulls me in the direction of the future and prepares the groundwork for that future to occur. Unlike expectation, anticipation specifically contains the sense of thrusting or pressing forward, where the past is called upon in this movement toward the future. If we return to our analogy of thresholds from the Introduction, we might see expectation as knowing that a spouse will be at home when we arrive in the evening, without having to ask. Anticipation, on the other hand, would be the conversation that we have with ourselves to explain the reaction that we believe the spouse will have when we arrive late. In the former instance, the future remains at a distance, even if we are relatively certain of its approach. In anticipation, however, we not only ready ourselves but also press forward into the future, enacting it and thereby pulling the future toward the present.

Ethnographic Anticipation

> Anticipation, anticipation
> Is making me late
> Is keeping me waiting.
>> Carly Simon, "Anticipation" (1971)
>> © Universal Music Publishing Group

This refrain about a futural orientation is one of the best known and most lasting in pop music history. The song is an ode to indeterminateness which was penned during a period of much anticipation: student movements that would change the course of the Vietnam War; a civil rights movement whose slogan became "We will overcome"; and a revolution in gender and sexual relations that would alter the way that we think of ourselves. Looking back, it was an epoch of great change, though for those who lived through the period, it was a time of hope tinged with uncertainty.

The song begins with that uncertainty, with the assertion, "We can never know about the days to come/But we think about them anyway." However, Simon then immediately turns around this seemingly forward movement by asking if she is really with her lover now "or just chasing after some finer day." Indeed, when Simon penned her song about a temporal orientation, she cast it in the mode of uncertain impatience, a lover whose thoughts and desires run ahead of the possible and the present. Although she tells him how right his arms feel around her in the moment, she admits that she had rehearsed the words the night before, "When I was thinking about how right tonight might be." This is a lover who can't wait for the future to come, who in fact lives so pressed against the future that her present suffers.

She ends the song with the possibility that they might not be together tomorrow, "So I'll try and see into your eyes right now/ And stay right here 'cause these are the good old days." In an interesting reversal, then, because the lover of the song is always running ahead of herself, the present is already in the past, "the good old days." And throughout the song, the refrain casts anticipation in the role of an actor, in fact the primary agent, which is always making the lover late and keeping her waiting. Anticipation, in this sense, acquires the affect of an external force driving her continuously past the present.

This popular song gives us a number of clues to how we might approach anticipation through ethnography. In particular, it illustrates the way that, in anticipation, there's a sense of being unable to wait for the future, instead needing to rush toward it. This may be either to greet it or to thwart it, or as in the case of the song's lover, to shape it. In the song, she describes how her experience of being in her lover's arms in the present is dimmed by already having rehearsed the words that she will say to him describing that experience. Because she has already moved toward the future, anticipation is "keeping her waiting" in the present.

How, though, may we transpose such individualized understandings of anticipation to the level of the collective? We suggest that at the level of the collective, anticipation helps us to understand a particular affective dimension of time that calls for collective response. We often talk about such "times" in the colloquial: a Time of Peace, a Time of War, a Time of Hunger, a Time of Crisis. These are "times" that require or induce collective responses.

To help us understand this, we may turn from pop songs to early social theory – in particular, to a little-known passage from the *Leviathan* in which Thomas Hobbes gives an explanation of time that is helpful for thinking about how, as anthropologists, we may study time's affects, and through them, anticipation. Writing at a particularly bloody moment in England's history, immediately after the English Civil War, Hobbes observed that war is defined not only by moments of conflict but more importantly by a period of time in which we may anticipate violence.

For WAR, consisteth not in battle only, or the act of fighting; but in a tract of time, wherein the will to contend by battle is sufficiently known; and therefore the notion of *time*, is to be considered in the nature of war.

(Hobbes 1962: 100; emphasis in original)

What Hobbes describes here is the particular experience of time that we ordinarily describe as a "Time of War." Although the phrase "a Time of War" may often be used to describe a period of history, Hobbes suggests that we may equally see a Time of War as a way of organizing time itself. The quote from Hobbes continues by comparing a Time of War with the weather:

For as the nature of foul weather, lieth not in a shower or two of rain; but in an inclination thereto of many days together: the nature of war, consisteth not in actual fighting; but in the known disposition thereto, during all the time there is no assurance to the contrary.

(ibid.)

What Hobbes suggests, then, is that Times of War are ones of immediacy and of a "known disposition" to fight, even if no actual clash takes place. The nature of war, in this assessment, is not simply violence but the anticipation of it.

We tend to understand "disposition" as an inherent quality, as in someone's "sunny disposition." Here, however, Hobbes refers to disposition as something situational – in other words, as a *dispositif*, an arranging or ordering (Ranciere 2010) that in this case signals a readiness for war. This arranging or ordering is orientational in two senses: both portending a possible future, and also attempting to forestall it. This "known disposition" to fight creates what Pradeep Jeganathan calls "the shadow of violence" (Jeganathan 2000). This shadow is figured by Hobbes as the looming clouds of foul weather.

However, there are also dispositions created through violence's anticipation. These would be the collective equivalent of Carly Simon's lover always living in the future. Jeganathan, for instance, deftly deploys the notion of anticipation to describe the ways in which "Tamil-ness" has been lived in southern Sri Lanka. "There is, in the shadow of violence," he notes, "a repertoire of signifying practices that is positioned in relation to that shadow" (ibid., 117). He calls these "tactics of anticipation," a repertoire of actions "produced in relation to a chronological series of events of violence" (ibid.). Such tactics include, for instance, Tamils learning to pronounce particular words in a Sinhala way (ibid., 118). A similar case from Bryant's fieldsite of Cyprus was Turkish Cypriots speaking English, rather than Turkish, when entering Greek Cypriot-dominated areas.

A "Time of War," then, is a time that casts a particular shadow, a time of a "known disposition to fighting" and an ordering that signals it. In the example with which we opened the chapter, a young boy described becoming aware of what his older brothers had already perceived and responded to: certain Greek Cypriot neighbors' preparations for violence. As a boy, he only gradually became aware of this shadow of violence, a "period of tension" that was short of war but required a response. We suggest that this affective dimension of time has the effect of appearing to foreshorten, forestall, stop, or start the future and thereby temporality. After all, there are periods when time may seem sluggish and others when it seems to move too fast. There are periods when we "have time on our hands" and others when we seem to run to catch up with the future. This affective dimension of time, we suggest, may manifest at the individual level – as in Simon's lover – but is often experienced collectively. We all live together through Times of War, Times of Peace, Times of Hope, and Times of Hunger. Although Simon's lover described her experience of time at the individual level, the song was written at a moment when youth seemed ahead of themselves, running toward the future.

The reader will notice that we here separate time from temporality. While, as we discussed in the Introduction, we bracket ontological questions regarding time, we are nevertheless concerned with how time may be collectively perceived. Above, we call this "affective time," to refer to the collective sense of living within a period that has a particular temporality. More precisely, however, we may refer to it as *vernacular timespace*, or how, collectively, we express the everyday ways in which temporality temporalizes.

We should keep in mind that for Heidegger, temporality temporalizes because the future "awakens" the present. In other words, our future-oriented actions shape our understanding of the present, and its relationship with the past. To understand our concept of vernacular timespace, however, we must return to Schatzki, who built an explicitly social model of what he calls activity timespace from Heidegger's project. Because Schatzki's model builds also on practice theory, it is particularly amenable to thinking through the gains of a future orientation for anthropology.

The "space" of Schatzki's timespace is based on his idea of a "site" – specifically, the "site of the social":

> Social life transpires through human activity and is caught up in orders of people, artifacts, organisms, and things. As such, it is not just immersed in a mesh of practices and orders, but also exists only as so entangled. The mesh of practices and orders is the *site* where social life takes place.
> (Schatzki 2002: 123)

A site, then, includes physical space but goes far beyond that to include all the other orders of people and things that are associated with human activities. For instance, the "site" of a factory would be not only the physical space of the factory itself but also the various orders of suppliers and their supplies, sellers and their vehicles and stores, consumers and their credit cards, advertisers and their newspapers or websites, etc., who are involved in the everyday activities of factory production. The social orders that define such sites are arrangements of people, artifacts, organisms, and things that "hang together" within a particular domain (ibid., 1). The importance of Schatzki's intervention is that although his "arrangements" bear resemblances to the "assemblages" of Deleuze and Guattari (esp. 1987), Schatzki emphasizes practices and human activity as key to creating such sites (2002: 92–95, 204–210).

The idea of timespace that Schatzki develops is one expression of his insistence that "agency is the chief dynamo of social becoming" (2002: 234). In this, he refers to social practices, by which he means "an open, organized array of doings and sayings" (2010: loc. 1341): "What people do is what makes sense to them to do for the sake of particular ways of being given particular states of affairs" (ibid., loc. 118). Activity timespace, then, "consists in acting toward ends departing from what motivates at arrays of places and paths anchored at entities" (loc. 1075).

What is important for us here is that this conception of timespace is open, indeterminate, and non-exhaustive. We never live in only one timespace, but different forms of activity open up different timespaces. The site of the social, for Schatzki, is a site of becoming within which end-oriented action is realized.

If we turn this to Hobbes's stormy description of a Time of War, we see that his invocation of dispositions also has a teleological character in the interdeterminate sense used by Schatzki. War, in other words, creates its own activity timespace. This is the timespace of both human and nonhuman living things, as well as the spaces and objects that draw them together. The activity timespace of war consists not only of soldiers on a battlefield or even the army that supplies them, but also of everything and everyone who may potentially be affected by or implicated in the battle. Weather, in this sense, is a particularly apt spatial metaphor, as a storm crashes down on all within its range. But weather also is a temporal metaphor, as Hobbes explicitly notes: "The nature of foul weather, lieth not in a shower or two of rain; but in an inclination thereto of many days together" (1962: 86–88). An impending storm, then, is an apt metaphor for the activity timespace of war.

We suggest that such activity timespaces, particularly outside the flow of "ordinary" time, are given vernacular expression through epochal thinking. Such epochal thinking is intended to express perceived differences in the temporalizing of human activity, in other words, in the ways that the future "activates" the present. Such epochal thinking may express a perceived shortening or lengthening of the relationship between future and present in our own lives (a Time of Crisis, a Time of Hunger, a Time of Peace), or it may express what we perceive as the difference between the relationship of future and present in our own lives and in that of ancestors, animals, or the universe (the Time of Ancestors, Environmental Time, the Time of the Cosmos).

Orientations at the communal level are based on such vernacular timespaces. In the case of anticipation, we find the temporalizing of temporality expressed by what Frank Kermode (2000) refers to as the "imminence" versus "immanence" of the future. While the former gives a sense of the future as *now*, the latter allows for a more "normal" flow of time, one in which the future is still in the future.

Hobbes's invocation of weather to describe war uses a metaphor of imminence: clouds have gathered, and as far as we know, the "storms of war" are on the horizon. It is this dimension of imminence, a foreshortening of the future, that we suggest creates anticipation as a disposition, or a mode of comportment. In Hobbes's description a "known disposition" to war casts a shadow of violence. In response to that shadow, however, other dispositions emerge that anticipate and respond to it. Such tactics of anticipation bring the future into the present, requiring us to "second-guess," or to act in preventative mode. The future is always possible now, at this moment, viscerally present in the act of anticipation.

In particular, this affective imminence of the future creates what we will call *thresholds of anticipation*, contrasting these with what Ricoeur and Koselleck, following Gadamer, call horizons of expectation. For Koselleck, "the horizon is that line beyond which a new space of experience will open, but which cannot yet be seen" (1985: 273), while for Ricoeur "the horizon presents itself as something to be surpassed, without ever being fully reached" (1988: 220). This sense of horizon contrasts with the horizon sketched by Hobbes for a Time of War: although a storm conjures horizons, a storm in fact may come directly to one's door. The threat of a storm is that it approaches, proclaims its imminence with thunder and lightning. It is this sense of approaching, of coming to one's very door, that makes the metaphor of a threshold more appropriate.

A threshold implies both the imminence of the future and the idea of pressing forward into it, potentially crossing into it. While not as apt for more mundane forms of everyday, individual anticipation, we find that forms of social anticipation often press toward the future in ways that imply crossing into another space of time and a radical reorientation of the present. This is in strong contrast to the image of horizon, in Ricoeur and Koselleck's sense, where the future is never fully realizable, always receding.

Perhaps the most thoroughly studied instances of such thresholds are apocalyptic times, which anticipate the destruction of the world as we know it and a radical reorientation of both time and space. Moreover, in messianic or apocalyptic time, the present is liminal, a "current situation" to be rectified by the "redemption" of the future (Baumgarten 2000; Bromley 1997; Kravel-Tovi and Bilu 2008; Robbins and Palmer 1997). Indeed, another reason to think of the orientation of anticipation as a threshold is this liminality of the present, where it is stuck on the "limen," or threshold, moving toward the future but not yet there. Life lived at a threshold of anticipation, then, may be said to be one of a liminal present, a temporary state that in Carly Simon's song was "keeping her waiting."

In such temporalities, the present is not simply a step on the way to the future but is a temporary anomaly that must be patiently endured, or that must be gotten past through action oriented toward the future. Such extended liminality at the threshold of anticipation appears to be what we mean by a "Time of War" or a "Time of Conflict." One of the ways in which we may understand this is that both in cases of war and in apocalyptic temporalities the vernacular timespace is imagined as coming to a conclusion through a radical reorientation of the present. Achieving peace is not only a matter of negotiating a political solution, just as apocalyptic histories do not end with Jesus' second coming. Rather, these foresee entering a new timespace, a "Time of Peace," or a "Time of Eternity."

In the next section, we explore in more detail what forms of comportment and intentionality emerge from socially produced anticipation, and how anticipation emerges ethnographically. In the final section, we will then examine what happens when there is a socially produced inability to anticipate, which we argue results in a "Time of Crisis."

Exploring Collective Anticipation

At the beginning of the twentieth century, the island of Crete had already experienced a series of revolts by Greek Cretans who wished to unite the island with Greece. The response had been counterattacks by Muslim Cretans who desired to retain Ottoman rule in the island. The period was one dominated by what was then called the Eastern Question, an effort by Western European powers to decide among themselves how they would divide up the Ottoman Empire. In 1898, an autonomous Cretan state under Ottoman suzerainty was founded, though it was protected by Western European forces, and its High Commissioner was Prince George of Greece. At the same time, there was continuing agitation to unite the island with the "mainland," leading one Ottoman newspaper in the island to proclaim in a 1906 headline, "Awake, Muslim people, we are losing Crete!" (Gökaçtı 2003: 43).

The eventual result of this turmoil would be the incorporation of Crete into Greece, and in 1923 the Greek–Turkish Population Exchange, the UN-brokered movement of around 350,000 Turkish-speakers from Crete and northern Greece, and more than one million Greek-speakers from Anatolia to the Greek peninsula. This would set the stage for a century marked by partitions and population movements, and it would become part of the political imaginations of large numbers of people around the world. Demands for partition quickly became a way for minorities to express an anticipation of violence.

We have argued above that anticipation is fundamental to everyday life and action. In its most basic sense, we must anticipate that a floor will not collapse in order to step on it. However, the spontaneous reactions required by anticipation are not so easily mobilized at the level of society. This seems to be why anticipation becomes the collective response to similarly collective senses of danger. What are perceived as "Times of Danger" – whether times of conflict, or times of impending disaster – produce anticipatory responses. These are the responses that project into the collective future, imagining a people's elimination through violence, either human-wrought or natural.

This projected life-shattering event has the threshold character that we discussed earlier. It is an event beyond which imagination falters, as the world will not be what it once was. Collective anticipation, then, becomes an attempt either to facilitate this radical alteration – as in Christians attempting to induce what they believe to be signs of the Apocalypse – or to forestall or change its outcome – "it is not a matter of *if* a disaster strikes, but a matter of *when*" (Choi 2015: 289; emphasis in original). The ability to understand or forecast the difference between *if* and *when* of course relies on prior knowledge, particularly collective experiences, hopes, and fears. As Vivian Choi remarks regarding disaster preparedness in eastern Sri Lanka, for the people she knew there "the possibility of a disastrous future depended on what they knew and had experienced in the past" (ibid., 299). This included not only the devastation of the previous tsunami, but also the violence wrought by state security forces in the province during the civil war – the same security forces later responsible for disaster management.

In the case of Crete, that disaster was a long time coming. We find a similar building of collective anticipation in cases such as the Partition of India, a project initially conceived as the forestalling of a minority's annihilation. Faisal Devji calls the project of Pakistan a "Muslim Zion," where he uses "Zion" "to name a political form in which nationality is defined by rejection of an old land for a new" (Devji 2013: 3). He argues that this uprooting was the product of "situations in which minority populations dispersed across vast subcontinents sought to escape the majorities whose persecution they rightly or wrongly feared" (ibid.). Unlike other nationalist movements, we may see these as anticipatory enclaving whose ends were not preordained. Some Indian Muslims had imagined a non-national state, while others had thought of sovereign enclaves of Muslims dispersed across the subcontinent. Zionist Jews had sought homelands in South Africa, Cyprus, and elsewhere before settling on Palestine as much by political accident as because of historical connection. The places where they eventually established states were, in this sense, what Devji calls "accidental countries," "settled by nations founded outside their borders not for reasons of sentiment as much as convenience" (ibid., 14).

Devji describes the ways in which this anticipation of their own displacement had penetrated to the realm of social imagination. We see this, as well, in the case of Cretan Muslims, the wealthier of whom began to move their investments to Istanbul and Izmir long before the population exchange forced them from their homes. Similarly, in Cyprus, as Bryant writes elsewhere (Bryant and Hatay 2019), the Turkish Cypriot imagination of *taksim*, or partition, was founded on what was, by the 1950s, the social imagination of partition as a political option. That was, of course, based on common knowledge of the Population Exchange and the partition of India, but it was cemented by a set of similarities that Turkish Cypriots saw between their own situation and that of Muslims in Crete and India. One close friend of Bryant's, for instance, described how in her childhood a neighbor who had spent part of her childhood in the island's north talked to the girl constantly about how she would one day return there. "She made plans about it, talked of selling her property," Bryant's friend told her. "When I asked her, she told me, 'But we'll all go there one day! We can't stay here.' That was the mentality then."

It is worth noting, moreover, that the realization of these three partitioning projects produced a radical reorientation of the present, and hence of the past. Partition was itself a threshold, one beyond which the present and past could no longer be the same. So for those groups who had not lived with the minority's extended experience of anticipating violence – in these cases, Greeks exchanged from Anatolia, Hindus exchanged from what is now Pakistan, and Greek Cypriots who fled from north Cyprus – the moment of division was inscribed in social consciousness as a trauma and relived and retained in poetry, stories, music, memoirs, and archives. The study of such memorialization has, of course, provided fertile ground for memory studies, a tentacular field that appears to have at its base the assumption of a "normal" time that has been marked or scarred by violence. This does not take into account what we have suggested here is a particular temporalizing of temporality by collective anticipation that marks the future as threshold and makes the present liminal.

The threshold character of the future may be seen in the ways that, in the three partitioning projects mentioned above, the minority groups who had long lived with the collective anticipation of violence later produced none of the stories, memoirs, songs, and poetry that memorialized loss for the other group. Indeed, Bryant argues elsewhere (2017) that conflict-related displacement may also contain gains that can outweigh losses. In the terms that we are developing here, we could say that crossing the threshold into the projected future leads to a radical reorientation of present and past. This meant, in these three cases, that it was not until a developing awareness of the moral imperative to remember the past – particularly following the burgeoning of memory studies in the 1990s – that these three collectively displaced groups began to write songs, stories, and memoirs about the places they had left behind.[1]

---

[1] In the cases of Cyprus and Turkey, one sees this also in the ways that Greek Cypriots and Anatolian Greeks immediately founded associations of displaced or exchanged persons. In the case of Cyprus, where Greek Cypriots consider the division to be an occupation and the result of an illegal military intervention, they have established municipalities in exile, while refugee associations play an important political role. In Turkey, no associations of exchanged persons were established until the late 1990s, when elderly exchangees and their descendants began taking tours to Crete. Turkish Cypriots began to establish their first associations, named after the villages from which they were displaced, in the early 2000s, after the opening of the checkpoints that allowed them to see the Greek Cypriot associations in the island's south.

That threshold character may also be seen, however, in the relation-ship between anticipation and a continuing Time of Conflict. In her research in eastern Sri Lanka, for example, Choi found resistance to the idea that the war was over. "People commented on my seeming naivete when I probed them about the end of the war," she remarks, "'Who told you the war was over?' asked Ravi, who had come home for just three months, on holiday from his job in Qatar" (Choi 2015: 299). Ravi, moreover, remained in Qatar because he felt that the east of Sri Lanka remained unsafe. Others remarked on the ways the government con-tinued to limit movement, while some speculated that the paramilitary LTTE (Liberation Tigers of Tamil Eelam) might rise again.

In a similar fashion, one of Sami Hermez's interlocutors in Beirut often asked him, "Sami, do you think there will be a war?" as a way of starting conversation, particularly about whether or not he should move to Dubai before the war started (Hermez 2012: 327). Reversing Toby Kelly's (2008) observation that even periods of violence are infused with the ordinary, Hermez argues that the anticipation of violence infuses what appears to be ordinary life with the threat of violence, and hence with the anxiety of uncertainty (see also Vigh 2011). This is what Jeganathan had called the "shadow of violence," and which Hermez calls an "absent presence" that "solidifies war as an inescapable compo-nent of politics" (2012: 330). This shadow or presence hovering over daily life, then, leads to thoughts of potential emigration, and in one case, to a discussion among neighbors about whether or not it was worthwhile to buy a generator, since there might be no diesel available for purchase when war started.

As Hermez describes it, this everyday, pervasive forecasting of war results in a collective sense of uncertainty, but one whose vocalization produces the laughter of anxiety. When his neighbors discussed whether or not diesel would be available in the coming war, they laughed anxiously because it was both a potential practical problem and one that seemed real when spoken. It was, Hermez observes, "the laughter of anxiety" (p. 335). There is an element of absurdity that seeps into such conversations – the absurdity of discussing as though real something that everyone still hopes will not happen. It is, then, this sense of a need collectively to anticipate war – a need that may lead to considering emigration or potential diesel shortages – that is how we recognize that we are not yet in a "Time of Peace." Indeed, other work has argued that "post-war" Beirut has been geographically ordered through sectarian and political difference, and that these "geographies are being produced according to planned and imagined geographies of local and regional wars 'yet to come'" (Bou Akar 2012: 151).

This life in the shadow of violence that is not itself violent has been called "not-war-not-peace" (Nordstrom 2004; Sluka 2009). Sluka refers to this as life in the "shadow of the gun," "a semi-permanent state of 'peace process'" that is neither peace nor war (Sluka 2009: 282). Sluka's invocation of the gun's shadow provides a contrasting metaphor with Hobbes's impending storm. Because guns may be hidden away, they may constitute what Mariane Ferme calls the "underneath of things" (Ferme 2001). It is in such a way that bringing what is underneath "to the surface" may result in the sort of nervous laughter that Hermez describes for Lebanon.

What shapes anticipations of violence in these cases is perceptions of imminence: if violence is still but a few clouds forming on the distant horizon, one may have hope that it will disperse. However, if one has lived through other instances in which such seemingly harmless clouds turned to a storm, one may nevertheless make speculative preparations. One may still hope against the realization of violence, but as Hermez remarks, anticipating violence "can provide a useful technique to inject certainty into the uncertainty infused in daily life in Lebanon" (Hermez 2012: 333). That attempt to inject certainty, to forestall or alter the future, obviously takes on urgency as the storm moves closer.

Anticipating, then, becomes a collective way of stepping into the future, of trying to transform one's own future or the future of the collective before it occurs. Collective anticipation is one that tries to forestall or alter the coming event that is itself expected to transform the life of the present. Anticipation, in this sense, works to relieve the anxiety of uncertainty and to "normalize" the present through a speculative imagination of the future.

What happens, however, when anticipation is not possible – when the future cannot be imagined, planned for, forestalled, or resolved? What happens to the temporalizing of temporality? It is these times, the next section will argue, that we describe as times of crisis, moments when anticipation, and therefore the alleviation of anxiety, are not possible, and when as a result the present becomes uncanny to us in its present-ness.

Times of Crisis and the Uncanny Present

The anticipation of violence, as we discussed it above, temporalizes temporality through a present lived with one foot in the future. Anticipation relieves the anxiety of uncertainty, giving us a sense of *what we should do.* What of those instances, however, when the parameters of life have changed so distinctly that the future is no longer imaginable? When anything or nothing could happen? We argue here that this is the circumstance that defines the vernacular timespace of a "Time of Crisis."[2] Whereas above we discussed thresholds of anticipation that imply "crossing into another space of time and a radical reorientation of the present" (Bryant 2012: 339), here we will discuss what we call *critical thresholds.* These are thresholds in which, unlike in apocalyptic narratives, the future is not one of anticipated rectification or reorientation of time and space but is rather uncertain and unknown.

---

[2] In her analysis of the recent proliferation of crisis discourse, in which it seems that everything becomes a crisis, Janet Roitman argues that "crisis serves as a transcendental placeholder because it is a means for signifying contingency" (Roitman 2014, loc. 320; see also Roitman 2011). In Roitman's reading, an event becomes a crisis because it shows that the world could be otherwise. While accepting this analysis, we also suggest here that one of the reasons such moments become ones that we call "crisis" is because they bring the presentness of the present to the fore (see also Bryant 2016).

If we return to our indeterminate teleological explanation of how temporality temporalizes, it is clear that we see the emphasis as being on the future. If the future "awakens" the present, action in the present becomes urgent or anticipatory when there is a future looming that must be forestalled or changed. What, however, if the future is unimaginable, unknown, and so outside the parameters of expectation that one is unable to anticipate? Thinking of Hermez's observation, above, that collective anticipation can work to relieve the anxiety of uncertainty in everyday life in Lebanon, we can see the problem when the future is unknown, unimaginable, unanticipatable. Bryant (2016) describes this phenomenon generated by a Time of Crisis as a critical threshold, a temporalizing of temporality that gives us an uncanny present, a present that is unfamiliar in its presentness. It is the present that suddenly seems to hover between past and future, taking on the burden of gathering the past and projecting it into the unknown future when the teleology that would ordinarily shape that temporal relation is lost.

During Bryant's Cyprus research, that temporality of crisis first took on urgency during the 2003 opening of the ceasefire line that divides the island, when the almost 200,000 Cypriots who had been displaced three decades earlier were able to visit their homes and villages, though not to return to them. After almost thirty years in which the present seemed stalled, never moving toward a future of reunification and peace, the opening produced unpredictability, the sense of being thrown into a new temporality in which the future was entirely unknown. For some, this gave a euphoric sense of freedom. But for many of the people with whom Bryant worked, who had gone on with rebuilding their lives after the division, the unpredictability of the future produced a period of crisis. This was a present that suddenly seemed uncertain and anxious, determining the future rather than being shaped by its ends. Both past and future took on a new immediacy and indeterminacy, even as many of the people with whom Bryant spoke in that period sought ways to control them. Unlike the sluggish time of previous years, then, the uncanny present was fraught with the anxious sense that the future was running out of control.

When the opening was followed only a year later by a referendum that would decide the future of the island, anxiety in certain quarters bordered on panic (Bryant 2010). Indeed, the sudden opening and the return of a past that had been put away seemed a jolt into an uncertain future, one that led them to seek a new anchoring in the present. As a result, Bryant (2010) describes the stories of the past that emerged in that opening not only as expressions of past trauma but also of disquiet, apprehension, and an unknowability regarding the future. The stories were inevitably coupled with questions: What do they want from us now? Will they want to take back their property? Will displaced persons really come back?

Affectively, all of these events are certainly critical ones in the sense used, for instance, by Veena Das, to refer to the annihilation and recreation of worlds (Das 1997, 2006). Moreover, Bryant's informants' view of these moments as "critical" echoed the original meaning of a decision or judgment, or its early modern medical meaning as a point in illness when the patient would either die or recover (Koselleck 2000, 2006; Starn 1971). Anxieties around the opening and referendum recognized that these events would reconstitute the everyday.

Particularly among Turkish Cypriots, who had long anticipated the island's division, movement to the north had been the start of a new time, and many people had chosen to "put the past behind them." For instance, when Bryant's Turkish Cypriot husband took a Greek Cypriot colleague to meet his grandmother after the opening, the grandmother suddenly asked him if he knew that there were seven missing persons in their family. When he said that he did not and asked her why no one had told him before, she replied, "Then you didn't need to know, but now you do."

The idea that one "needs to know" is about creating a particular intentional stance, a disposition, in the present. The idea that one "needs to know" now, as opposed to in the past, puts emphasis on the presentness of the present, the way that the present moment gathers the past and is decisive of the future. At the time of the opening and referendum, there was a sense that time itself had become weightier, that it bore a particular burden of the future. The moment was a crisis in its pathological meaning, as a terminal point in illness when the patient would either live or die, a period that acquired particular significance as a future being made *right now*.

This sense of the presentness of the present, its role as a node between past and future, is one that I do not normally experience except when I stop philosophically to reflect on the question of temporality. Sitting at my desk, I have no more sense of a "now" than I have of a "here." After all, where do "here" and "now" begin and end? But I may become aware of both in moments of what we call crisis, moments when contingency comes into play and interrupts my intentional relation to the world. In the *Phenomenology of Perception*, Maurice Merleau-Ponty referred to Husserl's intentionalities as ones that "anchor me to an environment. They do not run from a central I, but from my perceptual field itself, so to speak, which draws along in its wake its own horizon of retentions, and bites into the future with its protentions" (Merleau-Ponty 2012: 31; also Husserl 1964). Ordinarily, as we sit at a desk or go about our daily lives, we experience such an anchoring; only the interruption of this field of intentionalities would make us feel unanchored, adrift. This is what we referred to earlier as an interruption of the normal teleology of human activity.

The anxieties of an opening and referendum, then, derived from the uncanny present, the present whose presentness as a node between past and future had become viscerally immediate for them. We described this above as a "burden of the future," meaning that rather than the present being shaped by ends, the present becomes determinative of ends. It is in this sense that one may "need to know" a past that had previously been left unspoken. This was a call to mobilize pasts in new ways by recalling those aspects of the past that had remained as what Paul Ricoeur (2004) calls a "reserve of forgetting" – those aspects of memory and history that are forgotten but available to consciousness. This reserve of forgetting represented a past that had been foreclosed in the interest of particular futures but that in the opening many people began to recall in order to create particular intentionalities (see also Bryant 2014). For instance, the refrain of many Turkish Cypriots, that "We suffered, too," and "Greek Cypriots know nothing of our suffering," were often repeated as ways of creating intentional stances toward the return of a past that threatened the future.

While we have focused here on an example of a particular moment that could obviously be described as a Time of Crisis, Townsend Middleton (2013) shows how the anxiety of uncertainty may stretch crisis over longer periods of time or cause it to bubble up at particular moments. The uncertain future of the Gorkhas in India is one in which their ancestry in Nepal leaves them subject to the constant threat of deportation. These create what Middleton calls "anxieties of belonging," anxieties that are "fundamentally about being-in and being-of the nation-state" (2013: 612). Never quite certain of their future, crises reoccur, and the colonial and postcolonial past become part of an "underlying structure of feeling that subtends and spans these episodic emergencies" (ibid., 619).

As with the response to crisis that Bryant describes, what is significant about the use of symbols and stories of the past is the way that they orient us and provide us with modes of anticipation. Those symbols and stories may produce affects – a strong and unfocused sense of defiance, for instance – but what is important for the uncanny present is the way that they give us orientations, modes of action, and intentionalities.

Conclusion

This chapter has used a Heideggerian-inspired concept of indeterminate teleology to understand anticipation as a specific, and ubiquitous, way of temporalizing temporality. While at the individual level anticipation pervades the actions of everyday life, at the collective level we find that anticipation is linked to particular moments of uncertain or threatening futures. Anticipation, in these instances, is a collective way of addressing the anxiety of uncertainty, and of forestalling or altering something that threatens a radical revision of the present. In such Times of Anticipation, the past becomes a resource for rewriting the future in the present.

There are, however, moments when the future cannot be anticipated, when there are no resources to think about the future that might be. In such moments, the present becomes uncanny to us in its presentness, acquiring a weight of the future. These times are ones that in the vernacular we describe as "crisis," and that in the examples given here may be resolved through mobilizing "forgotten" pasts to develop a new intentional stance toward the future.

TWO

Expectation

> There would, without the future, be no more history, and there would be no more future, no event to come, without the very possibility of an absolute surprise.
>
> Derrida 2005: xiii

We had a good life in Syria before war took everything. I had a good job as a tailor. We lived a normal life, surrounded by family and friends. It was a hard moment the day I woke up to find our beautiful street in Aleppo, Syria, full of soldiers. The air force was overhead and bombs started raining down around us, destroying houses and killing people in our neighbourhood. I realised that day that my family was not going to find happiness again until we left Syria. Life as we knew it had been destroyed but it was very hard to make the decision to leave. ... We had to flee to Lebanon, there was nothing left, no future for my children.[1]

It has become a distressingly familiar story: that of "normal life" disrupted by violence, and the accompanying destruction of familiar anchors of the everyday. In his own narration of the loss that accompanies displacement, a middle-aged man named Darwich describes their decision to leave Syria as one prompted by the disappearance of a future. Moreover, the lost future is not only his own, but that of his children: the future of the future.

---

[1] www.dss.gov.au/settlement-and-multicultural-affairs/meet-darwich

Expectation

This chapter concerns the orientation of expectation, which we described in the previous chapter as a conservative teleology that gives thickness to the present through its reliance on the past. Throughout the chapter, we use the contrast of a Time of War and a Time of Peace to bring into relief the distinction between collective anticipation and collective expectation. For while these two vernacular timespaces, and the futural orientations that accompany them, are not commensurable, they are invariably invoked together as the contrast between the "storms" of war and a day of sunny weather. Although one of these terms does not make sense without the other, they offer us qualitatively different ways of approaching the future. We offer that the same may be said for anticipation and expectation.

We explore here the oft-used metaphor of expectation as "horizon" in order to understand a particular thickness of the present in relation to the future that exists when we live in vernacular timespaces that enable us to expect. This chapter will first explore philosophical and historiographical approaches to expectation in order to give us a fuller description of expectation as a futural orientation. Our aim here is to examine more fully what Schatzki calls the "teleoaffective structure of practices," or those "ends, projects, actions, and combinations thereof that participants should or acceptably pursue" (2010: loc. 1363). In particular, we use Schatzki's model of the "teleoaffect" – what we have called the futural orientation – as providing some clues to why expectation is one of the primary ways in which we define "normal life."

We examine both collective desires for "normality" and examples of the uncanniness of everyday life when the unexpected becomes routine. We ask how the "normal" is defined in these cases where people collectively perceive and describe themselves as experiencing a loss of the "normal." What we propose creates the "normal" in such descriptions is the expectation of expectation: the expectation that the horizon will remain open, unreachable, but visible. Much as a horizon defines the limit of the world as we know it, so, we argue, expectation defines what it means to *have* a future.

This does not mean that the unexpected does not happen. Indeed, we describe the ways in which the expected also contains the possibility that what we expect may not, in fact, happen. Like a promise that may be broken, so expectation may not turn out as we expect, and instead we may be met with surprise. It is surprise, moreover, that creates "the eventness of the event" (Derrida 1997: 2), something that may be prefaced by "perhaps" or "maybe" but that is founded on the unexpected. Looking at the relationship between the expected and unexpected at the level of the collective, we see how the unexpected may itself be routinized – how we may come to expect the unexpected. The concluding section of the chapter will then explore some of the uncertainties, anxieties, and losses of orientation that emerge when the orderings that enable us to expect are radically altered or swept away.

Theorizing Expectation

One of Bryant's friends in Cyprus was eighteen years old in 1974, the year that a Greek-sponsored coup d' état intended to unite the island with Greece provoked a Turkish military intervention, the division of the island, and the displacement of around 200,000 Cypriots. Before the checkpoints that divide the island opened in 2003, that friend, Alexis, sent her to Famagusta to try to take a photo of his house, now inside the Turkish military zone that is the hostage city of Varosha. In 1974, its white sand beaches and luxury hotels had made it the Monte Carlo of the Eastern Mediterranean. Her friend's father, a poor man, had saved money over many years by selling trinkets to tourists and had finally, only in 1972, managed to save enough money to build a modern house near Varosha's famous beach. He had also bought a bright yellow sports car for his only child, Bryant's friend, when he turned eighteen. The night before the coup, Alexis had used it to take a girl that he loved to the port city of Kyrenia. "We sat in the harbor," he said, "and the world was right. It seemed that the future was spread out before us. We expected it to last forever."

As with the refugee narrative with which we opened this chapter, narratives of war and the choices made during it are so often framed in terms of truncated futures. Bryant's friend described the coming of war as a shrinking of the future's horizon, which previously had seemed vast and open. Darwish described his family before war as living "a normal life, surrounded by family and friends." Such descriptions of life before war take on nostalgic overtones and so should be treated as *narratives* of life before conflict, rather than as reflections of the "real" conditions that prevailed then. Nevertheless, they give us insight into the ways in which a narrowing or truncating of future horizons is implicated in what it means to be in a Time of War.

In his work on historical time, Reinhart Koselleck refers to the future, any future, as a "horizon of expectation." Recognizing the indeterminate nature of his horizon metaphor, he uses a joke to drive home the ways in which the future's horizon is always just out of reach. In the joke, Nikita Khrushchev declares in a speech, "Communism is already visible on the horizon." One member of the audience does not understand the meaning of "horizon" and so once at home, looks it up in a dictionary. The answer that he finds is, "Horizon, an apparent line separating the sky from the earth which moves away when one approaches it" (Drozdzynski 1974: 80, quoted in Koselleck 1985: 273).

Koselleck uses this image of a receding limit to our world to describe the future. The etymology of the English "expectation" is in consonance with this landscape metaphor. In Latin, the root of *expect* has to do with sight, as we can see from other words derived from -*spect*, such as perspect, prospect, or retrospect (Junker 2000: 697). The Latin *ek* (out) + *spectare* (to see) becomes, in combination, "to look out for." However, Koselleck's metaphor also suggests a more literal possibility of seeing ahead of oneself. The horizon is always ahead of us, always just out of reach, just as, Koselleck suggests, expectation, and hence the future, can never be grasped. This sense of the future as almost but never quite visible, almost but never quite reachable, is one of the meanings of Alexis's statement that "The future was spread out before us."

In contrast, Koselleck calls the past a "space of experience," using "space" to indicate "the presence of the past as distinct to the presence of the future" (ibid., 273). For him, a "space" is a totality of many layers that are present simultaneously, encompassing both our own and others' experiences in much the same way that any "here," any present space, cannot be only mine, in other words, cannot be distinguished or partitioned from the "here" of others. Expectation, on the other hand, represents a "line behind which a new space of experience will open, but which cannot yet be seen" (ibid.).

For Koselleck, the categories of experience and expectation were both highly general and absolutely indispensable: "No expectation without experience, no experience without expectation" (ibid., 270). Indeed, "they resemble, as historical categories, those of time and space" and "indicate an anthropological condition without which history is neither possible nor conceivable" (ibid., 268). His conception of those categories is virtually indistinguishable from Husserl's intentionalities of retention and protention, though now elevated to the level of historical time. As with Husserl, Koselleck also argues that experience is the past dwelling in the present, events that "have been incorporated and can be remembered" (ibid., 272). Experience, similarly, is the "future made present" (ibid.) which restructures the present and so enters the space of experience "with retrospective effect" (ibid., 275).

Despite these similarities to the phenomenologists, Koselleck's concern is to understand the relationship between the experience of history and its writing. In particular, he focuses on historical time, or the way in which we experience the relationship of past, present, and future. His thesis is that this experience has changed in modernity, when history is no longer experienced *in* time but *through* time. "Time is no longer simply the medium in which all histories take place; it gains a historical quality ... Time becomes a dynamic and historical force in its own right" (ibid., 246). His conception of historical time, then, is related specifically to the timespace of modernity, with its teleology of progress, from which certain peoples and groups may be allochronically excluded (Fabian 1983).

We return to the Time of Modernity toward the end of this chapter. For now, it is worth noting that Paul Ricoeur, while influenced by Koselleck's metaphors of the space of experience and horizon of expectation, at the same time critiqued Koselleck's reduction of time in modernity to a time that makes us (as we inevitably pass through it) and that we are able to make. Ricoeur notes, for instance, that Koselleck does not distinguish between temporality and historical consciousness, or between the passage of time and our consciousness and even narration of its passage. Ricoeur argues that because Koselleck is concerned with a modernist version of history in which humans make it rather than being made by it, he cannot take into account the ways in which we are "affected by history" and "affect ourselves by the history that we make" (Ricoeur 1988: 213).

Ricoeur's critique of Koselleck offers some insight into how we might further our discussion of the relationship between vernacular timespaces and futural orientations. Noting that "nothing says that the present reduces to presence," Ricoeur asks, "Why, in the transition from future to past, should the present not be the *time of initiative* – that is, the time when the weight of history that has already been made is deposited, suspended, and interrupted, and when the dream of history yet to be made is transposed into a responsible decision?" (ibid., 208). The time of initiative, for Ricoeur, is a present of "acting and suffering" (ibid., 230), but one with an obvious impetus toward the future.

The significance for us of Ricoeur's intervention is that he emphasizes that at the horizon of expectation, "What happens is always something other than what we expected. Even our expectations change in largely unforeseeable ways" (ibid., 213). "There is no surprise," he notes, "for which the baggage of experience is too light" (ibid., 209), suggesting that experience always contains the possibility of surprise within it. Indeed, it is the possibility of the past *not* returning, or our expectations being flouted or our plans undermined that signals the very *futurality* of the future: expectation is always something yet to be made, and so something that may not be made, or may be unmade:

If, therefore, we admit that there is no history that is not constituted through the experiences and expectations of active and suffering human beings, or that our two categories taken together thematize historical time, we then imply that the tension between the horizon of expectation and the space of experience has to be preserved if there is to be any history at all.

(ibid., 215)

This tension is precisely the possibility that the expectations provided by experience must also contain the "perhaps," the "maybe" that opens them to the possibility of surprise.

For both philosophers, the metaphor of horizon indicates the openness and unreachability of the future as expectation. Expectation is, by definition, what remains in the future; to expect is, by definition, to look toward the future. In this sense, we may say that expectation defines the *futurality* of the future. To expect is to *have* a future, which is why Koselleck and Ricoeur understand it as fundamental to temporality.

Ricoeur's invocation of a time of initiative returns us to Schatzki, whose phenomenologically inspired practice theory, we have suggested, helps us make connections between timespaces and collective orientations. In particular, in *The Timespace of Human Activity*, Schatzki develops an idea that he calls the "teleoaffective structure" of practices, which we may link to Ricoeur's description of the present as a time of initiative:

A teleoaffective structure encompasses ends, projects, actions, and combinations thereof that participants should or acceptably pursue. It thereby encompasses existential futures that are enjoined of or acceptable for participants in the practice involved, as well as prescribed and acceptable places, paths, and regions. Participants in the practice tend to actuate subsets of the futures involved and to treat entities as anchoring subsets of the places, paths, and regions concerned.

(Schatzki 2010: loc. 1363–1370)

Put more simply, as anyone goes about his or her day, he or she participates in varied practices, and does so in different roles and for different reasons. This means that practices have an orienting effect through anchoring persons in different timespaces. "The timespaces of individuals are circumscribed by the teleoaffective structures of practices" (ibid.: loc. 1367).

Importantly for our purposes, Schatzki ties the idea of timespace to practice, and to the relations of humans, nonhumans, and objects that emerge within the "activity bundles" that characterize different types of practice. This allows him, he thinks, to avoid the Heideggerian error of characterizing Dasein as living in a single given world, with a single range of "tasks, ends, actions, and meanings" (ibid., loc. 1282). It is within such activity timespaces that human life "hangs together," and sociality emerges. However, in contrast to Heidegger's singular world, Schatzki proposes that "nets of interwoven timespaces are a pervasive and crucial feature of social life" (ibid., loc. 1341).

We have also suggested that timespaces emerge around particular future-oriented practices, very often described in the vernacular in epochal ways. A Time of War or Conflict, in other words, is the period in which we engage in particular kinds of anticipatory orientations to the future. Those practices have a teleoaffective structure in which, for instance, urgency appears to draw the future into the present. However, urgency is often experienced in more mundane timespaces; for instance, when together with colleagues we seem to condense time in order to meet a deadline. Those persons who exist within the teleoaffective structure of an oncoming disaster or an upcoming deadline could be said to share the teleoaffect of the same vernacular timespace.

It is noticeable that Schatzki's description of practices and the tele-oaffective structures that emerge from them relies on expectation. Indeed, as with other practice theorists, Schatzki's approach, while stressing the open-endedness of action, nevertheless "tends to fore-ground the content of practice at the expense of its inherently perfor-mative nature" (Nicolini 2017: 21) – though even critics who decry the lack of attention to performativity still emphasize that any practice theory should see practices as having "a perceivable normative dimen-sion" (ibid.). Indeed, the normativity of Schatzki's practice-oriented approach emerges when he defines the teleoaffective structure of prac-tices as the "ends, projects, actions, and combinations thereof that participants should or acceptably pursue" (Schatzki 2010: loc. 2824).

In this pursuit, he casts motivations such as desire, hope, and belief as "emotional activity" that is used to "put into words the future dimension of action temporality" (loc. 2824). Similarly, ceremony and ritual become "choreographies of action." Neither detract from what he views as open-ended action toward ends. Rather, they provide motiva-tion and form to activities whose open-ended teleologies suggest that they ought to be performed in particular ways to achieve particular ends. For example, one may have many motivations for making a cup of tea in the morning, but one expects that putting hot water and tea leaves into a pot will produce a cup of tea. In this, he appears to take expectation as the basic orientation toward the future and its ends, providing structure to the teleoaffect of human life. Activity timespaces emerge from the rhythms, sounds, scents, and feelings produced by these activities. Tea-making and tea-drinking – boiling water, waiting for the tea leaves to steep, waiting for the tea in one's cup to cool – produce, for those who share it, the sense of morning at home.

While we find this to be an effective description of the teleoaffective structure of timespaces that emerge from activity, we find it necessary to further pry apart the gap between the historical time or historical consciousness that concerns Koselleck and Ricoeur and the open-ended, everyday teleologies that Schatzki describes. In all three thinkers, the future from which the present acquires its form is imagined in the mode of expectation. If the present is constituted through practices, through what Ricoeur called initiative and Schatzki calls "activity bundles," all seem to accept that as we go about our activities in the world, the expectations that ground those practices are key to our anchoring in different timespaces. Expectation, then, is assumed to be the ground of the present in relation to activity.

We have called expectation a conservative teleology because of its implicit and assumed reliance on the past. We expect because of what the past has taught us to expect. Unlike anticipation, in which the present and past are awakened by the future, pulling me in the direction of the future, expectation does not contain the same sense of the future pulling me forward. Rather, it awakens a sense of how things *ought* to be, given particular conditions. It awakens the possibilities of our future presents, without in fact realizing those. Unlike anticipation, in which we rush toward the future at the same time that we pull it toward us, expectation instead defines what we have called the *futurality* of the future, which depends on the simultaneous acknowledgement that our expectations could be dashed, that all our plans could be tossed aside. Indeed, we may say that expectation *futuralizes* the future, in the sense that it creates for us the sense of something on the horizon – almost but not quite visible, and so still the not-yet-made that is open to becoming something else.

We see, then, that the image of the horizon that is simultaneously visible and yet not quite is based in the radical alterity of the future: expectation always points to the future as Other. We reasonably expect that tea leaves and boiling water will make tea based on past experience, but we can only expect that, since there is always the possibility that they won't. We can also expect that our friend who said that she will come to dinner will arrive, but she may have an accident on the way to dinner, or she may get busy at work and forget. Similarly, we may expect to finish work on time but find that we are unable to do so. As we discuss in the final chapter, what Jean-René Vernes (2000) calls "aleatory reason" allows us to make causal connections that at the same time leave room for contingency – what Hume called the "secret nature" of things (see Chapter 6), in which we may expect tea to come from tea leaves and boiling water but also recognize that something entirely different may happen. The senses of impatience, frustration, excitement, and yearning that so often accompany expectation are indications that whatever we expect remains always beyond our grasp or control.

Moreover, as we discuss below, it is precisely this element of "teleological necessity and surprise" (Malabou 2005) that, in the epigraph, Derrida describes as fundamental to the Event: there would be "no more future, no event to come, without the very possibility of an absolute surprise" (Derrida 2005: xiii). Indeed, Malabou's description of what she terms the *voir venir*, the "to see (what is) coming," is one that seems also to describe expectation as horizon. She emphasizes, however, the horizon's openness to the unexpected: "'To see (what is) coming' denotes at once the visibility and the invisibility of whatever comes" (Malabou 2005: 184). Like the horizon itself, which is always visible but not quite, *voir venir* is "to anticipate, to foresee, to presage, to project; but it is also to let what is coming come or to let oneself be surprised by the unexpected, by the sudden appearance of what is un-awaited" (Derrida 2005: ix).

Expectation, in this sense, depends upon the unexpected: the aleatory irruption into the known. We explore in the next section this "'maybe' inherent in contingence" (Derrida 2005: xiii), which also represents what Toby Kelly calls the "movement between the 'is' and the 'ought'" (T. Kelly 2008: 353). Kelly shows how Palestinians grapple with the relationship between the expected and the unexpected, which also opens up the possibility for us to understand expectation as a communal futural orientation. In the following sections, we explore expectation as definitional of the futurality of the future, often expressed as *having* a future. We argue that in collective terms, it is *having* a future, or the expectation of expectation, that also makes expectation definitional for the ordinariness of ordinary life.

The Future as Promise

In many English novels of the nineteenth century, the author plays on the gap that divides expectations from their realization. Much of this play centers, moreover, on the tension between love and the promise of marriage with "ten thousand per year." Thackeray's *Vanity Fair* or Dickens's many novels – including, most notably, *Great Expectations* – satirize the vainglorious strivings of their characters as they navigate the class divides of English society, where even a young man "brought up as a gentleman – in a word, as a young fellow of great expectations" (Dickens 2007 [1860]: 117) may in a single day find himself in ruin and his expectations dashed.

It is the female novelists, however, who drew the finest portraits of lives lived in expectation. The pace of these novels noticeably slows, taking us from the endless schemings of Thackeray's Becky Sharp, as she ceaselessly tries to manipulate her fortune, to the domestic rhythms of women cloistered in the house, or in a particular place in society. For instance, Jane Austen's careful portraits leave us with some of the most studied observations about expectation. At the beginning of *Sense and Sensibility* (1992), one of her first novels, Austen gives us a brief description of the sunny disposition of one of her characters that leaves the careful reader wondering if this was not a quiet rebuke of the Utilitarian theory that was so popular in her day. A bit more than twenty years earlier, Jeremy Bentham had published his first work of Utilitarian theory, which espoused maximizing happiness, a matter of promoting those things that "add to the sum total of his pleasures: or, what comes to the same thing, to diminish the sum total of his pains" (Bentham and Mill 1961: 18). In contrast, Austen offers us a more nuanced portrait of happiness in her character: "In seasons of cheerfulness, no temper could be more cheerful than hers, or possess, in a greater degree, that sanguine expectation of happiness which is happiness itself" (Austen 1992: 26).

In a single sentence, Austen gives us a sketch of future-oriented human nature, one in which the state of being happy relies not on present pleasures but on the projection of them into the future. Moreover, Austen describes this as a *sanguine* expectation, one that is optimistic in the face of adversity. In contrast to Bentham, then, she suggests that the discomfort of the present can be overcome through our orientation to future presents, to a horizon toward which one looks optimistically.

However, Austen also suggests that what makes expectation futural is its capacity to orient us toward the horizon while at the same time acknowledging that its distance calls our own predictive abilities into doubt. Much as we can be fairly certain that the man walking toward us down the street is our father, because he strides or shuffles in a particular way, there is also the possibility that it is, indeed, someone else. Expectation leaves open that possibility. Later in the same novel, Austen describes her heroine Elinor Dashwood's encounter with the difference between "is" and "ought" embedded in expectation when she realizes that the man she loves has married another: "Elinor now found the difference between the expectation of an unpleasant event, however certain the mind may be told to consider it, and certainty itself. She now found, that in spite of herself, she had always admitted a hope, while Edward remained single, that something would occur to prevent his marrying Lucy" (ibid., 200).

Here, Austen describes the difference between "is" and "ought" as the difference between the knowledge that something is likely to happen, indeed is expected or promised to happen, and the alterity of the future embedded in the concept of expectation that allows us to think it might be otherwise.

One also finds here, however, two related meanings of "ought." The first is "ought" in the sense of "should," as in, "I just had the car serviced, so it ought to run." The other is "ought" in the sense of a yet-unfulfilled desire, wish, or possibility: "He ought to be a better person." The first is what we might call the "ought" of promise, the second the "ought" of potentiality. While "promise" derives from the Latin *promittere*, which means to send forth, let go, or to throw, "potentiality" derives from *potentia*, which means a power or force. While the former implies already sending the present toward the future, the latter implies a present that is, as we say, pregnant with the future.

As we will see, there is often slippage between promise and potentiality, or between "the expectation of happiness that is happiness itself," and the potentiality that opens the horizon to hoping for it. We find, however, that it is worthwhile to make a heuristic distinction between the two, amongst other reasons, because promise creates a sense of *awaiting*, what Heidegger called "the future as coming towards" (1962: 372).[2] Both horizons and promises, both seeing ahead of oneself and sending forth or throwing, imply awaiting, staying where I am as the future that I cannot quite see approaches, even as I try to see or reach ahead of myself. Like a promissory note, it is expectation as promise that is the foundation for language's future tense: to say, "I will come to visit you today," is not to say that my visit is a possibility, a probability, or a potentiality, but rather that it is a promise, in the sense of sending or throwing into the future. It is to say what will be the present in the future, or to sketch the future present.

---

[2] We should note that for Heidegger, expectation or awaiting was an inauthentic mode of being, while the authentic mode is anticipation, in which Dasein "comes towards itself." With the idea of expectation as promise, we return then to our distinction between expectation and anticipation, which Heidegger had expressed as the distinction between awaiting the actualization of a certain future and taking responsibility for it (Taillefer 2017: 206).

To return to our claim that expectation defines the future's futurality, we can see even more clearly with the metaphor of awaiting the fulfillment of a promise why "having expectations" is the equivalent of *having a future*. To say that one no longer has a future is to say that all prospects and promises have been dashed. It is to say that one can expect nothing *in* the future or *from* the future.

Returning to our previous discussion of Schatzki, we also see in the "ought" of promise something that we already know: that expectation is the ground on which practices, orders, and hence the normative emerge. The normative, after all, is about "meeting expectations" – a phrase that also suggests a reach into the future. The normative is a standard for evaluation, for saying whether certain outcomes are good or bad, desirable or undesirable, according to those standards. As such, the normative relies on expectation: knowing what behaviors or outcomes may be expected in particular circumstances. If we consider Schatzki's practices and orders, or the descriptions of everyday action by other practice theorists such as Bourdieu or Giddens, we see an assumption of a "normal" state of affairs, and a range of practices that rely on predictability. One must know the appropriate way to accomplish certain ends in order to achieve them. A change in expectations may lead to practices being suddenly altered, reshaped, overturned, or impeded.

However, as we suggested earlier, the other facet of promises is that they may be broken. Things may always turn out differently than we expect. The idea of the broken promise returns us, then, to Derrida's epigraph and its assertion that there can be no future without the possibility of "an absolute surprise." If Elinor's hopes were dashed, this was because she had held open the possibility of the future turning out differently than she expected. (That it would later turn out in such a way might be seen as both an absolute surprise and the most satisfying gratification of her expectations.) Derrida suggests that it is this possibility of the broken promise that opens the future to the possibility of change: "[W]ithout the conjunction of the essential or teleological necessity and, *at the same time*, of the aleatory accident, of the 'maybe' inherent in contingence, no event would or could ever come forth or happen" (2005: xii).

There are several conclusions to be drawn from this discussion that will help us to think through communal expectation in the next sections. First, if to expect is to await, *what* we await can take the form of potentiality or promise. Second, however, it is *promise*, with its etymology of sending forth or throwing, that is closest to *expectare*, or looking out for. It is this sense of "expect" as promise, moreover, that is the basis for the future tense in language. Third, everyday practices also rely upon the sense of expectation as promise, as defining the future tense in language. For this reason, then, expectation is the ground on which the normative emerges. Fourth, because expectations are always still to be realized, they define for us the futurality of the future. After all, when our expectations are met, they already become part of history. To define the futurality of the future, however, is to define the possibility of broken promises, of the Event, and hence the possibility of change.

If expectation is fundamental to the normative orders of everyday life, however, this gives us little purchase on collective expectation where such expectation defines what we have called vernacular timespaces. While expectation would be fundamental to the sorts of activity timespaces defined by Schatzki, we have tried to distinguish these from the epochal thinking that defines what we call *vernacular* timespaces: a Time of War, a Time of Crisis, a Time of Prosperity. These are periods when we may individually experience culturally defined temporal orientations appropriate to particular kinds of activity. In addition, however, we collectively experience what Schatzki calls "teleoaffects" – anxiety, uncertainty, fear, joy – in relation to conditions that collectively affect us.

In order to think about this, we look in the next section at the ways in which expectation is entangled with what it means to have a future, and how *having* a future is imagined. Bryant's friend, discussing a period of "normal" life, described a future that seemed spread out before him, a time that would never end. The horizon that allows us to expect expectation and that defines ordinary lives is what Ghassan Hage (2009) refers to as "existential mobility," a sense that one is "going somewhere" rather than stuck in the mire of the present. We describe this as a future in which we can expect to have expectations, a future that, as we argue below, may be seen as the description of "ordinary" life, or one that in Times of War is used to signal a Time of Peace.

Exploring Collective Expectation

Conflict zones are often stricken by periods of time that disturb the course of everyday life. These are periods that are popularly understood as a "period" or "time" of negotiations, extended moments when the United Nations and its multiple arms descend, there is a flurry of interest in international media, and whatever peace plan is on the table at that moment is declared to be "the last chance." In Israel-Palestine, notes Julie Peteet, "horrific rounds of violence are interspersed with the periodic 'peace negotiations,' which predictably fail to change the status quo" (Peteet 2017: 205). During these periods, tensions are high, time seems to speed up, and public discussion focuses on the uncertain future. Then when negotiations collapse, as they invariably do, everyone sulks back to their own "side" and goes on with life – at least until the next "last chance."

In Bryant's fieldsite in Cyprus, a Time of Negotiations is one when the pace of political life noticeably quickens, and when debates on television or discussions in cafes are all about what various proposals would mean for the future. In a Time of Negotiations, the future is pulled into the present in the form of hope and possibility, as well as speculation and fear. Predictable parameters are up for discussion, and topics such as returning land to people and people to land create speculation and anticipation regarding possible futures. All of these different ways of orienting oneself to the unknown future in response to various plans can also make a Time of Negotiations highly volatile. Every statement made by a negotiator will be mined for meaning, swinging the public mood from hopeful, to speculative, to anticipatory, especially regarding the potential rekindling of conflict.

"Normalization" is the word that comes up most often to describe what people believe *should* happen after The Solution – the Solution here coming to stand for the threshold that they will cross into a new future free of abnormality. If you ask almost anyone in Cyprus today, they will tell you that the island is not at peace, despite the fact that there has been no armed conflict for forty-four years. This lack of peace, or "no-war-no-peace," is often expressed in public discourse as the abnormality of their situation and the need for normalization. Because that normalization can only be produced through a peace deal, it gives to any negotiations a liminal, and therefore unpredictable, character.

In this section and the next, we tease out such periods when ordinary life seems put on hold for what they tell us about expectation and its suspension. The demand for "normalization" and opining of the abnormality of their situation bears many resemblances to the desire for "normal lives" that has been the subject of a growing ethnographic literature, particularly emerging from post-socialist states (esp. Fehérváry 2002; Greenberg 2011; Jansen 2015). One thread that draws this literature together is the way that "the normal" is imagined as a separate timespace – either a remembered Yugoslav past, or a fantasized timespace of modernity, a European future.

Fehérváry finds this imagination materialized in American kitchens and luxury bathrooms, which stood for a bourgeois, "normal" life "that had long been imagined was being lived elsewhere" (2002: 394). This was contrasted with the perception, which she claims was common through-out the Soviet bloc under socialism, that "everyday life was generally 'abnormal' under conditions of constant material shortages, all-encompassing bureaucratic entanglements, and political anxiety" (ibid., 373). For Jansen and Greenberg, in contrast, the abnormality of the present emerges in contrast to the Yugoslav past, when the state "worked," and Yugoslav passports allowed them to travel easily. Summing up this way in which their informants seemed to "occupy multiple temporalities" and "mobilize latent chronotopes," several ethnographers working on "normal life" in the Balkans refer to the ways in which their interlocutors move between such temporalities to express future-oriented desires (Gilbert et al. 2008: 11).

The desire for "normalization" in Cyprus is a desire to move into a new future, what many describe as a Time of Peace. This imagined new timespace appears to be quite close to Bryant's friend's description of the future as spread out before him and a time that he thought would never end. It is imagined as a change in the "status quo," or the existing state of affairs. Greek Cypriots describe it as the Turkish army leaving, and a rescue from what they view as the continuing threat of violence. Turkish Cypriots, who live in an unrecognized state, use the word *belirsizlik*, or uncertainty, to describe their current condition, suggesting that normalization would bring a future that is predictable, or at least foreseeable.

What the uncertainties of "no-war-no-peace" and the desire for normalization suggest, then, is that "normal lives," or "a Time of Peace," indicate a timespace in which predictability, foreseeability, and expectation are the norm. In a time when the future is stretched out before one, it is possible to expect that one can expect – the expectation that things will continue this way forever. A Time of Peace, then, appears as the expectation of expectation – the foreseeable if open future. In such Times of Peace, all futures seem possible, as the present reaches toward them.

Like the imagined timespace of modernity or the nostalgic timespace of a former Yugoslavia, it hardly needs mention that a Time of Peace is more imagined than real, more hoped for than realized. What it indicates to us, however, is the perceived role of expectation in fashioning "the normal." One *should* be able to expect, one *ought* to be able to expect, e.g., a state that works, a certain standard of living, or that one can pass on property to one's children without legal challenge. One should not be subject to the whims and corruption of bureaucrats, shortages on the market, or negotiations that might overturn all one's investments. In other words, a normal life is one in which one can expect to expect.

The expectation of expectation as ground for the "normal" emerges, for instance, in a burgeoning literature on infrastructure, where the state is materialized through expectations of what a state "does" (e.g., Harvey 2005; Harvey and Knox 2012; Painter 2006). One also sees it in a growing literature on waiting (e.g., Auyero 2012; Crapanzano 1986; Hage 2009; Janeja and Bandak 2018), where the politics of waiting is defined around expectations of who will wait for whom. While one may expect to wait, however, this may not be defined as "normal." Rather, "abnormality" appears to be defined by timespaces in which everyday life requires expecting the unexpected.

One sees this in places such as the West Bank today, where 708 kilometers of reinforced concrete and wire fencing partition the landscape into segments where Israelis speed by on bypass highways that connect seamlessly to the cities, while Palestinians have their own time controlled through checkpoints, military barricades, and truncated roads. What Anne Meneley (2008) has described as "occupation time" and Julie Peteet (2018) calls a Time of Closure is the vernacular timespace constituted by the period since the erection of the Wall, the separation fence that Israel began to construct during the Second Intifada. As numerous scholars have documented, any encounter with the Wall requires waiting, as well as an expectation of arbitrariness (see S. G. Collins 2008; T. Kelly 2008; Meneley 2008). Israeli soldiers may suddenly shut a checkpoint or erect another one. They may arbitrarily hold someone at a checkpoint for hours without explanation.

Checkpoints are sites of potential danger, or simply delay, that require anticipation (Jeganathan 2000, 2003). This may include forms of behavior that are anticipatory but become habitual. It is possible to expect the arbitrary, as in the case of the Palestinian woman described by Meneley who invented "queuing socks" to relieve the stress to her feet caused by hours of waiting (Meneley 2008: 21). In a very different context, when discussing the temporality of modern ideology, Koselleck makes a remark that is relevant to the case of such normality within the scope of the arbitrary: "Modern political terminology is typified by its containment of numerous concepts (*Begriffe*) that are more exactly anticipations (*Vorgriffe*). These concepts are based on the experience of the loss of experience, and so they have to preserve or awaken new expectations" (Koselleck 1985: 263).

Koselleck is concerned with the predominance of "the new" in histories of modernity. He views this as a loss of experience, where the future may always be different from the past. As one commentator remarks, "Under conditions of *Neuzeit* we have need of anticipatory concepts precisely because our expectations are radically underdetermined by our experience" (Kompridis 2006: 265).

Returning to our discussion in the previous chapter, we could also say that Koselleck and commentators are suggesting that while expectation relies on a thickness of the past so that we know *how* to expect, anticipation requires that we recalibrate what parts of the past we will use. It preserves or awakens new expectations, meaning that anticipation can become expectation when the past is again thickened, when we again know how to expect, or when we again expect expectation.

Toby Kelly (2008) describes an arbitrarily erected checkpoint where soldiers, for no discernable reason, would force Palestinians off the road and into sometimes muddy fields, which they would have to cross to rejoin the road past the barricade. While Kelly himself attempted to resist this arbitrary demand, his Palestinian colleagues and friends shrugged and trudged through the muddy fields. Kelly describes this episode as an instance of Palestinian attempts to "go on" and to live ordinary lives in the face of Israeli restrictions, where "[t]he unexpected is therefore never entirely a surprise and the expected is always partly surprising" (T. Kelly 2008: 353).

What Kelly points to, here and elsewhere, is the relationship between the ordinary and extraordinary as it is defined through the expected and unexpected. In the Time of Closure (Peteet 2017, 2018), "Time, like mobility, is a heavily marked category, objectified and subject to calculation and control, on one hand, and uncertainty and loss of control, on the other" (Peteet 2018: 44). Kelly remarks that while in the First Intifada Palestinians resisted this "abnormal" state of affairs by refusing to participate in the activities of "ordinary" or "everyday" life, in the Second Intifada continuing "ordinary life" itself became a form of resistance, but one that required them to expect the unexpected. He remarks, "The unpredictability of the very things that in another context might be taken for granted as the background against which unpredictable events occur … creates a constant speculation on the nature of ordinary life. To paraphrase Stanley Cavell, the ordinary is distinctively uncanny" (T. Kelly 2008: 366).

What Kelly means by the uncanny here, is that the "is" of the everyday does not live up to its "ought" – in other words, the "ordinary" of their own lives did not live up to what they thought the "ordinary" should be. What the ordinary *should* be or *ought* to be, one of his interlocutors told him, was like life in Scandinavia, where "nothing ever happens." "In this sense, ordinariness represented a hope to live in an 'ordinary state', where life was benevolently mundane" (ibid., 365).

In the terms that we have developed here, we could say that the *ought* of the ordinary is the expectation of expectation: being able to await the future, rather than having always to anticipate it. This space of the mundane, where "nothing ever happens" and the expected as expectable, is also that which is familiar, unnoticed, or what Freud referred to as *heimlich*. If the everyday is uncanny or *unheimlich*, then, it is because it is no longer the timespace in which expectation can be assumed. The *unheimlich* "is a kind of limit in, or disruption of, the sphere of the familiar, the usual, the comfortable" (Withy 2009: 5). What Cavell (1988) calls "the uncanniness of the ordinary" is a sudden recognition of the meaninglessness of everything that we value, and all the norms that we hold dear. It is, in that sense, a moment when the ground of expectation is shaken. In what sense, then, can the uncanniness of the ordinary help us to understand the teleoaffective structure of expectation as an orientation, and the vernacular timespaces produced by it?

Losing Expectation

In his now classic work on the failure of modernist teleologies of progress in Zambia, *Expectations of Modernity*, James Ferguson describes how the country experienced first a period of rapid industrialization and urbanization that both Zambians and others described as "progress," only to be followed by a prolonged period described as "decline." "Urbanization," he remarks, "seemed to be a teleological process, a movement toward a known end point that would be nothing less than a Western-style industrial modernity" (1999: 14). As the mining economy in the country expanded, the industry's soot and smokestacks called up images of early British industrialization, "and everyone knew where *that* had led" (ibid.). Expectations, then, were built on analogy, despite the clearly different political and economic conditions of these historical trajectories.

Ferguson's starting point, however, was the sense of despair that accompanied a period of economic decline and IMF-imposed austerity. Mineworkers who could barely feed their families often reminded Ferguson that there had been a time in the not-so-distant past when they were able to eat meat regularly and when the better-off amongst them had even bought cars. "What had been lost with the passing of this era, it seemed, was not simply the material comforts and satisfactions that it provided but the sense of legitimate expectation that had come with them – a certain ethos of hopefulness, self-respect, and optimism that, many seemed sure, was now (like the cars) simply 'gone, gone never to return again'" (ibid., 19).

This narrative of progress and decline is a historical teleology of the sort that Koselleck finds defines the *Neuzeit*, when we do not simply exist in time but are made by time's passage. History moves forward, and we either move with it or are left behind. We would note that unlike our own use of "teleology," which is indeterminate and practice-based, this sense of teleology refers to historical time, to the Time of Modernity. However, this points us to a feature of expectation that is important for us to understand how it may become a communal orientation to the future: expectation appears to be the orientation most amenable to narrative in the mode of historical time. Rooted in what Koselleck calls the space of experience, we expect certain things based on what has come before. Indeed, we may return to Ricoeur, cited earlier, remarking that the two categories of experience and expectation, taken together, "thematize historical time" and that the tension between the two is necessary for history to exist.

However, it is not only that we need the future in order to have a past-present-future relationship, or to have historical time at all, but also that expectation makes the past into a resource, in other words makes it a livable or living past. Arguing that we must resist the temptation to view the past only as what is done and unchangeable, and the future as open and contingent, Ricoeur argues that in fact "these are two faces of one and the same task, for only determinate expectations can have the retroactive effect on the past of revealing it as a living tradition" (1988: 216). We see from Ferguson's example that this may also work by analogous reasoning, where what we expect may be based not on our own, but on others', experiences of the past-present-future relationship. Such teleologies by analogy, then, may be used to create a horizon of expectation in the context of rapid and otherwise unprecedented social change.

It is worth noting that Ferguson describes what he calls "eras" and which we might summarize, in our own terms, as vernacular time-spaces: a Time of Progress and a Time of Decline. Moreover, he notes that the former was defined by what we would call a teleoaffective structure characterized by a "certain ethos of hopefulness, self-respect, and optimism." These teleoaffects were anchored, moreover, in every-day materiality – in the clothes that people wore, the food that they were able to eat, and whether they walked or drove a car.

What we believe this shows us is the way that expectation, when translated into communal terms, often slips between the "ought" of potentiality and the "ought" of promise. We address potentiality in the next chapter. For now, however, it is sufficient to note that the slippage between the two appears to open up the expectations of the everyday to use in larger teleologies. It does this, moreover, because of what we have referred to earlier as the alterity of the future, or the ways in which expectation is always about that which is beyond our control. As Koselleck remarked, "Past and future never coincide, or just as little as an expectation in its entirety can be deduced from experience. Experience once made is as complete as its occasions are past; that which is to be done in the future, which is anticipated in terms of an expectation, is scattered among an infinity of temporal extensions" (Koselleck 1985: 272). Just as we *await* something because it is not (yet) in our grasp, so we *await* the future.

We remarked in the opening paragraph that expectation relies on the familiar anchors of the ordinary. Those anchors are the objects, humans, or nonhuman beings that make up the orders and practices of everyday life. Expectation enables us to make those orders and practices habitual, familiar, and this is what we meant by the "ought" of promise. However, those things that anchor everyday life and, through expectation, become familiar to us are also Other to us: they contain their own potentiality and the possibility of defying our expectations. As a result, expectation always contains an uncertainty, or the possibility of its undoing. This is the uncertainty that had left Elinor with a trace of hope, since in fact she wanted her own expectation to be incorrect. We refer to this capacity of other objects and living beings to bring other possible futures into our present as "temporal dynamism." The term *temporal dynamism* reflects the ways in which the potentialities of others elicit, evoke, or emit other possible futures. Or as Aristotle phrased it, "Everything potential is at the same time a potentiality of contraries" (*Metaphysics*, Book IX, Ch. 8; see Aristotle 1989).

We expect, then, that what is yet to come is still to be made. That is part of what expectation is about. This is also, we suggest, why communal expectation is so often expressed as teleologies of historical time: because they slip between potentiality and promise and give to temporal dynamism the affect of existential mobility.

One sees this, again, so often in its loss, or in moments when the everyday takes on a distinctly uncanny form. If we refer to our earlier discussion of a Time of Negotiations, Bryant's research has shown that the uncertainty of the future in such instances causes the objects and orders of everyday life – houses, property, the state in which one lives – to take on an air of the uncanny (Bryant 2010, 2014). Other futures, based in other explanations of historical time, are projected onto these objects and make them unfamiliar, extraordinary, suddenly subject to potentially being disrupted and overturned. Potential reunification plans would entail the return of houses and property to former owners and one's own or neighbors' displacement. They would entail a new state in which one's own would be reshaped, and the familiar parameters of bureaucracy, politics, and the everyday of "living with the state" would be disrupted. Even more importantly, all of these transitions would entail times of uncertainty and disruption, liminal times when a peaceful outcome was still unclear.

If the expectation of the unexpected is "abnormal," it is also very often perceived as something that will pass. At the communal level, it appears that times of uncertainty – what Knight (2016) has called "temporal vertigo" – are liminal periods of the sort that Koselleck summarized as ones in which we need to turn anticipation into new expectations. Because of the way that communal expectation lends itself to narrativization in the form of historical time, rapid social change, or failure to produce expected change, produce disorientation in the present because of a loss of the future. Psychology has demonstrated that disorientation can be produced by the liminal state of being without a home (Lollar 2010), while in turn the extended experience of "living loss" for the caregivers of AIDS patients (A. Kelly 2008), or age disorientation in Alzheimer's patients (Shomaker 1989), show the association between liminality and extended periods of uncertainty. If we return to our metaphor of anticipation as a threshold, it should not be surprising that what Koselleck describes as the need for new expectations would be lived at the limen, or as extended liminality.

Such extended liminality may in some cases become a "new normal" – the expectation of the unexpected. Quite often, however, it seems to be experienced as extended uncertainty, as a period that should be transitional but instead remains unpredictable. Liminality was used by Arnold Van Gennep (1909) and Victor Turner (1969) to describe the uncertainties and dangers that accompanied periods of transition. In political anthropology, it has been used to describe, for instance, how the transition from the one-party planned economy of the Soviet system to liberal democracy has been troubled in most former Soviet states and where the end point is not certain (e.g., Berdahl 1999; Sakwa 2009; Wydra 2001). While Knight has explored the "vertigo" of living with economic uncertainty, Bryant has examined the extended liminality experienced by citizens of unrecognized states, who are stuck between the political form they once were and the recognized body politic they wish to become. Her Turkish Cypriot interlocutors use the word *belirsizlik*, or uncertainty, to describe their state, their identity, and their quotidian existence.

Moreover, such liminality may give to everyday life an uncanny quality, in the way that everyone else going on with life seems uncanny to someone who has experienced a sudden loss. Uncanniness emerges in the friction between expectation and anticipation, or between the anchors of what we usually describe as "normal life" and the "normalization" of the abnormal.

Conclusion

In his extended rejoinder to Henri Bergson's influential description of time as duration, Gaston Bachelard develops what he calls a "philosophy of repose." "Pure consciousness," he says, "will be revealed as the capacity for waiting and for watchfulness, as the freedom and the will to do nothing" (Bachelard 2016: xii). In particular, he opposes the Bergsonian attribution of continuity to time, arguing instead that a sense of continuity is just that: a *sense* of something, a psychological state that is neither solid nor stable. Continuities "have to be constructed. They have to be maintained" (ibid., 20). Arguing instead that duration is built on discontinuity, Bachelard focuses on duration as an experience of repose, as a metaphor for balance and a synonym for happiness. However, he immediately reverses this explanation to remark, "There is just one snag in all this: no experience is self-sufficient; no temporal experience is really pure" (ibid., 110).

The harmony that we appear to experience, he avers, is actually an illusion of duration produced because it is something that *begins again*. For Bachelard, the prime example is music, the melody of which he describes as a "temporal perfidy" that constantly returns us to beginnings and gives us the sense that we should have predicted where it was going. What creates an illusion of duration in music, he argues, is expectation, which is negative in the sense that we are not aware of expecting. When a phrase repeats itself, "We shall not remember having expected it; we shall simply recognise that we ought to have expected it. Thus, what gives melody its light, free continuity is this wholly virtual expectation which is real only in retrospect" (ibid., 112). Continuity, he remarks, is not within the melodic line itself. "What gives this line consistency is an emotion more vague and viscous than sensation is. Music's action is discontinuous; it is our emotional resonance that gives it continuity" (ibid.).

Using the example of music, Bachelard returns us once more to Austen's description of expectation as promise: "the sanguine expectation of happiness that is happiness itself." The vague, viscous, and virtual sense of expectation is a teleoaffect, he suggests, of which we are aware only when it is realized or not. Just as it may only be in the repetition of a melody that we realize that we expected it, so it may only be in the loss of happiness that we understand that we ever expected it in the first place.

It is in such a sense, then, that expectation may ground the everyday through anchoring us with such "vague and viscous" senses of how things ought to be – the promise of the future tense that becomes a conscious expectation only in the past tense. At a collective level, then, this suggests that unlike vernacular timespaces based in the orientation of anticipation, expectation creates timespaces that are always a promise, always prospective, the never-quite-realized teleologies of our historical time. A Time of Modernity or a Time of Peace, where the expectation of modernity or peace is of something always just on the horizon.

If anticipation showed us, then, how temporality temporalizes, we may say that expectation gives insight into the way that the future futuralizes, creating a horizon in which the expectation of the future is the future itself. It is such a teleoaffect of virtuality, Bachelard suggests, that anchors "normal life."

THREE

Speculation

The age of speculation is truly upon us. Across Europe, a generation born into a world of political union, social liberalism, and economic prosperity have had seriously to reassess their futures owing to the effects of financial crisis, the political turn to the right, and return to ideologies of belonging based on the idea of the nation-state. In the ongoing fiasco following the Brexit referendum, for instance, confusion and speculation have reigned supreme. The decision to leave the European Union made by 51.89 percent of the British public on June 23, 2016 redrew the terms and conditions of collective futures that had previously been tied to a shared pan-European project.

Discussions amongst Remainers following the referendum primarily focused on the struggle to understand one's place in the future, raising questions of national/transnational belonging, multiculturalism, broken promises, and disillusion with decades of believing that relations with Europe were secure, mapped out, and predictable. For many, beliefs in what it meant to be a twenty-first-century Brit had been shredded, with people attempting to grasp what exactly this meant for their own life trajectories in the newly constituted sociopolitical arena. This led to what Knight (2016), drawing on his work in austerity Greece, has described as "temporal vertigo," the befuddled search for direction experienced by people in times of crisis. Confusion and anxiety set in about where people belong in overarching timelines of pasts and futures: if not European, cosmopolitan, multicultural, then what, where, how, do I belong?

In Chapter 1, we discussed the inability to anticipate the future as one that produced an enhanced sense of the presentness of the present, what we called there an "uncanny present" (also Bryant 2016). We briefly illustrated that in such circumstances, pasts may be repurposed in order to give some direction and orientation toward an uncertain future. What, however, of the case in which no pasts seem suitable, where all expectation based on experience has been shattered, and we do not yet know what anchors we may find to allow us to anticipate the next day? Remainers Knight has spoken to feel "dizzy" and "nauseous" after having their present reality, their future plans, shaken to the core. They report feelings of being lost, suspended, or trapped in time, being thrown backwards toward a "premodern," "pre-European" future (Knight 2016: 35, 2017a: 239). In the gap that has emerged from shattered expectations, an inability to anticipate, and a lack of historical anchors, speculation has flourished.

This chapter dwells in the space between expectation and anticipation, the moments, often infinitesimally small, in which worlds of speculation are born. As Frank Kermode (2000: 45–46) writes, "Tick is a humble genius, tock a feeble apocalypse." The space between is not empty but filled with expectation, anticipation, or in the absence of those, with speculation. Speculation fills the fourteen-minute time delay before receiving transmission from Mars that a space-rover has landed safely (Valentine 2018). It is in the moment that you expect to hear the voice of your three-year-old child playing in the next room. It has just gone silent. You start to worry but anticipate that a sound will come soon. It does not. You speculate as to why.

It is in the gap, interval, pause, delay where speculation resides. In the case of Brexit, the ineptitude of the political elite to provide a roadmap to an orderly exit has proved a hotbed for speculation. What will Theresa May say to her counterparts when she goes to Brussels? Will those counterparts snub her? Will they politely toy with her, since they know, and she seems not to know, that they have the upper hand? Media and daily newsfeeds dally in rumor, play on gossip, and build narratives around conjecture.

In order to understand speculation as a futural orientation, we first travel through an emerging branch of philosophy whose proponents have called it speculative realism or speculative materialism.[1] For our purposes, we find it significant that philosophers who have opposed post-Kantian anthropocentrism and have called for an object-oriented ontology have made speculation a primary mode of knowing. Thinking with what Graham Harman (2005, 2010, 2018) and Levi Bryant (2018) call the "withdrawal of objects" and the desire and fantasy that this provokes, we move to a discussion of speculation as a futural orientation based on ontological immanence. Building on this, we then further develop in this chapter the concept of temporal dynamism, mentioned in Chapter 2, which helps us to harness insights from speculative realism to think about how anthropology may approach speculation as a futural orientation. We then return to the Time of Brexit as well as energy futures to ask what we may glean from these for thinking about how ethnographically to study an orientation based on conjecture, as well as how the metaphor of a gap or interval may also transform into a precipice, with its associations of risk, danger, and even thrill.

Some Notes on Speculative Thought

"Mind the gap" is one of those serendipitous everyday phrases that has served well contemporary philosophy's critique of post-Kantian thought. "The gap," as articulated in different ways in Derrida's deconstructionism and in Slavoj Žižek's Lacanian-inspired post-Hegelianism,

---

[1] For primers in speculative philosophy see Siebers 1998, Stäheli 2013, Whitehead 1978.

expresses the inability of the signifier fully to express the signified. As Levi Bryant summarizes,

The point is that in all speech or utterances something *escapes*. When we utter something, we feel as if we never quite articulate what we wish to say. Indeed, we aren't even entirely sure what we wish to say in our own speech. On the other hand, when we hear another person's utterances, we're never quite sure *why* they say what they say. This is the gap that lies at the heart of all discourse.

(2018: loc. 2945; emphases in original)

We find the gap in discourse a fruitful place to begin thinking about speculation. After all, speculation emerges at the point where we ask why a lover or friend said what she said, or even why I said what I said, when actually I wanted or tried to express something else. In Levi Bryant's terms, "Within the Lacanian framework, the fantasy is not so much a wish for something we lack, but is rather an *answer* to the enigma of the Other's desire. Fantasy, we could say, is a hypothesis as to what the Other desires" (ibid., loc. 3147; emphasis in original).

The gap, moreover, is the starting point for critiques of the Cartesian mind-body dichotomy, in that proponents of object-oriented ontology or speculative materialism argue that it is precisely the presumed gap between the Real and human perception of the Real that has tripped up modern philosophy and caused it to confuse epistemology with ontology. Graham Harman, for instance, has asserted that the past two hundred years of philosophy have been obsessed with overcoming the singular gap between humans and the world. Quentin Meillassoux, discussed more in Chapter 6, calls the reasoning that emerges out of this gap "correlationism," or "the idea according to which we only ever have access to the correlation between thinking and being, and never to either term considered apart from the other" (2008: 5).

Harman, Levi Bryant, and others have claimed that the obsession with this gap has given us an ontology of presence, concerned with the ways in which objects appear to us, and with achieving a transcendental perspective from which we can overcome the gap and see all. Instead, they argue for an ontology of withdrawal, one in which all objects are equally impenetrable and equally strange to each other. For ontologies of presence, the withdrawal of objects is accidental or incidental, not a feature of being. An ontology of withdrawal, on the other hand, presents what Harman (2012) calls a "weird realism" and Timothy Morton a "weird essentialism": "According to weird essentialism, things are real but not insofar as they are onto-theologically more real than other things. They are real insofar as they are playful: they lie and tell the truth about themselves at the same time" (Morton 2015: 143).

The "weird" of this realism or essentialism comes from the word's original meaning of "fate" (discussed more in Chapter 6), but also something twisted or turned, often back on itself (ibid). This ontology of withdrawal, of things *not* appearing or making themselves known, may also be viewed as an ontology of immanence, one that treats "all of being as composed of a single flat plane in which *all* beings are subject to withdrawal" (L. Bryant 2018: loc. 4461).

Via immanence, then, we return in a somewhat weird or twisted way to speculation as futural orientation, one that comes to fill the gap between expectation and anticipation. In the first two chapters, we described the future as imminent: either storm clouds approaching or a future that we look out for on the horizon. Speculation, we suggest, by taking us into the realm of the gap, takes us into the realm of the unknown, the withdrawn, the immanent. The gap or interval is the point at which the weirdness of the world, our inability to penetrate and pin it down, leads to conjecture, fantasy, and imaginations of the Other.

We should open a parenthesis here to note that although we find it fruitful to think about speculation through insights from speculative materialism or object-oriented ontology, our own approach distinctly differs from ways that most proponents of the "ontological turn" in anthropology have approached this literature. In fact, we see our approach as much closer to that of speculative realist philosophers themselves, who generally want to keep inquiry into the relation between humans and objects or society and objects but who see such analyses as "regional ontology, not privileged grounds for ontology as such" (L. Bryant 2018: loc. 4810).[2] Hence, while we may sympathize with the project of de-transcendentalizing philosophy, from an ethnographic perspective focused on understanding futural orientations our concern here cannot be with the ontic. The reason for this is that our subject, the future, ultimately concerns human conceptions of the ontic, or how what we understand to be the Real shapes perceptions of the future, and hence temporality. Our concern, then, is with what Levi Bryant called "regional ontology," or in this case the ways in which the weirdness of the world may appear to us at times when the future recedes as a horizon.

In attempting to understand the orientation that is speculation, we find useful Timothy Morton's concept of the "strange stranger," which, in *The Ecological Thought*, he uses initially to describe animals: "Instead of 'animal,' I use *strange stranger*. This stranger isn't just strange. She, or he, or it – can we tell? How? – is strangely strange. Their strangeness itself is strange" (2010: loc. 548). Simmel (1971 [1908]), of course, had famously described the stranger as someone who has general but not specific similarities to us, while he remarks that intimate, erotic relations entail a rejection of the general in the enjoyment of a seeming uniqueness. In contrast, Morton focuses on the uncanniness, the inherent strangeness, that permeates all forms of relation, particularly the most intimate. Writing still of animals, he remarks, "Their strangeness is part of who they are. After all, they might be us. And what could be stranger than what is familiar? As anyone who has a long-term partner can attest,

---

[2] It is also worth remarking that the tendency in the anthropological literature to confuse the ontic with the ontological often makes reading works of the "ontological turn" something of a guessing-game as to whether authors refer to the Real as such or to the philosophy of the Real.

the strangest person is the one you wake up with every morning. Far from gradually erasing strangeness, intimacy heightens it" (2010: loc. 553). For Morton, intimacy produces the strangeness of the uncanny precisely because it is so close and familiar.

Despite the language of discovery in which Morton writes, he is effectively simply pointing out that anything familiar is ultimately strange because of what Freud called the unhomeliness that haunts the homely. Freud gives examples such as seeing one's own back in a mirror to show that it is precisely that which is closest to us that may also be strange to us in a way that is disturbing. Morton surely does not suggest that "strange strangers" are always strange to us, but rather that they become so at particular moments. Heidegger, for instance, had called the intimate places and objects of our daily lives the "ready-to-hand," things that recede from consciousness because they exist for us as part of the totality of our involvements in the world. He had also stressed, however, that the objects of daily life may become uncanny in moments of angst, when everyday certainties are dislodged, and, as a result, the world around us appears unfamiliar (Heidegger 1996: 188–190; on temporal sequence and objects see Kubler 1962).

In terms of futural orientations, we may say that uncanniness and the speculation that it breeds arise in moments when the familiarity of expectation is shattered. This should not be surprising if we return to our description in Chapter 2 of the way that expectation always contains the possibility that what we expect may not, in fact, happen. Like a promise that may be broken, so expectation may not turn out as we expect, and instead we may be met with surprise. Derrida (1997: 2) asserts that it is surprise, moreover, that creates "the eventness of the event." We suggest in that chapter, however, that it is the very possibility of the unexpected occurring that makes expectation the orientation that gives us the futurality of the future. After all, if all expectations can only be fulfilled, and cannot ever not be fulfilled, that would already make them actual, and hence part of the present or past.

In practice, however, we see the ways that we hold at bay the possibility of what we expect not occurring, allowing the world to be "ready-to-hand." The process of acculturating ourselves to particular expectations is a matter of socialization, maturation, and habit – in other words, making the world go on. However, we could say that the ready-to-hand, the process of making the unfamiliar familiar and masking the potential for the unexpected, disguises the ultimate alterity of objects. Indeed, what is most familiar to us always harbors the uncanny, argues Dylan Trigg (2012), because it masks what he calls the "dark entity" beneath it, namely, the fundamental indifference of the world to us.

The uncanny present that we described in Chapter 1 emerges in times when anticipation is blocked and when the sense of presentness that we do not usually experience is unmasked, becoming what Morton would call a "strange stranger" to us. This state produces anxiety, what Trigg, in a discussion of Heidegger, describes as "the sliding away of things which enforces the gradual recess of the unity of being from where we find ourselves stranded in a disembodied, and so placeless, sphere of groundlessness" (2006: 6). For Heidegger, we *hover* in anxiety (ibid.). Although Heidegger's anxiety was one of existential crisis, we do not have to return to a metaphysics of Being to take from this the fundamental link between the receding of the world, uncanniness, and anxiety.

Just as the gap in discourse is covered over in everyday life, so the gap between expectation and its realization that hides the "dark entity" of expectation's opposite remains for the most part unseen as we produce the present through expectations of the future. When those expectations are shattered and the present becomes uncanny, however, the gap emerges as a fruitful site for speculation. Paraphrasing Levi Bryant, we might say that speculation as a futural orientation becomes an answer to the enigma of the future as Other.

The Speculator and the Uncanny Present, or, How to Fill a Gap

In the mid-nineteenth century, there were few men as well known in the USA as William Thompson, a figure who sometimes went by other names but who inspired the label "confidence man." The swindle for which he became famous has resonances with present-day emails from Nigeria or the scandals of Wall Street. But whereas the latter play on baser instincts – the desire for an easy and quick million or two – the nineteenth-century swindle was one in which the original "confidence man" played on the desire to demonstrate good will. In the hustle, Thompson would casually strike up a conversation with a stranger in a park or cafe, eventually bringing the conversation to the subject of the lack of confidence and trust in fellow humans so rife at the time. If his interlocutor protested and expressed faith in fellow humans, Thompson would ask for a "demonstration of confidence" in the form of entrusting a watch or wallet to him until the next day. He would, of course, abscond with said item.

The confidence man emerged in the aftermath of the Panic of 1837, which itself was largely the result of speculative lending practices in the Western states and a consequent adjustment of interest rates. The editor of *The New York Herald*, James Gordon Bennett, however, also saw how the crisis had been intentionally precipitated by the Bank of the United States, which had lost its charter as the nation's central bank under Andrew Jackson. One commentator remarks that as the crisis got worse and worse, Bennett noticed how all sides of the conflict pleaded with each other to "restore confidence" (Seybold 2018). When, a bit over a decade later, William Thompson came to Bennett's attention, he wrote an editorial entitled "The Confidence Man on a Large Scale," in which he compared the confidence game to Wall Street speculation and asserted that if only Thompson had practiced his game in finance, he would have been a wealthy man. As one article that compares this period to the 2008 crisis describes, "It is the speculator and the stockbroker, Bennett argued, who are most 'occupied by this process of "confidence"', and who are therefore the 'real' confidence-men" (ibid.).

Indeed, in his history of fraud and scams in the nineteenth century, Michael Pettit argues for a history of deception that unravels what people consider to be deception at a given time. Pettit emphasizes the association made in the nineteenth century between fraudsters and capitalists:

Not only were corrupt political officials identified with swindlers, but practices of the marginal confidence man and the methods of captains of industry also became increasingly difficult to distinguish. For a number of their contemporaries, the capitalist enterprise writ large, especially in the form of the stock market and futures trading, operated like a kind of confidence game that threatened the political order.

(Pettit 2013: 44)

Giving the example of the ways in which the construction of America's railroad network depended on defrauding small investors (White 2003), Pettit remarks that what made deception different in the Gilded Age were new communication technologies like the telegraph and the availability of cheap newspapers in the age of yellow journalism. We would add that the availability of mass transport, such as steamboats and railways, made those the sites of many fictional descriptions of confidence games in the period.

The confidence man, then, was a nineteenth-century type, described by Mark Twain and Herman Melville, but one who fits into an array of such types in the period. He is often described as particularly American, his difference from ordinary thieves or hustlers being the ways in which he gains the trust or confidence of his prey, usually through incredible self-confidence. One commentator described him as representing the various types of mobility that characterized America in the period: "As a wanderer, the confidence man was eternally self-aggrandizing. Blessed with superior wit, skill in the use of resources, adaptability and enthusiasm, he was a one-man enterprise. . . . In the theoretically fluid, open social world of the Age of Jackson, the trickster emerged as the archetypal American because the trickster represented man-on-the-make" (Pierson 1962, quoted in Wyllie 2016: 4). However, this "man-on-the-make" also relied, as we noted before, on new developments, such as communication and transport, that were making their effects felt across the world, perhaps most strongly in Europe.

Indeed, we see from literature and other sources that Europe was also rife with such shape-shifting characters. The novels of Dostoevsky and Gogol show that in Russia of the period there was considerable concern over social upheaval and the capacity of certain persons to "trick" the masses.[3] In the Ottoman Empire, there were numerous figures who slipped in and out of roles, including, perhaps most famously, Friederick Milligen, also known in Istanbul as Kıbrıslızade Binbaşı Osman Bey, and in Russia as Vladimir Andrejevich, the adopted son of a grand vizier and author of several works that he called anthropology. We also know from the novels of Dickens and Thackeray that the swindler, hustler, or confidence man (or woman) could cross continents and use the British Empire as a stage. Thackeray's most famous character, Becky Sharp, for instance, engages in a shape-shifting that seemed to define the age:

Observing what was happening around him – the old morality breaking down, the inherited social forms in disarray, and the world changing almost too rapidly to describe – Thackeray presents us, in Becky Sharp, with a totally free soul. She is breaking loose to try an existence in tune with the caprices of fortune. No wonder she dominates the novel imaginatively and seems to "get away" from her creator.

(Henkle 1980: 89)

---

[3] As one commentator notes, trickster figures were also both widespread and wildly popular in the early Soviet period, showing that the "role of the real, not the fictive, center belong[ed] not to the ruler or the bureaucrat, but to the trickster – the artist and the philosopher of manipulation" (Lipovetsky 2011: 123).

If, as Bear *et al.* assert, speculation is "the making present and materi-alizing of uncertain futures" (2015: 387), then there could be no one so adept at this as Thackeray's Becky, a trickster for her times.

Indeed, in the recently emerging anthropological literature on spec-ulation, it is surprising that so little has been made of this obvious historical, and also contemporary, association of the speculator and the confidence man. In her work on what she calls "populist specula-tors," Laura Bear has described a conversational style that is highly reminiscent of the working methods of William Thompson:

> [F]rom my first meetings with them they confided secrets; revealed previous mistakes; unveiled what they claimed to be the real forces at work behind the scenes; and mooted potential schemes. At the same time they suggested that they should not be disclosing information in this way since they worked for a highly secretive bureaucracy. Later I realized that they had the same manner with all the clients that entered their offices.
>
> (Bear 2015a: 414)

What, indeed, seems better designed to gain confidence than presumed confession, and a conversational style that draws one into the scheme?

Such figures emerge, it seems, at moments of heightened liminality. Mikhail Bakhtin (1984) had, of course, long ago noted that tricksters emerge in moments of communal transition, liminal periods such as what those who experienced it perceived as such during the mid-nineteenth century. Arguably, the difference with actual states of limin-ality is that the rites of passage on which the theory is based presumably have a known end point, whereas, as we have tried to point out, spec-ulation emerges where the end point is not clear: "Speculation fuels, and is fueled by, a heightened state of anticipation in which routes of calculation are often suspended" (Bear *et al.* 2015: 388).

We see this in the Time of Brexit, when some people's authorship, ownership, of the future was rudely repossessed in a single referendum. A once unyielding version of Britain's future is now past, or at least on hold: a future tied to a particular kind of European cosmopolitanism, involving closer cultural integration, freedom of work and movement, tariffless trade, and imaginaries of boundless socioeconomic prosperity (Knight 2017a: 238). Knight's discussions with Remainers highlighted new anxieties and expectations, with people feeling that their futures were being held "hostage" or "in suspension." On the one hand, they questioned their past beliefs about the cosmopolitan project; on the other, they tried to predict scenarios for life outside the European Union.

As Britain attempts to negotiate a deal with the European Union post-referendum, a public once split between euphoric hope and dejected resignation now share in speculation about paths to the future. The lack of firm policy and the abounding rhetoric on all sides stoke the fires of speculation: what will happen with the Irish border? European Union citizens working in the United Kingdom? Tariff-free trade? Or, perhaps more pertinently to the majority of the populace, will the average Brit require a visa to vacation in Ibiza? And what will happen to all those European Premier League soccer stars? It is striking that in the halls of Westminster and Brussels, the future is up for grabs in a way not seen since the divvying-up of the continent after World War II, and speculation about all aspects of post-Brexit life covers the pages of newspapers and internet forums daily.

Some of this speculation is in the form of conjecture, the type of speculation that may also be made about the past. We might speculate as to why a decision was made, how a certain course of action was preferred to another, and what the resulting alternate set of circumstances and consequences might have looked like had we done something differently. There is speculation about what a person was thinking at a particular time or while partaking in a certain conversation – "we can only speculate about her motives." In speculating about the past of Brexit, its seeds may be said to have sprouted from initial reluctance to join the European Community in the 1970s or refusal to sign up to the European single currency at the turn of the millennium.

It is this meaning of speculation as conjecture that can also be applied to the present or past that makes "confidence" such an important term for marking out speculation as a futural orientation. Even as we write, Prime Minister Theresa May is faced with a potential no-confidence vote if she does not enact a plan to leave the EU customs union. May had already gambled on confidence in a snap parliamentary election in summer 2017, when her party lost votes, and she subsequently squeaked by a confidence vote with a narrow margin based on bargaining on other issues. In the UK system, a prime minister may be faced with a no-confidence vote specifically in the House of Commons, and so the PM must retain their confidence in her effective leadership.

Confidence, then, appears key to staving off the anxiety of uncertainty that comes with speculation. As one commentator remarked, "Confidence is what makes you continue to bet on black, even when you know you will inevitably see red. It spurs an irrational appetite for risk-taking. The 'state of confidence' aggregates many highly subjective and often only semi-conscious projections of the future" (Seybold 2018).

The phrase "state of confidence" is taken from John Maynard Keynes, for whom, as Seybold remarks, simple rational calculation could not make the economy turn, because in that case no one would take risks. Rather, a "state of confidence" was necessary, in which we assume that a state of affairs will continue, even though our experience tells us that it probably won't. What is particularly interesting for us about this word, confidence, is the way that it "stands, simultaneously, as a synonym for certainty and uncertainty" (ibid.). Like Bear's populist speculators, the confidence man is the one who creates "confidence" through presumed access to information and by himself displaying confidence.

The confidence man, then, claims to have particular knowledge of or access to the unseen, the "real forces at work behind the scenes" (Bear 2015a: 414). In this sense, confidence men not only display confidence or arouse it, but they also play on the other meaning of confidence as something that we confide. The confidence is also a secret, something that should be kept hidden. And it is in this way that we return to the ontology of withdrawal, and to the ways in which speculation relies upon these many meanings of confidence. And while speculation is always with us – we always speculate about why someone is late, or who will get a particular award – the trickster figure who is the confidence man or popularist speculator appears to emerge in periods of rapid social change and crisis. The vernacular timespace characterized by an uncanny present appears to be a moment particularly ripe for the emergence of persons who claim access to the unseen.

In the next section, we suggest that this unseen is not simply a good tip on the market; rather, it is a tip that opens up an array of other possible, hitherto unseen futures. We build in the next section on the claims of object-oriented ontology, based on an ontology of withdrawal, that humans and animals, as well, should be treated as objects insofar as they are also subject to withdrawal. We harness these claims to thinking through what Bryant (2014) elsewhere describes as objects' temporal alterity, or the ways in which objects are temporally other to us. We use that concept here to think in the larger scale, about how, in particular times of communal crisis or anxiety – the Time of Brexit, the Time of the Greek Crisis – we may come to imagine other temporalities through the hidden temporal power of objects.

The Temporal Dynamism of Energy

Between 2009 and 2011 three natural gas fields were discovered in the Eastern Mediterranean. Named Tamar, Leviathan, and Aphrodite, the revelation that 122 trillion cubic feet (tcf) of untouched reserves were just waiting to be tapped sparked intense political debate between Cyprus, Greece, and Israel, and later Egypt and Lebanon, over ownership and extraction rights. Cyprus and Israel were quick to commence negotiations, establishing an exclusive economic zone (EEZ) in 2010 that, in a bid to reduce costs, included a joint agreement on the extraction of natural gas by the American company Noble Energy. Europe requires 19 tcf of fuel per annum; Cyprus believes that its EEZ holds 60 tcf. Several factors point to oil and gas reserves, such as the discovery of thermogenic natural gas, working hydrocarbon systems, and the identification of fourteen hydrocarbon plays in the Cyprus EEZ alone. Licensing for the exploration blocks is expected to start at around 80 million euros per drillship. Suffice to say, Greece felt left out of the fun and games.

Amidst the political bickering and points-scoring that has marked the so-called Greek economic crisis that has raged since 2010, the Greek government lost sight of the potential of a major gas field on its doorstep. Only in 2013 did Greece sign a memorandum of understanding and in 2015 broker a deal to export gas to Europe. This was despite much public speculation about the potential benefit of natural resource extraction for the Greek public in the grips of chronic austerity. A news broadcast in late 2012 bemoaned the lethargic reaction of the Greek government in allowing Cyprus and Israel to get a head start on a matter that "might be the answer" to the financial problems of the Greek state. Their government, argued the presenter, was too interested in fighting amongst itself and its politicians focused on holding onto their seats in parliament. Rather, a longer-term view should be adopted to serve the future of the country. Cyprus, the audience was told, had the luxury of a consistent energy policy that was passed from one administration to the next. In Greece, with the (regular) change of government came a change in energy policy. It was back to the drawing board every two or three years as a new party swept to power. Greece was also painted as being under the illusion that it was the political powerhouse in the region and could broker a deal on its own terms whenever it wanted.

Amongst the general public there was an air of excitement, tinged with frustration and myriad conspiracy theories. Rumors, myths, and hyperbole concerning the extent of the discovery and the potential financial benefits of exporting energy reigned supreme in cafeterias across the country. Speculation as expressed through rumor and gossip, Stavroula Pipyrou (2018) argues, is a leisure activity that punctuates even the most morbid or anxious domain. Distorting the real proportion of information is a key aspect of speculation, often expressing concerns about power discrepancies in the community (Kroeger 2003; Pipyrou 2018: 255). Playing on well-established stereotypes, distortion, and hyperbole allows heightened visibility of crucial points of the story, including its origins, motivations, and responses. Rumor, as a vessel of active speculation, continually disassembles, evaluates, and reconstitutes the everyday world (Rapport 1998: 267). Participating in gossip feeds fantasies and conspiracy theories and as such should be considered as a form of communication about the future through which people in an ambiguous situation attempt to construct a meaningful interpretation by pooling their conversational resources (Pipyrou 2018: 255).

Since 2011, the Eastern Mediterranean energy field has been one of the main topics of conversation between Knight and his research participant, Vasilis, a sixty-five-year-old retired salesman from Central Greece. When he first learned of the potential gas fields, Vasilis felt that this was a great opportunity for Greece to become a major player in the European energy industry. He thought that the discovery might signal a way out of the financial quagmire, certainly on a national level, and that perhaps some benefits might even filter down to the everyday person, at least in the form of employment and cheaper energy bills. His son had just qualified as an engineer and Vasilis had dreams of him working the rigs and providing for his cash-strapped family. In the apparent emptiness of the present (see Dzenovska 2018a), with not much left to hope for – Vasilis had recently had his pension cut by 33 percent and both his children were unemployed – his mind was racing.

Over the years, Vasilis's optimism has turned from disbelief, to disillusion, to apathy. He has since started speculating as to why political consensus has not been reached and drilling has not started. In what could be classed as conspiracy theories, Vasilis believes that the USA and Israel will corner the market for energy extraction in the Mediterranean in an attempt to keep the Greek people in poverty, "in the same way that the United States broke up the Balkans into small countries – to have more markets to sell their McDonald's and Budweiser and keep the local people poor." He states that "our politicians could make this country rich by agreeing a contract to drill for gas and oil, but they are in this together with the Americans and the Jews. They [the Greek government] are as corrupt as the foreigners."[4] Vasilis is proud of what he terms "Greek natural riches," a category which includes the golden beaches, turquoise seas, famous cuisine, and now a major energy reserve. But his initial excitement which provoked him to dream of a better life for his family has now firmly turned to resignation that international power-games are set to conspire against the Greek people. His speculative future has collapsed, and he has shifted from the optimism of dreaming for a better future for family and nation, to cynicism and conspiracy about the colonization of the future by corporations and subversive political forces. Vasilis believes that this is a deliberate attempt by his own government and external forces to promote cynicism about the future and keep the population under control by making resignation "a dominant mode of political action" (Benson and Kirsch 2010: 474). His visions of a prosperous future based on the fruits of the energy industry may never come to fruition as he had once projected, but it still holds potential – evidenced by the physical existence of natural

---

[4] On tactics of blame and accountability in Greece, see, for example, Knight (2013) and Brown and Theodossopoulos (2003). For a recent example of conspiracy theories surrounding perceived Jewish involvement in the economic crisis, see Rakopoulos (2018).

gas under the Mediterranean Sea. Yet, for Vasilis, this potential was no longer a topic on which to speculate.

Knight has written at length on how the energy industry has been hailed as the savior of the Greek economy (Argenti and Knight 2015; Knight 2017b). Public speculation on the benefits of new energy initiatives has been quick to turn to narratives of economic extraction, neocolonialism and the punitive impact of excessive private investment on local communities. The complex and rapidly expanding vernacular timespace of the Greek crisis has notions of colonialism, occupation, and international conspiracies of blame at its very heart. In this epoch, energy has been at the forefront of two forms of speculation: public conjecture on an industry that might save Greece from the economic abyss, and speculative investment in the energy sector by multinational corporations, who often secure contracts at bargain prices. Here we wish to dwell a moment on the rhetorics surrounding renewable energy initiatives in austerity Greece, as the case helps emphasize the duel-aspect speculation at play in energy futures.

Originally initiatives aimed at repaying national debt and decreasing fiscal deficit through energy export to northern Europe, from 2011 there has been a remarkable surge in photovoltaic (solar) parks placed on agricultural land in central Greece and wind farms constructed in the Aegean Islands. Renewable energy developments provide a stable monthly income for disenfranchised farmers through feed-in tariffs and have presented new employment opportunities for local mechanics and salespeople who have diversified into the green economy sector. The movement toward the green economy has been hijacked by multinational corporations taking advantage of austerity-era policy that encourages a repetition of the same neoliberal model of privatization, short-term accumulation, rentier agreements, and resource extraction symptomatic of the relationship between the West and the new Global South (Knight 2017c; on morality and affect in neoliberalism see Muehlebach 2012; Muehlebach and Shoshan 2012). The appropriation of land and resources for food or fuel under the banner of sustainability and environmentalism has been termed "green grabbing," where "green" credentials are a façade for exploitative extractive practices (Leach 2012).

What is clear is that renewable energy infrastructures represent for most Greeks more than a promise of prosperity; they also represent futures that unfold in the space of the temporality of fuel. Although heralded by the Greek state and European Union as the future for year-round energy self-sufficiency, in fact renewables rarely generate enough energy even to serve local communities. As a result, as evening draws in on any cold winter day, thick smog descends over towns all over Greece as people light their open fires and woodburning stoves. Two seemingly contrasting energy sources – high-tech photovoltaic panels and open woodburning fires – have become local symbols of the livelihood changes brought about by economic crisis. Knight's research participants associate photovoltaics with clean green energy, futuristic sustainability, groundbreaking technology, ultra-modernity, and international political energy consensus. Open fires conjure images of premodern unsustainability, pollution, and extreme poverty. They report being transported back in time to another era of existence (Knight 2017b).

Contrasting energy solutions have provoked people to speculate about their temporal trajectories: are they part of a prosperous European future or destined to "go back in time" to some archaic premodernity? For people in Greece, the prominence of contrasting energy paraphernalia offering alternative versions of the future prompts them to rethink their worldview. One research participant, Sotiris, says that "the paradoxes of current energy technologies" with their intermingling allusions to a high-tech future and a low-tech past make people "reconceptualize their place in space and time ... do we belong to a modern Europe ... are we in the same time as Germany and France?"

In the context of São Tomé and Príncipe, off the coast of West Africa, Gisa Weszkalnys (2015) discusses the grassroots impact of oil speculation, where locals are quite literally building for a future that may never exist. Rumors over the supposed presence of an oilfield off the coast of the small islands sparked investment in infrastructure – roads, resorts, hotels for oil workers, website domains – that have since lain dormant for nearly two decades. The social and economic consequences of investing in speculative futures have drained the islands not only financially but also emotionally, as stories of dry wells that harbor "no oil" continue to be transformed in public rhetoric to "no oil yet" (ibid., 630). At a time when the Gulf of Guinea was consolidated as Africa's petroleum frontier and global oil prices peaked, there was much bafflement that São Tomé and Príncipe's oil exploration had not taken off as initially expected. Rather than asking why there is no oil, Weszkalnys queries the persistent notion that there might be, one day, if we wait long enough.

For Weszkalnys (2015: 621), "speculation about resource potential thrives at historical junctures characterized by the foreclosing of previous material possibilities while it opens others alongside new markets." Speculation comprises "a tangle of things," major socioeconomic events like financial crises, ideological struggles, technological innovation, and human actors sensing new commercial opportunities. The timespace for oil in São Tomé and Príncipe should be marked by emptiness. Move on. A barren desert. Next future please. But somehow expectations about plundering probably nonexistent potential persist.

As an observation of potentiality, speculation offers a mode of participation, based on games of risk and chance, in hypothetical futures. The creative contemplation of possibility is part of the temporal disposition inherent in speculation, which suspends the need for certitude in the desire for disproportionate gain (Weszkalnys 2015: 623). Oil exploration is based on speculative knowledge of indeterminate potential – knowledge that is incomplete, based on uncertain and partially obscured evidence, that occasionally makes "less than rational connections between means and ends" (Comaroff and Comaroff 2000: 310). It is an industry truth that oil reserves are composites of economic probabilities, technological feasibilities, and geological potentials: a complex assemblage of interwoven agencies. As outlined in the Greek case above, speculation in the energy sector is manifold, for along with societal wondering and political rhetorizing, corporate investment in oil is also speculative. For both the local people and the hard-nosed investor, speculation can be retrospectively justified based on profitability. This plays into the game of risk and chance-taking for investors and local residents alike. Risk is calculated from fuzzy lines on graphs and scientific ponderings not fit for publication (Weszkalnys 2015: 625).

On Saõ Tomé and Príncipe and in Greece, the energy sector is immersed in future-oriented speculative investment, often fueled by rumor and conspiracy theory. Local people and corporations buy into indeterminate futures – indeterminate both in terms of materiality and in terms of temporal distance. Nobody knows precisely what will be found (if anything); what the eventual social and economic benefits might be (if any); and when potentiality will be turned into actuality (if at all). A similarity in the two cases is that locals feel that they have very little to lose in pinning their hopes of future prosperity on shaky scientific evidence and/or political promises, for in both contexts economic crisis has been raging for years. The "Time of Oil" has been with us since at least the first Gulf War, and now a new extractive economy has joined the party in the shape of renewables, offering promises of futures filled with vast riches, but this time also accompanied by green morality. And it seems that people are queueing up to invest.

Speculation about natural resources by definition concerns what is hidden, buried, immanent, or potential. While solar power concerns a potential to be harnessed, oil and gas concern what is buried deep in the ground or disguised by the vast unknown that is the sea. Potentiality is the subject of our next chapter, but for now we can note that natural resources, like other objects, acquire a power to reshape the future not only because of the riches, hidden like a buried treasure, but also because, as we remarked in the previous chapter, objects have different "lifespans" from the human and so elicit other possible futures. While the solar energy studied by Knight is associated with technology and ultra-modernity, speculation in gas and oil connote geological time, a time incomparable to the human.

In this sense, objects, including natural resources, point to the possible, the potential, or the eventual in ways that may overlap with but do not necessarily correspond to what we know or experience as past, present, and future. We refer to this capacity of objects to bring other possible futures into our present as "temporal dynamism." In thinking about this capacity of objects, it is helpful to return to Aristotle's distinction between form as actuality and matter as potentiality (cf. Marx 1978: 143; also Althusser 1970; Harris 2009). Whereas the physical (form, actuality) appears to fix the object as a product and representative of a particular time, the material and its potentiality suggest that the object is always within time, always yet to be made. This is a distinction to which we return in the next chapter, for potentiality has been a much-debated subject in object-oriented ontology.

For now, we may note that potentiality becomes an important realm for speculation not because of form but because of matter – in the case of oil still to be found, not in the form of a few trickles that one may extract, but because of how these few trickles point us to potential. This is a potential that is both an inherent quality of oil and a facet of our relationship with it. In other words, oil does not realize its potential unless someone extracts it.

In many cases, then, we speculate on the realization of potential, bringing potentiality into actuality. That realization relies both on the materiality of the object – the geological conditions and span of time that it takes for oil to be created – and the conditions that would bring its extraction about. However, the way that speculation occurs around the hidden or "withdrawn" qualities of objects – those aspects that are not ordinarily available to us – means that when we speculate, we rely on information that is partial, conjectural, confidential. This also means that speculation often tips over into deception, or fears of it. If the prototypical figure of the speculator is the confidence man, we should keep in mind the observation, quoted above, that confidence "stands, simultaneously, as a synonym for certainty and uncertainty." It is that thin line between certainty and uncertainty contained in "confidence" that so often makes speculation a type of self-deception about possible futures.

Speculation/Deception

In his brilliant rereading of the emergence of psychology in early-twentieth-century America, Michael Pettit asks, "How did psychology take root in a culture fascinated by robber barons and confidence men, national brands and their counterfeit, yellow journalism and muckraking exposes?" (2013: 3). His answer takes us on a complicated journey through the emergence of mass consumption and the accompanying "deceptive landscape of modern life" (ibid., 8). Psychology offered ways to navigate this landscape that "ranged from self-help manuals for overcoming charlatans, scales for detecting the likelihood of trademark infringement, machines to detect liars, and therapeutic techniques to reveal self-deceptions. These interventions did not eliminate deception from the public sphere or private life but were instead predicated on acceptance of its existence" (ibid.).

Pettit traces the emergence of public deceptions to 1834, when P. T. Barnum began his career as a showman through the "artful manipulation of uncertainty" (ibid., 10) – uncertainty about whether or not the dubious persons or animals on display were "real" or concocted. Pettit links these dubious displays requiring faith or confidence on the part of the observer to the rise of confidence men, swindlers, and marketplace speculators at the end of the century. "From the late nineteenth to the early twentieth century," he notes, "the scientific study of potentially deceitful persons and deceptive things became closely linked to ways of being in, and governing, the marketplace" (ibid., 13).

The early twenty-first century seems to return us to a period rife with fears of deception. If P. T. Barnum and William Thompson defined an age of hucksters, charlatans, and confidence men, Nigel Farage and Donald Trump appear as the confidence men of our time. Gregarious and self-aggrandizing, they inspire "confidence" – a confidence which, in turn, finds its dark double in "fake news." In a technique perfected by P. T. Barnum, the label "fake news," as employed by Trump and his followers, refers to the sort of expert opinion or reporting that does not reflect the "reality" that can only be revealed speculatively.

Indeed, in an age of easy deception through trolls and vines on the Internet, we seem to have returned to the time of P. T. Barnum's early deceptions. As described by Pettit, Barnum's beginnings were his exhibition of a woman named Joice Heth, who claimed to have been George Washington's nanny. Barnum inspired confidence in her story first by questioning her legitimacy, then by declaring her genuine and asking the public to pay for tickets in order to decide for themselves. Moreover, Barnum's "artful manipulation of the uncertainty surrounding her authenticity" depended on "societal norms that placed relatively little value on the final authority of experts" (Pettit 2013: 10). It is certainly tempting to find in Barnum's techniques a predecessor of our current political climate.

What is particularly significant about the story Pettit tells of the period, however, is the way that he weaves developing sciences of psychology and criminology into a tale of deception and attempts to find certainty. In this tale, it is never entirely clear who is deceiving and who is deceived, just as in the age of the Internet persons who eschew mainstream media outlets in favor of sites that tell the "real" story may be both deceived and deceivers. Moreover, in order to overcome potential deception, psychologists, Pettit observes, "crafted an episte-mology particularly suited for the human sciences, the ideal of 'the unobserved but observing observer'" (ibid., 233). This was not a "'view from nowhere' but rather the perspective of a hidden or disguised undercover sleuth" (ibid.). Like a detective, the social scientist could often be ruthless in pursuit of truth, including deceiving those who would potentially deceive, or withhold information.

This story of Barnum, Trump, and the early social sciences returns us, then, to post-Kantian philosophy, which, as Meillassoux and others note, was intended to shore up knowledge against potentially deceitful representation. Speculation emerges in the gap between representation and certainty, the point where expectations prove futile and anticipation misleads. Confidence and deceit are two sides of the same speculative coin, because just as deceit blurs the distinction between deceiver and deceived, so confidence implies both certainty and uncertainty, both self-assurance and a secret entrusted. In communal terms, we have argued, these many meanings of speculation emerge in the gap between anticipation and expectation.

Conclusion

This chapter has taken us into the gap, interval, or pause between expectation and anticipation, the moment filled with conjecture, fan-tasy, and imagination between the time a spouse is late coming home and the sound of the key in the door. Speculation takes us down alternative temporal routes, other possible futures that may also be anticipatory. What if he was in an accident? We anticipate whom we will call. What if he's gone out with friends without telling us? We think about the argument that we could potentially have, and whether or not it would produce an effect.

At a communal level, we have suggested that speculation flourishes in moments of transition perceived as crisis, moments when expectations are shattered and the present becomes uncanny because we seem stuck in it, unable to anticipate the next day. The Time of Brexit is a good example of the teleoaffect of speculation produced when expected futures are truncated and other futures not yet imaginable. The projects, actions, and ends which it is now acceptable to pursue have changed. A range of discourses on immigration, nationalism, and sovereignty have come to the fore in public debate, and leaving the European Union is now a goal toward which the British government is headed. As a result, *something* has changed; as an epoch of affective time, Brexit Britain undoubtedly *feels* different than before.

Such moments when, as Heidegger put it, we hover in anxiety are ones when the ready-to-hand becomes uncanny to us, or when many aspects of our lives that had seemed familiar become what Timothy Morton calls "strange strangers." Suddenly, entities that are otherwise withdrawn reveal what Trigg calls the "dark entity" beneath them. We see that whatever our expectations, we've always known that things could be otherwise. In the moment of uncanniness, however, the "otherwise" becomes a source for conjecture and speculation on what will happen now.

Turning speculation into a productive futural orientation requires what John Maynard Keynes called a "state of confidence." However, as we know, confidence itself, like expectation, already contains its opposite. Moreover, "confidence" also refers to the confidential, the secret, or hidden. In such periods of anxiety, tricksters emerge, persons who know things that others don't know, persons who win our confidence. However, that confidence may also tip from speculation into deception, from positive potentiality into negative actuality.

In order to understand this better, we turn in the next chapter to the potential, and to the metaphor of being "pregnant with the future." What does it mean for our orientations to the future to find certain futures always immanent within us?

FOUR

Potentiality

In potential is where futurity combines, unmediated, with pastness, where outsides are infolded and sadness is happy.

Massumi 2002: 30

In the early hours of a mild mid-1980s spring morning somewhere in the south of England, a child was born. Let's call him David. Raised on the edge of a council estate, David excelled at school, regularly topping his class in history, geography, math, and the sciences. His English language and literature grades can best be described as "could do better." At the age of ten he was advised by teachers and family to decline a scholarship to a private educational institution to instead attend the local comprehensive secondary school, a place with a reputation as one of the worst performing in the region. It was then on a government watch list, and the headmaster had just resigned after suffering a nervous breakdown. Two weeks previously, his prized second-hand Ford Cortina had been set alight. But at least, David was reminded, the school was only a short walk around the corner on a bleak, damp, blustery English winter's day.

David was told from an early age that ambition, aspiration, and motivation were optional. The future would take care of itself, no matter where he was educated. Aim low, and you won't be disappointed. Perhaps that was right. Most students who attended the prestigious private school, his teacher suggested, would only end up in dead-end jobs anyway – and why would he want to get lost in a cohort with people who "were not really his type?" They played cricket and lacrosse, not soccer.

At the age of fourteen David visited the school careers advisor. What would become of him? The advisor flicked through his grades and asked him about his interests, passions, goals in life, then seemingly disregarded all and sat him in front of a whirring machine. A computer program would suggest his potential path. He entered: name, birthday, hobbies, lesson grades.

Parents' education: secondary level (left school aged 16)
Parents' employment: Father an unskilled laborer; Mother a shop assistant
Postcode: XX2 6XX
Computing, please wait . . .
Result. Your perfect job for life would be: *Golf course green keeper*.

David had entered that he enjoyed the outdoors, and working at a golf course could, one supposes, be considered a step up in the social circles where he might mix. The careers advisor recommended that he should take a Saturday job at one of the local courses to get networking ASAP.

Despite the computer projection, David continued to pursue something more, for he had known since the age of ten that he wanted to teach. Probably geography, maybe history. At what level and how to get there was unknown. On attending sixth form college from age sixteen to eighteen, encouraged by his tutors, he found the freedom to intellectually flourish, although despite his straight-A status he was still not invited to participate in the closed-door Oxbridge preparation sessions run twice weekly over lunchtime. Instead he clumsily searched the web for a university program that might appeal to his interests. He eventually went to study archaeology.

This is not a sob story of missed opportunities and deprivation in the British working classes, but rather a way to illustrate what Gilles Deleuze (1991, 1993, 1994) – following Henri Bergson (1994) – calls the "virtual" immanent within actuality. "The virtual," says Brian Massumi, "the pressing crowd of incipiencies and tendencies, is a realm of *potential*" (2002: 30; emphasis in original). As a press of potential, the virtual also orients us to the future. David had such incipiencies and tendencies, yet it was impressed upon him from an early age that his orientation to the future should not be ambition or aspiration, but rather a trust in his own destiny or fate that had already been written. He was of a certain class, a particular background, with preordained capacities, and all the potentiality in the world could not make up for circumstance of birth.

As a vessel of potentiality, David had the world at his feet but could have moved through life on a fateful course. He was "saved" by Greeks on his first day at university in 2003. They turned him from archaeology to anthropology, tutored him in life and instilled a self-belief that he was the master of his own future. As he progressed in academia, his background would make him a social alien, a freak of nature in terms of life-trajectory. He was taught to be the author, the owner, of his own future and to believe in his own potential to transcend his birthright future. One will never be able to calculate how much of his potentiality – in terms of relations, domains of career and family, ability to change the world – has been fulfilled. That remains in the realm of speculation.

This chapter is about potentiality as the future's *capacity to become future*, or the future as virtuality in the present. As Aristotle first noted, without potentiality there would be only actuality, and hence no possibility of a future. We often speak of potentiality as the present pregnant with possibilities, or what Giorgio Agamben refers to as "the presence of an absence" (1999: 179). The future is still to be born, nurtured in the present but not yet seen or realized. Potentiality, then, is the immanent, not-yet-actualized capacities of things, often not ontologically pinpointed (Strathern 1996: 17). As we will see, it is in the sense of encompassing all that is not actual that potentiality preserves the very idea of a future, those things that are immanent, present yet absent in the now, while at the same time being defined by being the otherwise-than-actual.

Potentiality

Because potentiality concerns the not-yet-actual, it also opens the door to surprise; as Aristotle was the first to emphasize, "Everything potential is at the same time a potentiality of contraries" (*Metaphysics*, Book IX, Ch. 8). This means that sometimes "potential" may be a weaker form of expectation, as when we say that a particular investment has the potential to yield 7 percent profit. Potential here represents a weak version of Agamben's definition of potentiality as "I can" – in this case in the sense that it can but may not happen.

However, potentiality may also remain dormant, invisible, or unknown precisely because unrealized. For instance, someone may have the potential to be a very good violinist but allow that potential to remain dormant and unknown because she does not like playing the violin. Demonstrating that potential would require its realization in action, a realization that would then point to "another side" of that person, one that even her friends did not know, but one that remains unactualized because she does not practice or regularly play the violin. It is this capacity or faculty, Agamben notes, that is Aristotle's primary concern, in that he emphasizes that potentiality is as much about the potential not to do something as to do it.

It is the dormancy or latency of potential – something present yet absent – that Massumi, following Gilles Deleuze and Henri Bergson, describes as a virtual realm, one that is real without being actual. Potential, in this sense, not only resides in recognizable capacities but also in what Massumi calls – following Spinoza – "intensities," or those aspects of experience that transcend the immediate sensations of the body and our capacity to express them. "The body," he remarks, "is as immediately abstract as it is concrete; its activity and expressivity extend, as on their underside, into an incorporeal, yet perfectly real, dimension of pressing potential" (2002: 31). In the first section of this chapter, we discuss Massumi's work in dialogue with Aristotle, whom he interestingly does not mention, and Agamben, who explicitly relies on the ancient philosopher. In particular, we use this dialogue to develop an understanding of potentiality as what we might call the otherwise-than-actual, a possibility that exists alongside the actual in what Aristotle described as materiality.

We then expand our previous discussion of speculative realism to confront the *potentia* of Aristotelian materiality as filtered through affect theory and object-oriented ontology. Like speculation, potentiality is about an immanent future, though this is one that may be already in the process of emergence. Potentiality is the always possibly realizable but never yet. Finally, we return to the pregnancy metaphor so often used for potentiality, which makes it a particularly fruitful starting point for thinking about biomedicine, in vitro fertilization, and debates over abortion.

The Otherwise-Than-Actual

In his highly influential *Parables for the Virtual* (2002), Brian Massumi returns us to one of the defining problems of ancient Greek philosophy: whether or not the Real is capable of change. For Parmenides, existence itself was unchanging, because it is simply "what-is." For Heraclitus, the universe was ever-changing, hence his famous observation that we never step in the same river twice. For Zeno, best known for his paradoxes, movement could only be understood as an infinitesimal series of points, ultimately making, for instance, a moving arrow motionless. Responding particularly to Zeno's paradox, Massumi asserts that it has haunted metaphysics and even contemporary cultural theory, which pins bodies down in "positionalities." Instead, Massumi builds on a term briefly employed by Michael Foucault, *incorporeal materialism*, "the real incorporeality of the concrete" (Massumi 2002: 5). Massumi suggests a Bergsonian fluidity, one that incorporates movement rather than positionality, and that in doing so integrates potentiality into a theory of becoming. The incorporeality of this materialism is best described as an affect, a felt bodily intensity, or for Massumi, "the feeling of having a feeling, a potential that emerges in the gap between movement and rest" (Rutherford 2016: 286).

In the previous chapter, we discussed the gap between anticipation and expectation where we claimed that speculation resides. The gap between rest and movement, on the other hand, is one filled with potential. To understand this, we may employ the example of a ball game that Massumi, Michel Serres, and Bruno Latour all use. A soccer player in the midst of a game acts in relation to the ball, which in turn creates a field of potentialities. The player scans the field for potential blockages, potential passes, potential ways to score. Moreover,

When a player readies a kick, she is not looking at the ball so much as *she is looking past it*. She is reflexively (rather than reflectively) assessing the potential movement of the ball. This involves an instantaneous calculation of the positions of all the players of the field *in relation to each other* and in relation to the ball and both goals.

(Massumi 2002: 71; emphases in original)

This vague and instantaneous perception of the field is one in which potentialities are sensed.

The player's subjectivity is disconnected as he enters the field of potential in and as its sensation. For the play, the player *is* that sensation. . . . Sensation is the mode in which potential is present in the perceiving body. The player does not play on the ground. He looks past it and past the ball to the field of potential – which is insubstantial, real but abstract. He plays the field of potential directly.

(ibid., 75)

Potentiality, then, comprises the "incorporeal materiality," the unseen capacities of other people and objects, that is always present and sensed by us, shaping the course of our actions.

For our purposes, it is important to emphasize that this is a field of potentiality rather than of possibility. While perceptions of both potentiality and possibility rely on prior knowledge and experience, potentiality refers to a capacity or faculty. Unlike possibility, potentiality "is not simply non-Being … but rather *the existence of non-Being*, the presence of an absence" (Agamben 1999: 179; emphasis in original). It is this present absence, Agamben remarks, that we refer to as a faculty or power. It is like the difference between the instantaneous calculation of the potential speed of another player and her distance from one before kicking the ball, and the possibility that something might fall from the sky and hit the other player on the head while in play. While the former is part of the field of potential and must be calculated before making a move, the latter falls into the realm of fantasy, speculation, or hope.

The conflation of potentiality and possibility has often been used to critique object-oriented ontology, where the theorization of the withdrawal of objects appears to introduce contingency and infinite possibility. As Levi Bryant (2011) notes,

Some people seem to conflate the concept of potency, power, virtuality, or potentiality with *possibility*. In these cases, it seems it is asserted that the advocate of potentiality is introducing something spooky into ontology, claiming that it is possibilities that are really real. Yet there is a massive difference between the *capacity* of gasoline to burn, and the *possibility* of a president named Barack Bush that would be a strange synthesis of democrats and republicans. Around the former you take care when smoking a cigarette at the gas station, around the latter you merely entertain the possibility of what the world would be like if such a being existed. Barack Bush has no potentialities, whereas the gasoline is rife with all sorts of possibilities. Potentiality is the reason that we wear pressure suits when we ascend to altitudes over 50,000 feet. Potentiality is an entirely *real* dimension of objects, whereas possibilities are not.

The difference between an object possibly falling from the sky and a player potentially blocking my kick, then, is that potentiality is a capacity, faculty, or real dimension of the player, one that constitutes a present absence. So, while potentialities are also possibilities, not all possibilities are potential.

Potentiality

The present absence of potentiality is what we called in the introduction to this chapter the "otherwise-than-actual." Our reference to the actual returns us to Aristotle's triangulation of potentiality, actuality, and privation. For Aristotle, form is actuality (*entelecheia* or *energia*), or what exists at any moment. Privation, on the other hand, is the absence of form. These represent stasis, or what Massumi referred to as positionality rather than movement, existence rather than emergence. For something to emerge or change, one certainly needs form and its absence; however, one also needs something more. As one commentator remarks, Aristotle's

> basic consideration is that once it be recognized that all change requires that there be a something that changes, it must also be recognized that, in order for it to change, that something must be such as to be able to change or become different. And it is such an ability or capacity or potentiality for being other and different that Aristotle calls matter.
>
> (Veatch 1974: 33)

In other words, when a ball player scans the field of potential, she is not only looking at the positions and condition of the other players at that moment, but also sensing their potential to run, block, jump, or otherwise impede a move.

Within speculative materialism and object-oriented ontology there has been a lively debate about whether or not potentiality is a real quality of objects, and how or whether to distinguish it from the virtual. While we do not have room here to engage fully with this debate, it is worth noting that despite the rather commonsense assumption that potentiality must surely be effectively synonymous with what it means for objects to withdraw, Graham Harman has in the past contended that what we call potential is already actual, because for him objects are simply "anything that cannot be reduced either downward or upward, which means anything that has a surplus beyond its constituent pieces and beneath its sum total of effects on the world" (Harman 2018: 51).

In this sense, potentiality is already present in the object and so is already realized, if not actualized in Aristotle's sense. In particular, in earlier work (Harman 2009), Harman had asserted that a theory of potentiality undermines the possibility of novelty, because it makes it seem as though the acorn already contains the oak that it might become.

The most vigorous response to Harman's (and Latour's) critique of potentiality has come from Levi Bryant, who in *The Democracy of Objects* (2018) describes objects as split between the actual and the virtual. Moreover, for Bryant, as well, the virtual is a realm of potentiality. Returning to Spinoza's concept of affect on which Massumi builds, Levi Bryant asserts that there could be no affect without potentiality. He quotes Spinoza as saying, "By [affect] I understand the affections of the body by which the body's power of activity is increased or diminished, assisted or checked" (Bryant 2018: loc. 1881). Bryant then remarks,

What makes Spinoza's concept of affect so interesting is that it doesn't restrict affect to what is *felt*, but links the concept of affect to the *capacities* of an object. ... And these affects consist of both an entity's "receptivity" to other entities and the various capacities an entity has to act. ... Those nerves must have the *capacity* of being excited or stimulated.
(Bryant 2018: loc. 1875–1885)

It is in this sense of capacity, discussed earlier, that Bryant uses the concept of potentiality in responding to Harman: "[I]t cannot be said that the acorn already contains the oak tree. What the acorn contains are acorn powers or attractors, and while these powers or attractors are entirely determinate, their actualization is a purely creative process producing new qualities and eventually a new object. ... The virtual dimension of objects is *concrete* without being *actual*" (ibid., loc. 1885–1894).

This absent presence that is capacity or faculty – what Agamben calls the "I can" – is given the name "incorporeal materiality" by Massumi but for Aristotle was simply *dynamis*. This word has been translated as "matter," but the word obviously is at the root of words having to do with strength or vigor, such as *dynamic* or *dynamism*. For Aristotle, *dynamis* had two meanings: both the power inherent to a thing, and also the potential for that thing to be in another state. "It is as one who is building to one who can build," Aristotle remarks, "and as one who is awake to one asleep . . . and as something framed out of matter to matter itself" (*Metaphysics*, Book IX, Ch. 6). While clay is a form or actuality, it has potentiality in the two senses of *dynamis*: as something that may be molded, and as something that may specifically be molded into a bowl that will be glazed with drawings of Hermes.

Moreover, Aristotle places the distinction between actuality and potentiality in time, noting that potentiality precedes actuality and conditions it. This, then, gives to any thing or person a temporal dynamism that is part of what it means to *be* potentially. Judith Butler observes that in both Latin and Greek, the word "matter" refers not simply to "brute positivity" but rather "is always in some sense temporalized." In Marx, as well, she notes, matter is understood "as a principle of *transformation*, presuming and inducing a future" (1993: 31). We would note, however, that Aristotle, at least, did not see this potentiality as applying only to objects and things, but also to people: "We call even a man who is not studying a scholar, if he has the ability to study, though the opposite is actually true" (*Metaphysics*, Book IX, Ch. 6). The kithara player still maintains his ability (*potenza*) even when he does not play (see Agamben 1999: 45). And like Elinor's description of expectation in Chapter 2, Aristotle's apparent view of the non-industrious scholar is that although one shouldn't expect that he will apply himself, one can still hope.

We can see, then, how potentiality and actuality, in Aristotle's vision, are necessary to any theory of time. While the actual is what exists now, the potential is what might be, or what might have been. The potential, for Aristotle, is what guarantees change, and hence time itself. Moreover, if potentiality and actuality ever coincided, "no genesis or decay would be at all possible . . . and it would be a lie to speak of future things and past ones" (Aristotle 1862: 10–14, quoted in Virno 2015: loc. 915). As Paulo Virno (ibid.) observes, the actual is that which is no longer potential (but once was): earlier/later, preceding/subsequent, past/present, or for Kuber or Kermode, the tick-tocking of a clock continuously actualizing the potentiality of time as it pushes into the future.

In short, as we remarked in the introduction to this chapter, potentiality gives us the future's *capacity to become future*. Potentiality is what stops the whole space-time continuum collapsing, prevents everything from happening at once. For Aristotle, potentiality and actuality cannot simultaneously exist, and this is what structures time. It is also important, Aristotle reminds us, that if potentiality is to have its own consistency and not always disappear immediately into actuality, it is necessary that potentiality be able *not* to pass over into actuality, that there should be potentiality not to do/be, or as Aristotle puts it, that potentiality also be im-potentiality (*adynamia*) (Agamben 1995: 45).

As an orientation to the future, then, potentiality, like anticipation, permeates the everyday. However, while anticipation is an orientation of imminence, potentiality is one of immanence. As Italian philosopher Paolo Virno observes, if potentiality and actuality also structure a "before" and "after," this presents us with the question of whether they do so *in* time or whether they structure time. Returning us to our Heideggerian observations of the first chapter, Virno asks, "In brief, are they *temporalised* or do they *temporalise*?" (2015: loc. 927). Virno's answer is that they do both, simultaneously existing in time and ordering it. However, for Virno, what is temporally significant about potentiality is that it never coincides with actuality and so is "the persistent not-now." In temporal terms, what is also "not-now," he notes, is time as a whole, "all-embracing time, the entirety of time within which succession and simultaneity take place" (ibid., loc. 1003).

Potentiality

We may turn this final observation to thinking about ethnography. In ethnographic terms, we may ask in what way potentiality orients us as social actors, as well as how potentiality may orient us as groups. In other words, in social terms, what does it mean for potentiality to represent the otherwise-than-actual? In social terms, what does it mean for the otherwise-than-actual to represent the future's capacity to become future? While Massumi has described a soccer player's movements in a field of potentialities, it should be clear that the concept of timespace that we have heretofore utilized is also one structured by potentialities. Indeed, as will become clear below, the very concept of a vernacular timespace relies on potentiality, on what has the capacity to happen but has not happened yet. The orders that weave together a social site depend upon potentiality, while the anticipatory, expectatory, or speculative actions that we take rely on the otherwise-than-actual. One of the clearest examples to demonstrate this is the practice and ethic of reciprocity, which, as we show below, is structured around the not-yet that is potential.

Potential Relations and Timespace

In previous chapters, we have built on Theodore Schatzki's discussion of social sites, which argues that forms of sociality emerge out of the indefinite teleologies structuring practices and orders. For any given practice, Schatzki argues, participants "tend to actuate subsets of the futures involved and to treat entities as anchoring subsets of the places, paths, and regions concerned" (Schatzki 2010: loc. 1363–1370). We gave factory production as the example of a social site. Factory production consists not only of the factory itself, its workers, its machines, and its products, but also of the trucks that carry goods, the shops that sell them, the salespeople that hawk them, the banks that finance them. All are ordered around the production and sale of a particular product. Moreover,

"The timespaces of individuals are circumscribed by the teleoaffec-tive structures of practices" (ibid.) – e.g., by the time, rhythm, and urgency of production, shipping, and sale. We extended this analysis to argue that particular common social experiences may produce epochal understandings of temporality understood to have their own affects. As we mentioned earlier, those persons who exist within the teleoaffective structure of an oncoming disaster or an upcoming deadline could be said to share the teleoaffect of the same vernacular timespace. A Time of War, a Time of Closure, or a Time of Brexit all produce affects associated with the futural orientations of anticipa-tion, expectation, and speculation.

The ongoing game on a playing field described by Massumi and others would constitute a similar timespace, with its own teleology structured by the time of play. What the introduction of potentiality makes clear, however, is that the sinews that hold a social site together as a teleoaffective structure rely specifically on potentiality: what *can* happen must precede what could, should, or must happen. As such, then, potentiality gives shape to any timespace by defining its limits and prefiguring the possibility of social relations.

An ethnographic example should make this clear. In a special journal issue exploring the relevance of Marcel Mauss's *The Gift* (2001 [1925]) in the twenty-first century, Stavroula Pipyrou (2014) provides a nuanced example of relations that are not relations, where gifts will not be returned, and yet where the very fact of potential relatedness creates a particular timespace. Her case is the connectedness created by gift-giving from mafia affiliates to other social actors in South Italy. In principle, gifts given by members of the Calabria mafia (the 'Ndrangheta) to non-affiliates do not bind recipients, yet they are imbued with the potential of a relation. The examples of gifting that she gives are favors – finding a stolen car, or preventing an eviction – where there is no expectation that the recipient of the favor will ever return the favor.

This "non-relation relation" (Konrad 2005) is the outcome of giving gifts framed as free and altruistic. Nevertheless, Pipyrou notes, "The free gift has a potential to become a vincolo; a chain, link, or restraint, despite the fact recipients will never be obliged to reciprocate" (Pipyrou 2014: 414). As a result, even though the relation will absolutely, definitely, never be activated, the potential for relatedness still will never cease to exist, in some cases being carried from generation to generation. Pipyrou concludes,

Even when gifts are intended to be altruistic, actors fill the void with notions of obligation and potential reciprocity, in this case the vincolo. Although recipients know that the gift will never be repaid, they are bound by the ever-present potentiality of reciprocation; they can never be truly "free" from the gift.

(2014: 424)

In this way, vincoli are always potential relations that connect actors, institutions, and other parts of society across space and time. A gift given in Reggio Calabria, on the toe of Italy, can generate a potential future relation in Duisburg, Germany. Kin and future descendants of the donor are linked to those of the recipient.

There are two conclusions that we can draw from the Calabrian example. We see, firstly, through an example of "free" gifts – ones that have not been reciprocated and have not created social relations – that the social site (in Schatzki's terms) is defined not through the connection of actualized reciprocity but rather through the potential of relations in the future. Schatzki had pointed out that all practice is teleological, that the practice of maintaining social relations is itself always oriented toward the future. In cases of actually existing gift-giving relationships, such practices might be oriented toward their reproduction and maintenance. We see in the Calabrian example, however, how never-actualized potential relations may also influence both the perception of one's trajectory toward the future and the affective nature of this movement. Simply the existence of potential relations acting on the conscience of both donor and receiver influences how one acts toward the future. There is a never-ending argument circulating in the minds of the actors: The gift is free from obligation. But the relation itself means a bond. But the relation will never be activated. But it still exists. This potentiality concretely influences activity in the real world.

Returning to Virno (2015: loc. 1247–1254), we may agree with him in a qualified way that "[p]otential, properly speaking, is also the *world*, if by 'world' we mean to say . . . nothing other than the *perceptible context* to which the being devoid of any definite environment belongs. A context surrounds and envelops, remaining for the most part unperceived; it is not *in front of us*, but always and only *all around us*" (emphasis in original).

Like Massumi, Virno is arguing that the world as we perceive it in any given moment – what Heidegger would have called thrownness – is perceptible in its totality not as actuality but as potentiality. Our qualification is that, as both the practice theorist Schatzki and the onticologist Levi Bryant have argued, we never exist in only one world at any moment. Returning to our example of birdcalls and washing machines from the Introduction, various materialities in our environments and everyday lives engage us in multiple timespaces with their own teleoaffects. What Virno's remarks add to this is that the "world" of those timespaces is perceived and defined through potentialities.

Through an example of unfulfilled relations, then, we see how potentiality circumscribes the site of the social and thereby the shared timespace that emerges from it. This example shows us, secondly, how potentiality is not only necessary for change – as Aristotle observed – but is necessary to define the future as such. For Aristotle, "matter is simply potentiality; and potentiality, in turn, is always construed as a potentiality for something or other" (Veatch 1974: 34). Moreover, as we noted earlier, *dynamis* had two meanings for Aristotle: both the power inherent to a thing, and also the potential for that thing to be in another state. The importance of this distinction to our own discussion becomes clearer when we turn to Hegel's exposition of these two notions of potentiality. In her analysis of Hegel's concept of plasticity and its relationship to his philosophy of history, Catherine Malabou observes that Hegel builds upon one of these two types of potentiality. She quotes Hegel's discussion: "We can speak of some being as a knower either as when we say that man is a knower, meaning that man falls into the class of beings that know or have knowledge; or when we are speaking of a man who possesses a knowledge of grammar. Each of these has a potentiality, but not in the same way" (Hegel 1971: §401 quoted in Malabou 2005: 49).

To use Aristotle's distinction, we may say that the person who emerges from ignorance into knowledge is completely changed from one state to another, while the person who knows a language and uses it is actualizing a disposition. Hegel concludes, "There is one change which is privative; and another which acts on the nature like a permanent energy (force and habit, εξις)" (Hegel 1971: §402).

A person who has not had a chance to use a language that she knows and that finally, upon going abroad, exercises that capacity would be a good example of what Malabou means when she notes, "The accomplished act confirms a presence that has pre-existed, albeit withdrawn into itself. . . . This withdrawal or suspension of being is the other name of εξις" (2005: 49). Malabou's invocation of what she calls "presence in a state of withdrawal" returns us, then, to object-oriented ontology and to Levi Bryant's remark that "[t]he virtual dimension of objects is *concrete* without being *actual*" (2018, loc. 1885–1894). We find important the idea that the virtual dimension of objects defined by potentiality can be concrete – i.e., sensible in the world – while remaining withdrawn, a "permanent energy" that may be sensed by others.

It is this virtuality constituted by potentiality that we have called the "otherwise-than-actual." In terms of a futural orientation, then, we may agree with Virno, who extends his argument about the necessity of potentiality to create "the world" when he argues that potentiality "does not fall *in* time" (emphasis in original) and that its texture is "fully temporal, but not at all chronological" (2015: loc. 995). Virno expands, moreover, on the idea of potentiality as nonchronologically temporal: "[T]he 'always' of potential does not mean that it is perennially present, but rather *that it is perennially unable to coincide with actuality.* The potential is the persistent not-now against which each *hic et nunc* is defined, the unmovable latency which constitutes the horizon (or context) of each dateable event" (ibid., loc. 1005; emphasis in original). This persistent "not-now," we noted earlier, is what Virno refers to as "time as a whole," which is also the "never-actual."

To return to Pipyrou's vincoli, we can see how actual relations between residents of Reggio Calabria who have received gifts from members of the 'Ndrangheta are circumscribed not by actuality – respect, avoidance, or silence, for instance – but rather by virtuality – the always-present and always-perceptible potentiality of reciprocity that all know is unlikely ever to be demanded. Or to return to the ball game example, we can see how the activity timespace of play is constituted of all those animate and inanimate objects who are part of its "field," in other words who have the potential to influence the trajectory of the ball and the outcome of the game. Indeed, precisely because Schatzki's definition of activity timespace is teleological, it relies on potential to sketch out its scope.

We have seen, then, how potentiality circumscribes both the scope and the temporality of activity timespaces. Like anticipation, potentiality has a structuring role in all futural orientations. But also, like anticipation, potentiality may, at certain junctures, become a shared way of understanding the future – in other words, a teleoaffect that emerges from the sort of epochal thinking that we have called vernacular timespaces. In the previous chapter, we discussed Gisa Weszkalnys's study of oil speculation in São Tomé and Principe, in which she remarks that an empirical and ethnographic approach to potentiality "differs quite markedly from contemplating it philosophically." Instead, she approaches potentiality as "constituted historically and implicated in social praxis" (Weszkalnys 2015: 617). The next sections draw these approaches together, by examining both the historical and social constitution of potentiality as a teleoaffect, and also how we may relate an ethnographically based understanding of potentiality to philosophical debates.

The Emergence of Ethnographic Potential

In September 2011, exploratory drilling began off the southern coast of Cyprus, in the Aphrodite gas fields within the country's exclusive economic zone. The EEZ lies immediately west of Israel's Leviathan gas field, and indeed, only a year earlier the two countries had signed a treaty delimiting their zones. All of this had happened despite the vociferous protests of Turkey, which claimed that the Republic of Cyprus was encroaching on its continental shelf. In response to the drilling, Turkey sent out a rather aged vessel, the *Piri Reis*, to engage in its own explorations off the island's northern coast. Despite technical difficulties because of the age of the vessel, making it the butt of social media jokes, both sides of the island were abuzz with discussions of what would happen next. On the one hand, there seemed to be potential for national riches in the form of what some experts at the time suggested would be enough gas to secure the economic future of the island. On the other hand, there was the potential for war, concretized in a creaking vessel that despite its age represented Turkey's willingness to defy its regional and international partners on what it considered to be an important national issue. A very few hopeful souls even speculated that the riches that gas appeared to represent presented the potential for peace.

In a single example, we find three culturally and historically specific, shared understandings of potentiality: the potentiality for natural resource wealth, the potentiality for war, and the potentiality for peace. In their introduction to a special issue on potentiality in biotechnology, Karen-Sue Taussig, Klaus Hoeyer, and Stefan Helmreich identify three meanings of potentiality in everyday language that interestingly map onto these ways in which Cypriots have understood the potential of undersea gas:

The first [meaning] denotes a hidden force determined to manifest itself – something that with or without intervention has its future built into it. The second refers to genuine plasticity – the capacity to transmute into something completely different. The third suggests a latent possibility imagined as open to choice, a quality perceived as available to human modification and direction through which people can work to propel an object or subject to become something other than it is.

(2013: s4)

Certainly, Cypriots have understood gas as a hidden force, something with a future that only needs to be tapped. That hidden force, moreover, is composed of wealth, a wealth that only needs to be harvested. However, that hidden force may also transmute into something else, namely the impetus to conflict. But human choice and intervention may redirect that force to realize another potential, which is the potential for peace, a potential that some persons believe is latent but impeded, needing another push or motivation to realize it.

All of these types of potentiality may exist simultaneously, with persons and groups slipping from one to the other. In social media responses, discussions slid from economic to political calculations, from fear to hopefulness. The same persons or groups variously or even simultaneously experienced a fear of war, a hope for wealth, and a yearning for peace. As we will discuss below, what all of these tele-oaffects share is what in recent years has come to be known as *emergence*, what Bob Simpson, following Ernst Bloch, refers to as "the being of becoming." Using ethnographic examples of assisted reproductive technology, Simpson notes that "the being of becoming lands us in the province of the possible, the not yet, the unbecome" (2013: s93; see also Edwards 2009). The being of becoming is certainly a felicitous way to describe the plasticity of incipient life or as-yet-untapped or -untested natural resources whose only Being is precisely their potentiality both to be and to not be.

To understand the significance of the potential to not-be, we should return to our earlier delineation of the distinction between possibility and potentiality. Massumi had separated the two by remarking that "Possibility is a variation *implicit in* what a thing can be. . . . Potential is the *immanence* of a thing to its still interdeterminate variation, under way. . . . The distinction between potential and possibility is a distinction between conditions of emergence and re-conditionings of the emerged. Conditions of emergence are one with becoming" (Massumi 2002: 9–10).

If we return again to our example of the soccer field, we had suggested that as we play, we assess the potential of a player to intercept a pass, given her location and capacity for speed. The potential of a player to intercept, calculated instantaneously on the basis of capacity and distance, is one that is immanent and indeterminate, and could be similarly calculated depending on conditions (a muddy field, a sprained ankle) for any field of play. The possibility, on the other hand, that something might fall from the sky onto the opposing teams' players is a possibility implicit in playing on an open field, with no protection, though admittedly a highly unlikely one.

What characterizes the "being of becoming" of potentiality, then, is that anything that has not yet been actualized is immanent but still emergent and so retains the potential both to be and to not be. The observation that im-potentiality is part of the becomingness of potentiality dates back to Aristotle, who emphasized the necessity for potentiality to also take the form of im-potentiality (*adynamia*). For Aristotle, "what is potential can both be and not be. For the same is potential as much with respect to being as to not being" (Aristotle 1998: 10 in Agamben 1999: 45). What is important, then, is that potentiality *is* potential precisely because it may not happen. This is, however, different from the only possible, which has a different relationship to non-being. While potentiality is an immanence, an absent present, the not-yet that may never be actualized, possibility is not in a relationship to the impossible in the same way. While potentiality always harbors impotentia, impossibility cancels possibility.

Moreover, we see that the potential not to happen is what makes potentiality an important facet of social becoming. Through the potentiality not to be actual, we see new social forms emerging. In Pipyrou's cases, the potential to not become actuality is an important facet of the relation, indeed structuring it through its virtual presence. For this reason, Taussig *et al.* (2013) and others have argued, potentiality is political, working on and through morality in the present, encouraging us to act in certain ways with very concrete results. On the one hand, potentiality presents us with new or emerging moral dilemmas brought about by new technologies and discoveries in, for instance, biomedicine. The Human Genome Project is one such instance, they observe:

In public representations and contemporary scientific research, it is said that gene therapy has the potential to intervene in genetic conditions; genetic testing has the potential to reveal aspects of individual pasts and futures; pharmacogenomics has the potential to deploy new knowledge of human biological variation to develop personalized medicine tailored to the specific susceptibilities of particular individuals; stem cells have the potential to regenerate human tissue to treat spinal cord injuries, diabetes, or Alzheimer's disease; and not yet identified organisms have the potential to yield novel and useful genetic sequences.

(Taussig *et al.* 2013: s3)

Rich in potentiality, biomedicine skirts the thin line of judgment on the moral responsibilities of creating life itself.

The potentiality of biomedicine instigates moral claims to universal human rights – to reproduce, for instance – and plays on the conscience of people in need of medical intervention to "do the right thing." This is to say that now that technologies exist to intervene in the basic functions of nature, such as childbirth or a once terminal illness, the public feels the moral obligation to partake in medical procedures.[1] In turn, the financial benefactors become moral players in other people's futures and corporative initiatives claim ethical ground, ripe for political exploitation.

The reason these technologies present these choices, moreover, is because they offer potential that might not be realized without such intervention. As Lynn Morgan notes in her genealogy of the concept of potentiality in abortion debates, "Claims about potentiality are strategies that people deploy to enliven or erase certain life worlds, because potentiality – amongst its many other meanings – is a discursive device that can be used to formulate, activate, or resist particular imagined futures. . . . [P]otentiality debates can function as politics by other means" (Morgan 2013: S22). In this sense, then, the power or *dynamis* of potentiality is intimately entangled with the power of politics, where debates emerge over whose potential is to be realized, and the responsibility of realizing potential that remains unseen, untested, and emergent.

If potential offers emergence and change, the future as such, what happens when potential is not actualized? What happens, at the collective level, when potential turns to *impotentia*? What happens when potential gas is dry, when anticipated conflict simmers in antagonism, or when no one makes the choice to realize a potential for peace?

---

[1] One might also note here a speculative element, insofar as biomedicine inspires confidence. "Products" are sold based in confidence in the treatment and the potential to cure the problem. As a result, the public not only feels moral obligation to participation in treatment but also the confidence to do so.

Potentiality Defeated

In austerity Greece, exhaustion is the primary orientation to the future. After nine years of economic crisis (now best termed "structural austerity"), apparently without respite anytime soon, imaginations of scenarios for a better future have been defeated; interest in the postapocalyptic is a bridge too far for exhausted people. For many people, the future was all about potential – potential for social and material progression, investment, accumulation, and networking. Now, feelings of resignation and helplessness are expressed by both younger and older generations; the future of potential has been firmly defeated and, importantly, there is no preparation for a future that the next generation can find. Older people know that they will not be around to live the postapocalyptic future, and exhausted youngsters have written themselves out of the future, which they see as overpoweringly based on distrust, contempt, apathy (Knight 2016).

There is also a sense of déjà vu, something that Virno claims is inherently related to potentiality. Not only are people in Greece witnessing what they believe to be a repetition of past scenarios of hunger, occupation, and poverty, but the déjà vu of emergence, of potentiality collapsing. The future *is* déjà vu. In summer 2014, the then Greek prime minister, Antonis Samaras, made a bold statement that got Knight's research participants contemplating the potential futures of a postcrisis nation. That May he triumphantly announced, "There is growth (*anaptiksi*). ... We have come out of crisis. ... Greece can once again borrow money. ... We can get loans. ... we did it together, we have officially emerged from the crisis." Intended to incite hope for better things to come, speculation about what a society emerging from a prolonged period of turmoil might look like, an excited anticipation for a potentially better life, the prime minister's words instead provoked fear, resignation, and a sense of déjà vu of unrealized potential.

Being "suspended in time" in a "crisis that has lasted a lifetime," a dominant collective voice in central Greece suggests that people have learned to cope with decreased living standards and tighter budgets; they have managed to contain the crisis situation and fear the prospect of an emergent postcrisis nation. There is tolerance of the current circumstances (see Dzenovska 2018b). Furthermore, many locals report having become "accustomed" and "habituated" to the idea of emergence as a never-ending cyclical process. The intimacy felt with the crisis situation that has engulfed their lives 24/7 for eight years and the incessant anticipation of emergence has fed into the idea of being stuck in a never-ending cycle, unsure of their temporal trajectories. Are they heading forwards or backwards or are they caught in a cyclical uncanny present, an extreme spin cycle that leaves them struggling to walk straight? Many state that the only potential outcome of any social change will be to emerge into the past. A conversation Knight had with a thirty-three-year-old waitress, Vaso, is representative of how people have become overfamiliar with the idea of emergence and no longer anticipate it: "We have heard it so many times. The crisis is over. The economy is improving. One experiences déjà vu, it is a physical feeling of repetition. It makes you dizzy, gives you palpitations. Emergence-crisis, emergence-crisis, emergence-crisis." Vaso says that people now "know what they need to do to survive" and, fearing that "one neocolonial program" of dispossession will simply be replaced by another, she remarkably says that she is "happy to remain" with the current status quo. Exhausted by six years of crisis talk, the inability to project imaginations for potential futures has bred a kind of Stockholm syndrome, an uncomfortable comfort with the present and a fear of what lies over the threshold.

Despite its indexical relation to newness, Sam Collins (2008) argues that the trope of emergence tends to recapture its own potential, to foreclose the possibilities of futures by containing it within the "past–present relation." For Collins, the key problem is that there is usually little surprise in what emerges; typically, neoliberal projects emerging in their own image (see Valentine *et al.* 2012: 1018). This all adds to the sense of temporal vertigo experienced in Greece today, confusion as to where and when one belongs, culminating in reports of feeling "dizzy" and "nauseous" – the "elsewhere" and "elsewhen" of being "lost in time" (Battaglia 2005b: 4). Vaso concludes that there is nothing new in this world, that all the (individual, financial, material) possibilities of precrisis Greece have been annihilated, and that life is now full of repetition, of déjà vu.

In a fascinating account of already collapsed futures and seemingly insuperable potentialities, Morten Nielsen (2014) discusses how alternative futures might be accessed by manipulating the probabilities for the likely, albeit unwanted, outcomes of current actions. He presents material gathered in Maputo, Mozambique, showing how potential futures are proactively altered in the present. Nielsen (2014: 170) states that the future "wedges itself within the present moment as a transversal movement and establishes temporal differentiations without indicating a progressing trajectory." People seeking a future that they know has already collapsed – such as a man laying claim to land which does not belong to him in order to preempt his looming failure to secure the property through bureaucratic channels – seek to actualize full potentials of the future without converting virtual reality into physical materiality. They elicit desired futures in negated form.

In contrast to the Greek case presented above, in Maputo collapsed futures do not always discourage people from enacting the future in the present and laying claim to impossible potentialities. The man claiming the disputed land knew that he would lose out in a forthcoming legal battle, but also realized that he could potentially gain something by constructing the foundations to a house. People engage in potential futures that they know will never follow the present, and through the recognition of impossibility the future invades the present and itself is liberated. That which will never be is already there. The result, Nielsen suggests, is a set of virtual becomings, some of which may, at a long shot, be actualized as concrete possibilities (2014: 178). We agree with Nielsen (2014: 170) that "the future exists as an unstable transformative potentiality." Force-feeding the impossible future into the present opens up a new set of potentialities not generally seen in the context of Greece, for instance.

Conclusion

Like anticipation, potentiality is pervasive in our everyday orientations to the future because, as Aristotle first noted, potentiality must precede any actuality. Potentiality is the basis for action, and in that sense it precedes any could, should, or would. As Paolo Virno observes, however, the relationship between potentiality and actuality is temporal but not chronological, as potential always exists alongside the actual as its possible future in the present. Potentiality may remain dormant, unrealized, or unrecognized, as in the case of David, who was conscious that he wanted something particular from life but was unaware of how to achieve his goals. The oft-used metaphor of a present pregnant with the future captures potentiality's present absence.

The existence of potentiality alongside actuality is what we have called the "otherwise-than-actual," a time that is beyond time and a virtuality that defines the limits of any timespace. The orders that weave together a social site depend upon potentiality, while the anticipatory, expectatory, or speculative actions that we take rely on the otherwise-than-actual. One of the key features of potentiality, furthermore, is that potential may never be realized; potential is always at the same time *impotentia*, the possibility not to be. As we have seen in the case of the vincolo, relationships may remain within the realm of potential, never reaching actuation. Nevertheless, a relationship imbued with potential in a past act of gifting maintains a weighty existence as it is dragged through the present and shapes the future, despite the fact that all parties concerned know that the potential will never be realized. The complexity of potentiality conveyed through gifting reflects the paradox of the gift itself, as argued by Pipyrou, which is at the same time "free" and entangled in indeterminate future obligation.

The emergent aspect of potentiality, the possibility that it may still not manifest itself, may not come to fruition, also makes collective potentiality inherently political. Choices must be made to realize it. Ignoring or refusing to realize potential may have ethical consequences. Once knowledge or technology are available to correct illness, do we not have an ethical responsibility to do so? In what ways are we ethically responsible for creating or preserving life when the potential to do is in our hands? In what circumstances, then, may potentiality serve as a proxy for a politics that directs our future on the basis of a present absence, a virtual not-yet?

Moreover, what happens when potentiality is not realized? When emergence, the "being of becoming," never results in the intended or anticipated future? We suggest that the future may take the form of emptiness (Dzenovska 2018b) and exhaustion (Knight 2016) when potential does not materialize as expected or desired. Like the dry wells of São Tomé and Principe, it may lead to abandonment and apathy. However, as should become clear in the next chapter, it is the failure of potentiality to be realized that may also lead to hope and yearning.

ꭏ

Hope

Athens, Greece, January 2015. "*I Elpida Erxetai*" ("Hope Begins Today" or "Hope Is Coming") read slogans held aloft by the thousands packed into Syntagma Square. The same motto appears regularly on television screens and on freeway billboards across the nation. There is a palpable thickness to the air as a country is caught up in something that feels extraordinary, a new beginning, a becoming, a wave of positivity and anticipation. There is buoyancy while travelling through Greece; one feels as though one were enclosed in a large bubble, bobbing up and down on a sea of optimism. Even the sceptic, the opposition supporter, might admit that something special is about to happen. "*Makari*" (I wish [it be successful/bring change]), he might reply.

The epicenter for the seismic ripples of hope expanding beyond the borders of Greece and shaking as far afield as Germany and Spain is the charismatic young leader of the Greek left-wing Syriza party, Alexis Tsipras, who is coming to power at a canter based on a message of hope. Over five years on from the onslaught of crushing fiscal austerity in 2009/10 and with a country now on its knees, this radical coalition of leftists promises to fight internationally imposed structural readjustment measures, build a sustainable economy based on radical ecological policy, give back to the people much of what they have lost, and restore hope and pride to a nation that has taken a very public beating. The election of Syriza is most certainly a vote against Troika (European Commission, International Monetary Fund, European Central Bank) austerity and the two-party political establishment that has run Greece since the fall of the junta in 1974. Standing up to the injustice of Troika austerity is a popular position, but other policies, such as reintroducing "14 wages per year" and increasing the minimum wage, and the promise that people will be able to return to the living standards of precrisis years are of obvious concern to some citizens (Knight 2015b: 243; 2017c). There is a collective feeling that Greece is entering a new era, an emerging timespace with different teleoaffects. Syriza is driving toward an alternative, although indeterminate, *telos* and there is overwhelming hope that it must be better than what has gone before. A new era of prosperity is just over the horizon.

Chicago, USA, 2008. Now iconic posters are held aloft by a crowd straining for a glimpse of presidential candidate Barack Obama. "Hope." "Progress." "Change." The official Democratic Party campaign slogan reads "Change we can believe in" (often accompanied at rallies by the chant "Yes we can" and parodied at opposition marches as "No you can't" [Haugerud 2013: 25]), and Obama is carried into office on a message of hope – hope for political change in Washington DC, for economic and healthcare reform, for energy independence, for a reassessment of US military involvement in Iraq. His charisma has captured more than just the hearts and minds of the American voting public. Like Tsipras years later, the world is captivated by the striking difference between the ineptitude of the previous government and the optimism being offered. In this case, the controversial and turbulent stay of George W. Bush in the White House is coming to an end, a change that is likely to impact the entire world. Bush's tenure has seen the September 11th terrorist attacks, wars in Iraq and Afghanistan, Hurricane Katrina, and the onset of recession. Obama offers a horizon of hope, clarity, and cosmopolitanism, and the global public has a new set of expectations.

In these two examples, we see hope as a swell of emotion, an affect of positivity, appearing to push the crowds toward a better future. This is not the future of dream, but rather the future of blocked or unrealized potential. In both cases, this is the potential to capture something that certain segments of the public saw as lost: in the case of Greece, the living standards that they enjoyed before the crisis, and in the case of the USA, a sense that the country had begun to slip from its position as "leader of the Free World" (a problem discussed more in Chapter 6). These were potentials that still existed, could still be mobilized and actualized in the future toward which the crowds were pressing.

Hope, we argue in this chapter, is a form of futural momentum, a way of pressing into the future that attempts to pull certain potentialities into actuality. Hope is not the only such form of futural momentum, but unlike other forms, we argue that hope emerges in the gap between the potential and the actual, between matter and its not-yet form. Hope is about something that doesn't presently exist but potentially could; hope is based on more than a possibility and less than a probability. In that sense, hope is a way of virtually pushing potentiality into actuality. The potential is never actualized in all the ways that are possible; the remainder, we argue, always breeds (new) hope.

In order to make this argument, we turn first to the limited philosophical and more extensive anthropological literature on hope to think about this teleoaffect as a form of futural momentum. Building on the previous chapter, we argue that hope is a way of handling the indeterminacy of potentiality, of harnessing its remainders for momentum into a future that navigates the otherwise-than-actual. If the otherwise-than-actual always exists alongside the actual, hope is the affective result of trying to bring particular "otherwises" into actuality. We then examine how this takes place collectively, through the mobilization of political rhetoric, technologies of the imagination, and utopian thinking. Finally, through examples of sporting events, we discuss how hope often flourishes in a different form of vernacular timespace, where beginnings and ends appear more neatly defined.

Hope as Futural Momentum

In his seminal work *The Principle of Hope* (1986 [1938–1947]), Ernst Bloch provides a critical exploration of the possibilities of utopian futures – fundamentally future-oriented and indeterminate "not-yets." Bloch introduces the idea of the not-yet-conscious, man and universe existing in anticipatory consciousness about the yet-to-come, anticipation exaggerated and perpetuated by way of "wishful images" consumed in fairy tales, fiction, theatre, and travel journals. These images make up part of the affective timespace that influences action toward the future; the images are both part of a range of acceptable or known teleoaffects and readily accessible technologies of imagination that provide momentum toward an indeterminate *something*. Akin to the electoral propaganda presented at the start of this chapter that provides influential images of what potential not-yets might look like, Bloch contends that popular images produced, consumed, shared in the mass media project visions of the "not-yet" and encourage affective contemplation in the realm of the "could-have." Wishful images invite people to imagine not-yets from the potentiality of the present, providing momentum toward the actuation of aspiration. "Only with a farewell to the closed, static concept of being does the real dimension of hope open. Instead, the world is full of propensity towards something, tendency towards something, latency of something, and this intended something means the fulfillment of the intending" (Bloch 1986: 18).

Bloch asks us not to focus on the current state of social relations, but on what they might become. Indeed, Bloch argues that hope opens contemplation to the future by allowing us to think about what might be, what is not yet. Contemplative knowledge, he notes, "is by definition solely knowledge of what can be contemplated, namely of the past, and it bends an arch of closed form-contents out of Becomeness over the Unbecome" (ibid., 6). Contemplative knowledge, for Bloch, can only consider actuality and has no room for potentiality. Hope, in contrast, opens up to the tendencies or latencies of things, what Massumi would call their virtuality and which we have called the otherwise-than-actual.

We argue below that hope as a futural orientation bridges the gap between potentiality and actuality. Hope emerges from what Bloch calls the Unbecome, tendencies or latencies that are as-yet-unrealized potentials. We have seen in Chapter 4 that a core aspect of potentiality is the potential not-to-be, to remain otherwise-than-actual. The immanence of as-yet-unrealized potential, however, becomes a resource for hope. There are opportunities in the everyday, Bloch proposes, to identify and activate dormant potentialities that will benefit both the individual and community. When a potential is not yet realized, or when a potential's realization is thwarted, then, hope has the possibility to emerge, providing momentum to mobilize potential for a push into the future actual. The activation of potentiality stimulates a form of movement toward an undefined but qualitatively different future.

More than any of the orientations discussed in this book, hope is perpetually in motion, a movement that is, as Bloch contends, a propensity, a tendency, *towards* something. If potentiality emerges in the gap between rest and movement, the moment where there is still the possibility to not-be, the seeds of hope are planted where there is the emergence of indeterminate potential breaking forth into the realm of the actual. Echoing Massumi, we suggest that hope acting on potentiality illustrates movement rather than positionality in a theory of becoming. Hope drives us into the future at a speed, captured, for instance, when social movements or election campaigns are said to be "gathering momentum" or in the metaphor of "the snowball effect" where something initially insignificant builds into an unstoppable force. What might start out as collective wishful thinking gathers momentum to bring improbable desires from the realm of potentiality to actuation. In this sense, hope is the *pursuit* of materializing the otherwise-than-actual.

To this end, we must locate hope, Bloch asserts, in the "world process," in everyday moments of emergent potentiality where potential "has not yet been defeated, but likewise has not yet won" (1986: 340–341). Innumerable unrealized potentialities are waiting to be discovered in the everyday, potentialities "in flux" (Thompson 2013: 3) that become vessels of hope as we push toward the future. Phillip Mar (2005: 365) has proposed that "hope accesses a temporalized sense of potential, of having a future," placing potentiality in time and space and thus allowing a consciously foregrounded anticipation of a possible future time, cementing belief in future's capacity to become future. Reinforcing potentiality in the historical timeline is a key aspect in the ability of hope to mobilize and collectivize. Bringing the hoped-for one step closer to the actual allows people to project into the future, to imagine, to dream – part of the reason why many scholars, including Bloch (1986) and Taussig *et al.* (2013), have argued that hope, like potentiality, is an overtly political orientation.

Bloch implores us to harness the not-yet-conscious – a liminal state where new ideas are fostered – and to pursue the not-yet-become – the time of activity that follows the emergence of a new idea and its sedimentation into history[1] (McAllister and Ruggill 2010: 47). Sometimes the momentum of hope is slow and plodding, when the future seems to be a strong headwind blowing into our face. In the struggle to actualize potential, momentum might carry us down alternative or unintentional paths to futures that we had not previously considered or planned for. On other occasions hope is our snowball, the unstoppable force, propelling us rapidly into a future dramatically different from what has gone before. Either way, hope encompasses an element of positive movement, in navigating toward the future,

---

[1] For Bloch, history is "thought in the wrong tense" (Wieseltier 1986).

providing a drive, harnessing and producing a captivating energy, stimulating emotional response, operating at different speeds in the pursuit of actualizing potentiality.

Momentum toward What?

If hope thrives on indeterminacy (see Miyazaki 2004: 69ff, Miyazaki and Swedberg 2017), then, this is an indeterminacy rooted in the not-yet – and possibly not-yet-ever – of potentiality. In Bloch's terms, hope's momentum is built on the infinite potential to create not-yets through realizing the "otherwise." For anthropology, one of the more interesting facets of Bloch's analysis is his focus on disappointment, or the ways that potential is always only partially actualized. In disappointment, he notes,

The first underlying factor here is that the Here and Now stands too close to us. Raw experience transposes us from the drifting dream into another state: into that of immediate nearness. The moment just lived dims as such, it has too dark a warmth, and its nearness makes things formless. The Here and Now lacks the distance which does indeed alienate us, but makes things distinct and surveyable. Thus, from the outset, the immediate dimension within which realization occurs seems darker than the dream-image, and occasionally barren and empty.

(Bloch 1986: 180–181)

The hoped-for in the realm of the virtual is unlikely to be a carbon copy of what emerges in the actual. Disappointment, then, is the recognition that actualization never realizes all potentials, or the paradox that can occur "that the dream appeared firmer or at any rate brighter than its realization" (ibid., 181).

What hope builds on, however, is precisely this: "In each fulfilment, in so far and in as much as this is even possible totaliter, there remains a peculiar element of hope whose *mode of being* is not that of the existing or *currently existing reality*, and which is consequently left over together with its content" (ibid., 186). It is precisely this left-over potentiality that Bloch argues produces a futural orientation as such, in other words, provides for what Miyazaki calls motion, Massumi calls movement, and which we named its temporal momentum. The subtle difference between momentum and motion or movement is that momentum is by definition teleological, i.e., it is always an impetus *toward* something.

We suggest that the concept of momentum allows us to retain the indeterminacy of potentiality – the possibility for it both to be and not to be – while still incorporating the idea of ends – the sort of indeterminate teleology that we have argued is essential for any anthropology of the future. Miyazaki appears to conflate teleology with determinate futures in *The Method of Hope* (2004), where he forcefully argues for hope as an indeterminate future orientation and method of living. The people of Suvavou, Fiji, who were displaced from their land in the 1880s, continue to seek government compensation in the face of continual rebuttals and failures. Through his ethnographically led theory, Miyazaki draws on Bloch's indeterminacy to critique the underlying philosophical assumption about humanity captured in the Greek notion of history as a teleological course of disclosure of the truth about the essence of life. The future will not unfold according to a plan, or by way of fulfilling an immanent teleology, but rather "the future will astonish and exhilarate" (Rorty 1999: 18 in Miyazaki 2004: 15). Indeterminacy is at the heart of Miyazaki's theory of hope as method.

More recent work, however, has begun to argue, as we do, for a more ethnographically nuanced alternative to the holistic indeterminacy of hope proposed by Miyazaki. Stef Jansen (2016) has contended that generalizing about hope as open-ended and optimistic overlooks the concrete contours of hope as it emerges in particular sociohistorical timespaces. Suggesting that hope is not always solely an indeterminate affective attachment to a potential future, Jansen recounts his Sarajevan informants' desires for the national team to win a soccer match; they have focused hope, attached to a specific object, with a particular temporal end point. In his case, the imagining of a soccer team winning an important match is not indeterminate, utopian, or over/under-optimistic. The soccer fans exhibit a distinct preference for particular futures rather than any genuinely open-ended multiplicity as Miyazaki's theories of hope might have us believe.

Jansen makes a useful analytical distinction between intransitive and transitive modalities of hope, describing the former as primarily an affect, i.e., "hopefulness" (2016: 448), and the second as a modality with an object. As illustrated by the example of the Bosnian soccer match, one may experience both modalities at the same time, being both generally hopeful and hoping specifically for a victory. In particular, in response to Miyazaki, Jansen suggests that looking into the historical circumstances of the production of hope, and its duration in shorter, rigid, epochal timespaces, does not forego the future-oriented qualities, but rather better contextualizes and helps us understand ethnographically why and how people hope for certain futures.

Jansen's critical overview of the ethnographic literature on hope is a useful starting point for thinking about the anthropological analysis of this futural orientation. In particular, Jansen makes four proposals for understanding what we mean when we speak of hope, and here it is worth taking a minute to dissect these for our own purposes. First, he argues that hope is a disposition that conditions practices (ibid., 7) – what we have called, following Schatzki, a teleoaffect. In Schatzki's sense, a teleoaffect mobilizes a set of practices that encompass a number of associated actions and ends which people acceptably pursue. Indeed, we argue that all future orientations are teleoaffects. In other words, while Jansen gives the example of a soccer match with its own teleology structured by the "practice bundle" of a ninety-minute game, we may also speak in more epochal terms of vernacular time-spaces that have ends that are simultaneously concrete and indeterminate. The hope experienced by Tsipras supporters or Obama fans created a bubble of time that could be described as hopeful – a period when people walked on the streets differently, talked to each other differently, and dreamed differently. Because the disappointments later experienced were potentiality unrealized, they were felt as what Levi Bryant called (referring to potentiality) concrete without being actual. They were real, and really determinate ends; at the same time, they were "only" potential and therefore always had the possibility to not be. And like Bachelard's description of expectation, they provide a "vague, viscous, and virtual sense" (see Chapter 2) of which we may be aware only when it is realized or not.

Jansen also poses that hope is pushing us toward the future and thus exists in linear time. The historical context of the production of hope is essential for knowing the focus, development and trajectory of hope over time. Here we would suggest that hope is teleological, thus freeing us from the need for linearity since we have previously demonstrated that understanding teleology as unilinear is associated with modernity and is simply one way of viewing time – a stance we do not necessarily have to accept (see, for instance, Stewart 2012). Teleology is instead about open and indeterminate ends. When we hope, we hope *for* something and in this sense, hope is about change. It is about wishing, believing, focusing on the possibility to actualize potentiality – although, as noted earlier, after undergoing the process of actuation the realized version of the hoped-for may only vaguely resemble its potential form.

Jansen's third proposal is that while hope may not be wholly positive, "a blanket feel-good word" (Kleist and Jansen 2016: 388, also Dzenovska and De Genova 2018),[2] it nevertheless needs to have a positive charge, "a

---

[2] Dace Dzenovska and Nicholas De Genova (2018) argue that hope may not be located in things that anthropologists find politically or morally agreeable, particularly when it comes to desires for the continuation of capitalism or the promotion of right-wing ideologies. Hope swells in the oppressive present, they argue, on both sides of the political spectrum, with left-wing activists and with right-wing nationalists trying to reorient political trajectories (2018: 2). Hope attaches to political formations that promise to deliver people from disaffection and dispossession, but also from the domination of so-called liberal, multiculturalist, and cosmopolitan elites.

degree, however hesitant, of expectant desire" (Jansen 2016: 454). While it seems indisputable that as futural orientation hope always contains an element of the positive, it is important to us how that positivity is socially constructed and what its momentum pushes us to do. Hope is not always about Bloch's "good society," and Jansen notes that we may be inconsistent in our hopes or may have hopes that are socially unacceptable or politically questionable (Jansen 2016: 453). What does a neo-Nazi hope for? Can this be viewed as positive?

For anthropology, an important problem presented by the teleoaffect of hope is how to understand the mobilization of virtuality at the collective level. While anticipation and expectation are grounded in the space of experience, hope often appears at the moment when experience is frustrated, when what we experience is less than what we desire. This is why, Bloch suggests, hope is often the realm of daydream, collectively mobilized through images, mass media, fiction, and technologies of imagination.

The final point for Jansen is that, echoing Miyazaki, hope is indeterminate and its outcome uncertain. We have framed this indeterminacy that accompanies hope here as the knowledge that many potentialities do not become actualities. Building on that observation, however, we may add a fifth element to Jansen's list: hope as futural momentum. Hope as teleoaffect emerges collectively in its various forms (optimistic, pessimistic, filled with certainty, filled with yearning) when people mobilize to push potential into the future actual. Hope, alongside such associated orientations as faith and love, operates to produce change, bringing fragments of potential otherwises toward indeterminate ends. This is never more so the case than during election campaigns or soccer matches where there is collective investment in virtual futures, a dimension of potentiality where there is an "energy" that can be collectively sensed. Hope harnesses this hidden but profoundly felt energy – the "incorporeal materiality," the unseen capacities of other people and objects – shaping the course of collective action. In the next section we will examine cases where collective urgings reveal momentum toward a potential that is not yet realized. It will be shown that vernacular timespaces of hope are often defined, quite neatly, by very specific beginnings and ends, as collective endeavors to actualize potential reach their climax.

In a Time of Hope

A recent companion to Bloch's work on hope, Peter Thompson and Slavoj Žižek's (2013) edited collection *The Privatization of Hope*, advocates the relevance of Bloch in the twenty-first century. The overall argument of the volume is that Bloch's musings on the future can help us to escape from construing hope solely on individual terms, as personal desires and wants, and to start pursuing hope collectively. In his conversations with Theodor Adorno, Bloch had begun to reflect on the "terrible banalization" of utopia, with Adorno adding that "utopian consciousness" is "shrinking" with people "sworn to this world as it is," obstructing the consciousness of possibility (Bloch and Adorno 1988: 3–4). Being offered an increasingly limited range of teleoaffects in a top-down fashion, the "crisis in hope" has meant that humanity has "lost its capacity to hunger and hope" collectively (McManus 2015: 18). In this section we contend that collective hoping is alive and well and is integral to such vernacular timespaces as election campaigns and sports events. Here we wish to offer insight into how collective hoping is facilitated through political rhetoric and technologies of the imagination that promote possibilities for alternative futures and cultivate collective hope to facilitate social change by actualizing potentiality.

Let us go back to Athens, Greece, January 2018. Three years on from Syriza's election and hope has turned to disillusion and frustration. Satirical slogans now read "*I Elpida gamithike*" (Hope Was Fucked) accompanied by the logo of Greece's most popular pornography site, and "*I Elpida Skouriase*" (Hope Rusted). The dramatic turnaround in public opinion is marked by the continuation of unforgiving austerity, the U-turn on a definitive referendum vote to "say no" to more tough Troika bailout measures (61.31 percent voted to reject the terms of a new bailout deal which the government then duly accepted), pension reform and taxation rises, the selling-off of public assets in the haulage, aviation, and energy industries, and most recently the controversial efforts to "resolve" the naming of the Former Yugoslav Republic of Macedonia. A Time of Hope has turned to disillusion, at best, and at worst, rage and fury at unkept promises to bring forth the potential for radically different political futures. Public expectations have not been satisfied, and the new timespace that was offered by the incumbent Syriza government in 2015 has not unfolded – or rather, it has unfolded in a manner that runs counter to public hopes and expectations. Optimism has dissipated, the conservative New Democracy party is leading the poles once again. Hope-fueled momentum is lost in the first few months of government, as hard-nosed European bureaucrats are blamed for derailing the drive toward an alternative future.

Chicago, USA, 2015. Six years on and Obama still clings to his message of hope, refusing to give in to anger and disillusionment. But it is becoming hopeless. Policies are watered down and blocked in Washington. Many American leftists criticize Obama for failing to govern as the transformative progressive his inspiring campaign promised he would be. But where potential has failed to be actualized, new hope can be found: new social movements such as Occupy Wall Street in 2011 and Black Lives Matter in 2013 grew in strength, spirit, and creativity during the Obama years due, principally, to the gap between what most moderate Democrats and leftists had hoped his administration would accomplish and what actually took place. As one of Knight's interlocutors in Chicago put it in 2015, "Hope has changed to compromise, but that is better than what we had before. Compromise is better than despair. . . . One still feels like we [the USA] are moving in the right direction, but just a bit slower than expected in 2008." The ardent

Obama supporter might say that his momentum was curtailed by others – Republican senators, those intent on sabotaging his policies. After the 2016 presidential elections, Obamatime is succeeded by the Trumposcene, Donald Trump coming to power on his own hope-filled message for a different audience, "Make America Great Again."

These two examples of electoral campaigns demonstrate the ability of hope to galvanize and unify public opinion through optimistic rhetoric, promises of change, and the generation of a set of expectations with powerful affects. After all, the poetics and politics of hope are powerful aphrodisiacs (Battaglia 2017: 273). For a confined period of time, messages of hope feed into wider technologies of imagination that promote alternative teleoaffective structures. Hope here is very much a collective concern relevant, in Thompson and Žižek's terms, to twenty-first-century desires. It is collective, also, in the sense that seemingly bounded timespaces of election politics transcend national borders and, as we will see, become concerns for transnational publics affectively invested in futures of global consequence.

This section discusses how rhetoric and technologies of imagination are employed in political campaigns as vessels of hope to provide a collective sense of futural momentum. Election campaigns provide the quintessential snowball effect as selected messages provide momentum to candidates with very definite goals. Evident at political rallies and in media coverage, energy swells in campaigns built on hope for change, reaching a crescendo on election night where a whole nation might be glued to the television set. In these vernacular timespaces, hope is a key teleoaffect that mobilizes toward specific goals. As demonstrations of collective momentum toward a potential not yet actualized, collective experiences of hope are held within particular limited timeframes which, in terms of duration and concrete boundaries, differentiates them from many of the timespaces we have so far discussed.

Technologies of imagination – the social and material means by which particular visions of the future are generated (Sneath *et al.*

2009: 6) – are key to the successful accomplishment of collective future-oriented goals. Where there is the desire to implement wide-scale political and economic change, technologies of imagination help galvanize public opinion, making sure that people invest in governmental visions of the future and promote the benefits of change. In short, technologies of imagination make sure that everyone is pulling in the same direction, that momentum is maintained.

In India, Laura Bear (2015a) provides an example of how technologies of imagination were key to transforming a national economy. The path toward market liberalization was built on a message of speculative hope fed from central government, providing a sense of collective momentum toward a new economic model that promised material accumulation, redistributed wealth, and social responsibility. The message was simple: the market economy had the potential to transform the lives of everyday people, and this was a future worth buying into. Throughout the 1980s and 1990s, successive governments attempted to build ties with influential business groups and strategically leaked information of economic reform into the public domain (Appadurai 2011, 2013; Bear 2015a; Holmes 2013).

Central banks, rating agencies, and government ministers possess the power to influence public opinion and stimulate interest from private investors through carefully placed words and hearts-and-minds advertising campaigns, altering the teleoaffective structure of what is emotionally and materially deemed acceptable to pursue. As we have seen with the Syriza and Obama election campaigns, these words and phrases offer glimpses, what Davina Cooper (2014) calls "tasters," of what it might look like if the otherwise-than-actual was realized – another version of Bloch's wishful images.

Douglas Holmes's (2013) groundbreaking study of central banks deals expertly with how "the bridge to the ephemera of expectations, to sensibilities in the future, is constructed through language, technical modelling and 'the economy of words'" (2013: 9–10). He argues that the economy should be viewed as a field of communicative action and that linguistic modelling of the future is imperative to the functioning of global capitalist markets. The words of policy statements endow the future with discernible features, sensibilities that shape expectations, and show how potential might be realized. The policy intentions of central banks that are aimed at the future are assimilated into the personal hopes and expectations of the layperson (you and me), and we act upon them accordingly, changing our shared teleoaffective expectations of the future. Through an intricate communicative field, banks thus recruit the public to fulfil their modelling of the future in a form of self-fulfilling prophecy. By introducing the public to new hopes for a future based on economic projections that in the present only exist in the virtual, the idea is that people will invest (both emotionally and financially) in the vision, and the future will materialize as financial institutions desire. Strategically placed words create the desired affect amongst the public who actively seek, somewhat impatiently, to pull the promised future toward the present.

This reminds us of *The New York Herald* editor James Gordon Bennett's comparison of Wall Street and confidence men, discussed in Chapter 3. By claiming access to specialized knowledge and playing on people's desires, bureaucrats and bankers play the role of the confidence man, gaining public trust and convincing people of how best to speculatively invest in the future. Of course, there is usually a significant discrepancy between what is depicted in bureaucratic rhetoric and actual working conditions on the ground (Bear 2015b); potential is not always realized as might be expected or desired. Technocrats do not make visible the instability, temporary infrastructure, and dangerous labor generated by public-private investment initiatives and government schemes of permanent austerity. Instead, they promote "the politics of possibility" – teleoaffective structures of thinking, feeling, and acting that increase horizons of hope, expand the field of imagination, and create greater equity in what can be termed "the capacity to aspire"

(Appadurai 2013: 295). In India, the technologies of imagination are a complex and highly influential nexus of people and institutions who deliberately produced a set of shared teleoaffects that encouraged private speculation and ignited hope-filled momentum toward the actualization of futures promised in political rhetoric. For Bear, technologies of imagination invoke an invisible realm – the unknown future – and make it visible to the public eye through promises of bountiful prosperity for nation and individual. In this sense they highlight the potential for the future to become the future; by offering "expert insights" projecting a future where potential has been actualized, there is a collective feeling that the future is within touching distance.

In the case of the Syriza election, imaginations of ushering in change from the what-has-gone-before became infectious and spread far beyond the borders of the nation-state. At the dawn of Tsipras's election in January 2015 there was hope in Spain, also suffering financial collapse, that the radical left may sweep to power now that the Greeks had shown the way. Rumors abounded in the European mass media that the European Union was trembling at the thought that left-wing revolution would catch on like wildfire and engulf Europe's southern shores – being termed "contagion" in the popular press. This felt like the moment of ultimate momentum, a collective push toward a transformed political future, an epidemic of hope facilitated by the press and social media.[3] Anti-austerity protestors on the streets of Madrid held aloft banners with messages of solidarity written in Greek and waved the Greek flag. Across borders, publics had been mobilized to back an alternative vision of the future, one that broke free from neoliberal economic and bureaucratic relations.

[3] The collectivizing nature of hope to push people toward new possibilities of being has long been part of the anthropological discourse on dreaming (Edgar and Henig 2010; Reed 2011; Stewart 2012). For instance, in Stewart's (2012) accounts of Naxiot dreaming the future is materialized through collective faith in visions. Often the dreams are counterfactual – running against the grain of historical circumstance or contradicting official Orthodox religious beliefs – but have the power to collectivize and mobilize.

Likewise, in 2008 the world was waiting in cautious but distinctly optimistic expectation that Obama would bring something new, a breath of fresh air, a level-headed stability to the global political scene, and a new trajectory in American politics. After eight years of George W. Bush and the associated "war on terror" in Iraq and Afghanistan which had global consequences, the world waited with bated breath to see what the new political era might bring. The future was very much the primary concern of the present, swelled by public concern about the vernacular timespaces of armed conflict and austerity that occupied the recent past. In 2009 Obama accepted the Nobel Peace Prize for fostering a new era of peaceful international relations. Obama had at that point only spoken of his intentions to deescalate the global conflicts that marked the Bush presidency – the Nobel Prize seemed as much a marker of collective relief to move on from the previous time-space as it was about actual change. With the USA still involved in two wars, Obama's Nobel Prize seemed to confirm as already actual something that was still very much only potential.

Both Syriza and Obama offered a space for people to invest collectively in "micro-utopias" of hope that signaled change from previous timespaces. In Cooper's terms, micro-utopias can inhabit the present as temporary "tasters" of the future, reinforcing hope for change.[4] In the campaigns, new vernaculars were constructed around events that were generally perceived as ruptures on the global political scene. The Syriza victory came with talk of defiance, upsetting the long-established political order, and with ideas of egalitarianism and victory for the little person against the Man. It offered a "taster" of what Europe might look like in a postcapitalist, postcrisis era. With Obama came a "we can do it"

---

[4] Jan Jonathan Bock (2016) picks up on this idea when discussing the micro-utopias emerging in the arts after the 2009 L'Aquila earthquake in central Italy. With the historic city destroyed and inhabitants living in makeshift camps, small arts and performance groups provided escapism, hope, and a space to build utopian imaginations of the potential future. Perhaps ironically, the emergent spaces in which to imagine the future were populated by people's desires to return to the nostalgic (pre-earthquake) past.

attitude, a sense Americans were now showing their liberal cosmopolitanism, while there was talk of change, honesty, progress. In both instances, the collective vision of the future had changed, giving rise to new optimistic vernaculars. Here, hope transcended the gap between potential and actual, projecting a distinctly different timespace before and after "the event" of a political election.

In the confined timespace of an election campaign people share, circulate, and exchange hope (Hage 2003: 9). Hope is carried in political rhetoric, by technologies of imagination, or delivered by those experts "in the know." Often, the promise is a clean break from vernacular timespaces of the past – Bushtime to Obamatime to the Trumposcene or a Time of Crisis to a Time of Stability.[5] The associated teleoaffects of previous timespaces, timespaces of failure, are emphasized and hope for change foregrounded as an alternative. In campaigns the goals are clearly defined, transitive objects of hope in Jansen's sense, and as such there is a focused momentum driving them forward. However, as Angelique Haugerud (2013: 34) notes, once an election campaign is won, it is quite another thing to deliver on promises, to actualize the potential to which hope was pinned.

Reorienting the future in real terms requires more than the technologies of imagination deployed through the fancy words of election-trail rhetoric. The "tasters" of the future offered on the campaign trail usually return to the realm of the otherwise-than-actual, to remain dormant as momentum fizzles out. This is why we say that such timespaces are often more clearly defined than, for instance, Times of Peace or Times of War, which tend to have indeterminate end points. Election campaigns are, in Cooper's (2014: 44) terms, "pockets of non-standard social practices," domains of "optimism and freedom," and after a relatively short venture into the excitement of something different, momentum is lost as the

---

[5] Although scholars such as Felix Ringel (2014, 2018) have countered that in some contexts hope may be a direction toward maintaining the present as the future (also Dzenovska 2018a).

energy dissipates and people return to daily routine. We now wish to turn to a brief analysis of the capacity of these timespaces, with seemingly defined beginnings and ends, to influence wider social change.

Limited Timespaces of Hope

One place where one can easily experience such restricted vernacular timespaces of hope are sporting events. Not only are there definite goals and palpable energy as fans drive their team toward victory, but these targeted hopes, transitive in Jansen's words, spawn general intransitive hopefulness that transcends the timespace of the match. The cases we discuss below illustrate how specific hopes pinned to the achievements of a national sports team are linked to general hopefulness for political change and the opening of a new timespace, namely a Time of Peace. Beyond the hope and excitement surrounding overcoming the opposing team, the games could be said to have the capacity to incite momentum toward social change well beyond their duration on the playing field. Yet, like the election campaigns above, once the timespace of the event has closed and the team is knocked out of tournament, hopeful momentum slows and eventually fades. The matches provide micro-utopian bubbles of hope, "tasters" of the otherwise, the could-be in Bloch's terms.

Throughout the 2000s, the Afghanistan cricket team had remarkable success on the field while the country was in the midst of a decade of war. The team was formed in the refugee camps of Pakistan, where young Afghans who had fled their war-torn country spent their days playing cricket with sticky tape balls and tree branches. Some have gone on to become national heroes, role models who ply their trade in the world's top cricket leagues. In an area of the world where it is often said that cricket is a religion and cricketers take on God-like status, Afghanistan qualified for the 2012 ICC World Twenty20 cup competition, 2015 ICC Cricket World Cup, and 2016 ICC World Twenty20, where they beat the eventual winners, the West Indies, and another top side, Zimbabwe. In 2017 Afghanistan was granted Test status, the ultimate accolade in the world of cricket, joining the likes of England, Australia, and India in the elite band of twelve top-class nations. The story of the rise of Afghan cricket has led to headlines such as "Afghanistan cricket team: A team called hope"[6] and "Afghanistan: The bringers of hope and joy."[7]

A similar case seemed to be taking shape in the form of the Syrian soccer team's bid to qualify for the 2018 World Cup held in Russia. Playing their "home" matches abroad (mainly in Malaysia) because of the war, Syria beat the odds to come through their qualifying groups, only to be defeated by Australia in the final play-off round. In Syria there were calls for a national holiday on the dates of the play-offs, the streets of Damascus were transformed by a "festive atmosphere," and there were reports that "relief had been found" in the distraction of soccer. Sales of replica strips also skyrocketed.[8] Mowaffak Joumaa, the head of Syria's Olympic Committee and Sports Federation, told The Associated Press in Damascus that "every citizen has become a soldier in his own profession. . . . We are hopeful that they will achieve a good result . . . and bring happiness to all Syrians."[9]

In the cases of the Afghan cricket and the Syrian soccer teams, sport has brought micro-utopias of hope. This is a targeted hope that belongs to a very limited timespace – ninety minutes on a soccer field, a Tuesday evening in September, 240 balls of cricket (in the case of a Twenty20 match). But from that determinate transitive hope springs an affective bubble of hopefulness for a potentially better future. As well as the "epoch of peacetime" that provides escapism or a micro-utopia for the duration of ninety minutes or 240 balls, the energy provided by these

[6] www.espn.co.uk/cricket/story/_/id/22066142/team-called-hope
[7] http://afghanconnection.org/rise-afghan-cricket
[8] www.firstpost.com/sports/fifa-world-cup-2018-qualifiers-syrias-hopes-of-making-finals-bring-relief-but-reveal-divisions-among-fans-4128279.html
[9] www.si.com/soccer/2017/09/04/syria-world-cup-qualification-2018-hopes-war

events spills over into rhetorics of hope for wider societal change, providing hope for epochs with alternative teleoaffective structures than the Time of Conflict.

Hope here is a feature of struggling to cope with the strains of the present, the renegotiated expectations of the future, in the yearning for "normal lives" (see Jansen 2014; Narotzky and Besnier 2014). According to Berlant (2011: 14), hope in the face of crisis is "a scene of negotiated sustenance that makes life bearable as it presents itself ambivalently, unevenly, incoherently." It is thus often a short-term coping strategy that bridges the present and the near future. In a positive sense, we may see that if potentiality is defined by its indeterminacy, always presenting us with the possibility that something that has not yet happened may yet, the ambivalence and incoherence of crisis opens the door to hope through creating such an affect of the indeterminate, something that may well happen, even though it seems it shouldn't or won't.

We would agree with Berlant that in a Time of Crisis hope is an important gateway to a micro-utopia of the "otherwise," offering a modicum of relief from the pressing demands of everyday life (see also Muñoz 2009; Pedersen 2012). However, we would contend that in these circumstances hope is often experienced in a coherent and direc- ted manner, in practices with clear definitions and goals. In the cases of Afghan cricket and Syrian soccer, we see that in providing escapism from the everyday and a portal to futures of potential otherwise, the bubble of hope has very specific spatiotemporal parameters. Further, it is part of a coherent vernacular timespace: government ministers com- ment on it, the hope-filled event is used for political propaganda, and the wider world seems alert to the potential for hope on the field of play to kick-start positive societal change. We agree with Berlant that in a Time of Crisis, hope stabilizes and familiarizes the present, but it does this through collective mobilization, a momentum that focuses on specific targets, from which generalized hopefulness springs. When crisis is the norm, what Berlant (2011: 10) calls "crisis ordinariness," hope is part of the teleoaffective structure that assists in negotiating suppression, destitution, the unknown. But the confined vernacular timespace of a sporting event also lends itself to an examination of hope and hopefulness as momentum not limited to crisis situations.

In 2018, the England national soccer team reached the semi-finals of the World Cup for only the third time ever – and a feat not achieved since the infamous loss on penalties to West Germany in 1990. A pre-tournament headline read "To Russia with Hope,"[10] though expectations of success were very low owing to an inexperienced team and unconvincing performances in the qualifying tournament. Another headline quoting one of England's greatest former players, Gary Lineker, advised fans to "write off" any hopes of doing well and focus on potential success "in four years" (at the next tournament).[11] Yet, over the course of three weeks, hope swelled to the extent that even those usually disinterested in the sport were gripped by football fever. It provided a welcome break from the endless talk of Brexit – which no longer felt like such a divisive topic – and nostalgic comparisons were made with the affects of that ill-fated 1990 campaign: both summers were unusually hot, the eerie silence on the streets during game time, grown men in tears.

Although not nearly as telling as the Afghan and Syrian sporting endeavors in providing visions of potential futures with social unity, positivity, and peace, the 2018 England World Cup campaign offered a glimpse into the underestimated potential of eleven men on a pitch to actually win a soccer match and how a divided nation came together in a bubble of hopeful expectation. With a sense of collective momentum, diehard fans and occasional spectators alike seemed to be pushing toward the same goal, a date with destiny in the final in Moscow on July 15th. After eventual defeat, fans were left in a state of hopeful

[10] www.theguardian.com/football/2018/jun/09/england-hope-russia-world-cup-2018
[11] www.independent.co.uk/sport/football/world-cup/world-cup-2018-england-squad-gary-lineker-write-off-hopes-blood-youngsters-a8353541.html

anticipation: just think what this young side, so full of potential, could achieve in 2022!

In the final group game with Belgium, having already qualified for the knockout stages of the competition, manager Gareth Southgate fielded a weakened side. England duly lost 1–0, causing meltdowns in the press and in bars across the country, lamenting England's "loss of momentum." After the semifinal defeat to Croatia, debate focused on momentum with a different temporal horizon: could the feel-good factor produced by England's performance be maintained, capitalized on for the future? Aristotle tells us that hope is a disposition that leads to flourishing (Cottingham 2016: 18), and there were cries in the press to harness the palpable positivity to generate future sporting success. How can we best facilitate this? Surely, it was suggested, this moment should be a catalyst for addressing serious problems of grassroots infrastructure required to nurture the next generation. Investing in the future of the game at this time would help capture the potential of both the landmark moment in the sport and the full potential of up-and-coming players.[12] There was collective anxiety, verging on desperation, about how organizations and funding bodies could capitalize on the euphoria of this three-week event and best help young sportspeople to realize their potential.

Sport seems to be ideally suited to Bloch's ideas of hope existing in everyday activities, often only to slip tantalizingly out of grasp as life returns to normal. Sports events at first seem nicely confined to their own neat timespaces with teleoaffects of hope, anticipation, anxiety aimed at definite ends. In this sense they ideally fit the concept of micro-utopias, bounded activities that provide escapism from the realities of the everyday through "tasters" of how things could be otherwise. Yet ultimately the object-focused hope is accompanied by an intransitive hopefulness for societal change. Further, the events discussed above all

[12] www.telegraph.co.uk/world-cup/2018/07/12/english-football-urged-use-world-cup-momentum-catalyst-grassroots

encourage futural projections and "what ifs," contemplating the otherwise-than-actual in the future tense. What-if we can capture this hope to build for future success on the soccer field? What-if we let this opportunity pass us by? We must maintain the momentum created by hope. Could a collectivizing event such as a victory for the Syrian soccer team lead to a national holiday and the ceasing of violence, even just for one day? These hopeful futural projections are constructed on double-aspect potentialities – how to get the best out of eleven players on a sports field to win a match and the potential impact of that success to animate alternative futures.

Conclusion

In 1963, Martin Luther King, Jr., asked those gathered in Washington DC to look not to today or tomorrow, but to the dream of "one day." This "one day" would be reached, he preached, through unyielding faith and hope to transform the potentiality of a dream into actuality. Dr. King's words mobilized a collectivity toward realizing the otherwise-than-actual by focusing on a specific set of goals. His use of dreams provided directionality to hope, binding hopeful desire with prediction, and an unstoppable momentum for social change (cf. Reed 2011). As we have seen, political rhetoric and technologies of imagination have the ability to mobilize across vernacular timespaces; well-chosen words placed by economists in India may lead to self-fulfilling prophecies of how potentiality materializes on international markets, and the radical policies of Greek politicians that imagine the future otherwise trigger rallies on the streets of Madrid.

For our purposes here, election campaigns, like sporting events, have been analyzed as vernacular timespaces with well-defined beginnings and ends, where hope crescendos. Through technologies of imagination, including Blochian wishful images, catchy slogans, and media endorsements, the public is offered glimpses of utopias that are just over the futural horizon, in the "one day." The propaganda of the campaign trail captures the potential near future in the present and provides a reason for people to invest in future-making projects. Elections represent intense vernacular timespaces with their own tele-oaffective structures that enchant us for a limited period before broken promises ultimately lead to disappointment. This is the space where new hope takes root.

We maintain that hope is at once one of the most abstract and most common orientations to the future that draws the not-yet into the present and motivates activity in the here-and-now. It drives potentiality toward actuation in the process of becoming. Rather than more passive forms of futural momentum, such as yearning which implies helplessness to produce change, hope always incorporates an aspect of positive movement, although we must be sensitive to how this is socially constructed. While handling the indeterminacy of potentiality, hope is the momentum toward realizing particular "otherwises."

SIX

Destiny

I cannot think the unthinkable, but I can think that it is not impossible for the impossible to be.

Meillassoux 2008: 42

On a hot August morning in the late 1960s, in a Texas city most famous for an eponymous television series, a girl was born out of wedlock. Let us call her Rachel. In fact, her mother had given her a different name, but she would not know that until decades later, because at one month old she was given to a young couple with a decent education and strong religious leanings. While she was still a toddler (and so unaware of these things), her adoptive father would return to school and, against all odds, receive a master's and then doctoral degree in English literature from a small Texas university. His own parents were primary school graduates who had farmed and worked in a grain mill, and they were puzzled by the trajectory that their son's life had taken. Her father always aspired to more than the hard-scrabble life of his own upbringing, and he gradually filled their home with antiques, paintings, and books.

It was the books that were a solace to Rachel when, at the age of seven, she moved with her parents to a small town in the Mississippi Delta. She spent her first year there at the back of the classroom reading, because she had already learned everything that her teachers were teaching. She had moved from a small school in a wealthy Texas hamlet to the depths of the rural South, where people viewed too much book learning with considerable suspicion. Always the outsider, she gradually developed a particularly American idea about her predicament: that she must be destined for something greater. Her teachers called her that ambiguous word "gifted," and surely the fact that she was so far ahead of her peers, that she got As without studying, were indications of a great destiny?

Fueled by such a belief, and imagining all sorts of goals for herself, she dropped out of high school and went to a famous private university. Unconcerned about problems of the immediate future, such as how she would later pay back her student loans, she focused on fulfilling her destiny, when surely all such problems would be set right. She struggled at the famous university and gradually came to realize that no amount of destiny had prepared her to be there. But her lack of preparation had to compete with the umbrage she felt when her professors dared to give her Bs rather than As in her courses. When she became the famous writer that she was destined to be, they would regret their mistake!

For her entire life until that point, Rachel had been told by those people she trusted or to whom she chose to listen that she could be whatever she wanted. If she felt compelled to do certain things, like write or play music or read philosophy, that sense of compulsion was directing her toward the path that she could take. Because everything was possible, it was up to her to fulfill her destiny.

Like the story of David earlier, Rachel's story is not only one of an awkward teen with dreams and longings, but is more particularly one of how those dreams and longings are shaped within an overarching narrative of the yet-unfulfilled future. Rachel had plotted her future; she thought she knew what her destiny was supposed to be; and she had acted in ways that she thought would realize that destiny. Stumbling blocks along the way had to be seen as part of what was necessary to reach that destiny. In classic Romantic fashion, she assumed that suffering and struggling were part of what it meant to become a great writer. Indeed, without yet having read Nietzsche, she adopted an *amor fati*, what he called his "formula for greatness in a human being": "that one wants nothing to be different, not backward, not in all eternity. Not merely bear what is necessary, still less conceal it ... but love it" (Nietzsche 1989: 258). This is what Deleuze and Guattari (1994: 158) called "becoming the offspring of one's own events." The "fatefulness" of this attitude is that it requires one to think of present events as what will make one into what one is supposed to be.

In small-town, rural America of the 1980s, it was still possible for a girl to believe in fulfilling her destiny despite the odds. Even if her own sense of destiny was peculiar by the standards of her class and upbringing, it remained part of what it meant to grow up white, middle class, and American in the period. It was a timespace in which America still had a destiny to bring "freedom" to the world, and when Rachel was also "free" to fulfill what she was meant to be. In fact, in the way that the concept of freedom was taught to her, it was very much based in the Enlightenment idea that the ultimate freedom was the freedom to pursue one's destiny. Although by that time high school students could critically view the USA's supposed Manifest Destiny as a scheme for land grabs, the idea of Providence remained strong. Even if one did not understand Providence as God's hand guiding one's actions, the way that early settlers did, one could still see America as somehow blessed by history, the heir of a progressive current that would lead the world to its anticipated, freer future.

This chapter concerns destiny as an orientation to a future beyond the horizon, a future that is not visible, not even expectable, but is nevertheless immanent in the present. Because of its immanence, it can sometimes be divined or glimpsed, but we can never know when it will be manifest. This immanence of the future is usually expressed not as the indeterminate teleologies of everyday life, but as the sort of teleology that Aristotle called a "final cause," that for which something is made, its purpose. As we will see, however, unlike potentiality, where the future is an absent but virtual presence, this particular immanence of the future is what Frank Kermode (2000) calls "the sense of an ending," the idea that we need a sense of an ultimate end to orient our lives. That orientation, however, relies upon the finitude of Time. In particular, it relies upon the relationship between the horizon of expectation and what lies beyond it.

We have earlier said that anticipation temporalizes temporality and have claimed that expectation futuralizes the future. In addition, we have argued that potentiality gives us the future's capacity to become future. All of these orientations contain both a particular disposition toward the future based on the past (what *ought* to happen) and a simultaneous knowledge of the aleatory. This chapter applies these ideas to the temporal limits of life itself, the point at which the horizon ends.

Unlike our other orientations, which take form within the limits of that horizon, destiny is defined by what is beyond the horizon: it is our part of the infinite that defines the finite. One sees this in the older meanings of the word "temporal," which referred not to time per se, but rather to time's passage, and therefore to its end. In the language of the Church, to speak of "temporal gain" or "temporal power" was to speak of things that were "of the world," and things that would pass away. Not only is this a recognition in our language that all matter is by definition temporal, but also that everything is temporary. Not only is all matter within Time, but it is so because the world is corruptible: everything passes away.

This means not only that our own destiny is shaped by the inevitable end of life, but also that conceptions of communal destiny have imagined endings. Those endings might be the end of history as we know it: the conquest of the world, the reign of freedom, the defeat of capitalism. Or communal destiny might be circumscribed by endings in which time ceases to exist as we know it: an apocalypse, a Second Coming, the return of the Mahdi, the overthrowing of or triumph of capitalism. Moreover, signs in the present foretell those endings, often leading believers to acts of provocation. Even in traditions defined not by apocalyptic endings but by eternal returns, the finite is in a relationship with the infinite such that destiny takes place as a series of finitudes. In the perceived temporal flow of the present, then, destiny is the immanence of our own finite horizon.

We call this *the untimeliness of the temporal* to point to the immanence of the beyond-time as what temporalizes our own lives. If fate or destiny is often portrayed as a force outside us, we argue, it is because this image describes the potentially actualizable future within us. If we are, as Deleuze and Guattari suggest, the offspring of our own events, this means that we are always pregnant with our own future selves. Unfortunately, the birth of that future self spells our own demise; it is a birth that we will never see.

This chapter explores what it means for the temporal to be untimely, for the passage of life to be shaped always by a conception of a time that is beyond time. We call this the untimeliness of the *temporal* to describe the ways in which the untimely is always already a part of how temporality temporalizes itself. Rachel, for instance, might not have received the grades that she expected to get, but she might perceive this as part of what Aristotle called the *peripateia*, or winding trajectory, of her life that would eventually lead her to her foreordained end. The pregnancy of her own potentiality seemed a destiny waiting to be born, one that would gain sustenance from the trials of the present.

Rachel was concerned not by what she was or what happened to her in that moment but by how that moment helped her to realize what she was *supposed to be*. In Medieval logic, the Latin *supponere* meant "to act as a subject," but when applied to the future may be seen to imply the uncertain necessity of becoming the offspring of one's own life. Whereas in Chapter 2, on expectation, we explored the gap between the "is" and the "ought," here we examine the movement between the "supposed to be" and the "bound to be" as a mode of orienting oneself to the future that contains both teleological necessity and openness to the aleatory.

Before exploring the ethnographic possibilities of supposition, however, we take a detour into causality, debates over which we see as directly linked to a particular puzzlement within modernity over the relationship between destiny and free will, or between fate and fatalism. This has infected anthropology, as well, we argue, which has similarly puzzled over how a belief in destiny can accompany agentive action. Examining more recent work that has attempted to suture this gap, we then return to think through the future's "dual aspect of being determined according to teleological necessity, yet at the same time, experienced as an aleatory accident" (Jeffs 2012: 43). If temporality temporalizes and the future futuralizes, we argue, they do so in relation to their limits, to the untimely that shapes their horizon.

The Anti-Philosophies of Fate

In most histories of philosophy, the modern is born from contingency. More specifically, it was in response to an argument made by a then-unemployed university dropout that some of the greatest philosophers of the Enlightenment launched a strident attack on ways of knowing that do not submit to what were known as the "laws of reason." In *A Treatise of Human Nature*, his first work, David Hume critiqued the fundamental principle of causation to argue that inductive reasoning is actually a result of custom, habit, and what he called the "constant conjunction" of events.

Although Hume's appeal to custom and habit – and thereby to anthropology – is interesting in itself, what is relevant for our purposes is the way in which Hume makes clear the temporal nature of what were otherwise regarded as natural laws:

We have said, that all arguments concerning existence are founded on the relation of cause and effect; that our knowledge of that relation is derived entirely from experience; and that all our experimental conclusions proceed

upon the supposition, that the future will be conformable to the past. . . .
From causes, which appear similar, we expect similar effects. This is the sum
of all our experimental conclusions.

(2000: 31)

Causation, he says, is not a type of law, but rather a type of expectation.
It is something that we impute to objects, a type of causal fetishism that
exists only in our own inferences, not in the things themselves.

Indeed, we can see the imputation of causation, he says, in the fact
that we are only slightly surprised when things turn out otherwise.
As we discussed in Chapter 2 on expectation, the orientation contains
within itself an uncertainty, the possibility of something happening
besides what we expect. In an observation that seems to be an early
summary of speculative materialism, Hume notes,

In vain do you pretend to have learned the nature of bodies from your past
experience. Their secret nature, and consequently, all their effects and
influence, may change, without any change in their sensible qualities. This
happens sometimes, and with regard to some objects: Why may it not
happen always, and with regard to all objects? What logic, what process of
argument secures you against this supposition?

(2000: 33)

Hume's famous example is a billiard table, where we hit a ball with the
expectation that it will act in a particular way, even though, in the end, it
may jump, spin, or go in a different direction than we expect. It is the
possibility of the unexpected within the expected that shows us that
what we consider to be a natural law is in fact only our repeated
observation of the "constant conjunction" of two objects. He concludes,
"All inferences from experience, therefore, are effects of custom, not of
reasoning. . . . Custom, then, is the great guide of human life. It is that
principle alone, which renders our experience useful to us, and makes us
expect, for the future, a similar train of events with those which have
appeared in the past" (2000: 37–38).

Hume's relativist anthropology describes a connection that we make from experience but denies the necessity of its conclusion. As we know, it was Kant's reply to Hume in the *Critique of Pure Reason* that set the stage for an entire history of Enlightenment thought that attempted to found a new world on the "laws of reason."

Beginning with Hume, Jean-René Vernes asserts, it is the confusion of what Vernes calls aleatory and deterministic reason that has led to Western philosophy's "unconscious refusal to take into account the unusual nature of random phenomena" (Vernes 2000: 32). Hume had reflected on the ways in which we use probability to control the always expanding limits of possibility, accepting that the possible outcomes of any throw of the dice or game of billiards are in fact infinite, even if probability limits these. It is this everyday use of probability to predict or expect a particular outcome that Vernes has called "aleatory reason," or the type of reason that we use when we calculate the statistical probability of turning up a particular number on a die more than once. Vernes opposes this to determinant reason, the reason used in, say, geometry, where the conclusion necessarily follows from the premises. He argues that it is the confusion of these two, or rather the reduction of aleatory reason to determinant reason, that characterized the "classic conception" of reason in the Enlightenment and after. It is aleatory reason to which Hume appears to have referred when he uses the word "supposition" in the passages above (e.g., the supposition that the future will always be conformable with the past).

This discussion offers us two important insights for a study of fate and destiny that hopes to go beyond merely describing ways in which, in various societies, people attempt to divine "final causes." The first insight is analytical and discussed in this section, while the second is metahistorical and outlined in the next.

The analytical insight is into what we referred to above as "causal fetishism," or the tendency to attribute cause to things themselves in modernity. If we say, "The deer leaping into the road caused the accident," what seems a very simple case of mechanistic action and reaction becomes much more complicated when we realize that, like Hume's billiard balls, the result could have been otherwise. Causation is something that we can attribute only after the fact, and as part of our understanding of how deers and cars don't mix rather than as a necessary property of the deer relationship to cars. In other words, Hume shows that causation is inherently temporal and can only be demonstrated when the expected future result is already in the past.

This concept of causality not only points to a notion of cause that goes beyond action and reaction. It also points to the temporal nature of our concept of causality itself, to the way that cause is always indebted to its effect. Hume shows, for instance, not only the elision of possibility with probability and of probability with necessity, but also the ways in which these are plotted in time. His examples make clear that causation is a principle that relies on expectation: as a "law of nature," it is not about what has occurred in the past, but rather about what we can expect will occur in the future. While we think of causation as depending on the cause, then, Hume shows us that in fact it depends on the effect: it is only through what is produced that the causal link is found. Or, as Giovanni da Col and Caroline Humphrey observe of the aleatory reason that explains luck or fortune, "The crucial point is that the 'after' makes the 'before' what it 'already was'" (da Col and Humphrey 2012: 13).

Interestingly, however, even as Hume was making his critique of the laws of reason, he did so by reducing all forms of causation to one: what in the Aristotelian lingo is known as the "efficient cause." For Aristotle, there were four primary "causes" (*aitia*) at work in the world: material, formal, efficient, and final. An oft-used example will illustrate: wood would be the material cause of a table, while having four legs and a top would be its formal cause. Its efficient cause would be the carpenter who builds the table from wood, while its final cause would be dining. All of these, for Aristotle, were causes of the table coming into being in its present form. When we think of our own concept of causation, however, we tend to refer only to the efficient cause, or the carpenter's sawing and hammering of wood. It is these, we say, that are the cause of wood becoming a table.

In a very useful volume that traces the history of our concept of causation as lawlike regularity (Schmaltz 2014), authors show how such concepts of multiple causation stuck around for centuries until the "Humean moment." Already prefaced by the works of Bacon, Hobbes, and Descartes, all of whom sought efficient or mechanical rather than final causes, Hume explicitly dismissed the idea that there could be any causes besides the efficient: "[A]ll causes are of the same kind, and ... in particular there is no foundation for that distinction, which we sometimes make betwixt efficient causes, and formal, and material... and final causes" (1949: 171). He is in search, then, of what makes efficient causes *necessary*, or how we can know that they have a lawlike regularity.[1]

While Hume appears to have reduced all causes to the efficient, Kantian and post-Kantian philosophy took up the challenge to prove causation necessary while accepting this singular definition of causation. We find, then, that in the period of the early Enlightenment, "cause" acquired a necessary, lawlike relationship with "effect," while "causation" became an expression of that necessity.

This brings us, then, to our metahistorical observation, discussed in the next section, which concerns historical and ethnographic attempts to understand other forms of what we call "causation." Causal fetishism, we have tried to show, has a particular history, and one that relied on rejecting Aristotelean concepts of cause and accepting only an instrumental understanding of causal relations. However, in many ways it is

---

[1] We should note that while Hume doubted our capacity to understand causal necessity, he appears never to have doubted that it exists. As Meillassoux observes, for Hume, "[W]e may well be able to uncover the basic laws that govern the universe – but the cause that underlies those laws themselves, and which endows them with necessity, will remain inaccessible to us" (2008: 90). In other words, what appeared to be an intellectual attack on our capacity to understand causality had the paradoxical effect of reinforcing the reduction of cause to the efficient.

quite unfair to blame the history of causal fetishism on Hume, who clearly no doubt understood that the English word "causation" was quite a departure from Aristotle's original *aitia*, which had a more complex meaning than simply "cause." Instead, as many commentators have noted, it meant "being responsible for" something, a meaning that may also have resonances of the use of the word *aition* in the courts of Aristotle's period.

Indeed, there are clues in Hume's text pointing us to another interpretation, one that may have preserved the sense of *aitia* while still challenging our human capacity to understand causal necessity. He observes, for instance, that we cannot learn the nature of bodies from past experience because "[t]heir secret nature, and consequently, all their effects and influence, may change, without any change in their sensible qualities" (2000: 33). This sentence could take us in many theoretical directions, as Hume widens the gap between things and their representation and opens the possibility for nonhuman agency. What is interesting for our purposes here, however, is that his argument is based on the possibility of contingency. He says that it sometimes happens that the secret nature of bodies eludes us, and they do things that we can't predict. "Why may it not happen always, and with regard to all objects?" he asks.

There is something strange in this passage, which suggests that experience is always potentially misleading and that the future is in fact unpredictable. Indeed, Hume's entire argument rests on the idea that in the future, the impossible might be possible because everything harbors a "secret nature" that we cannot know through the probabilistic reasoning that he calls "custom."

It is this "secret nature," the Other of experience, to which Quentin Meillassoux refers in the epigraph to this chapter. While in the future, the unthinkable remains unthinkable – particularly our own death – the "secret nature" of things shows us the possibility that the impossible could be. Meillassoux (2008) calls this "the necessity of contingency," which, as we will discuss in the next section, opens the door for both hope and destiny: the recognition that causes are never final or certain, and that the laws of nature, seen by Western science as necessary to keep the world running, may also be contradicted. While experience leads to expectation, it also leads to the knowledge that things may turn out differently than we expect.

In previous chapters, we have argued that this possibility of expectations being thwarted, a completely contingent surprise occurring, or potential never being realized ultimately makes the future Other to us insofar as it is something that we can never know. In the next sections, we see the concepts of destiny or fate as ways of coming to terms with the unknowability of one's own *telos*, the uncanniness of contingency, and the *weirdness* of the future's uncertainty. After all, it is only in the future that "it is not impossible for the impossible to be." Every other supposed impossibility has already passed into the realm of the possible, becoming a part of history where, as David Graeber puts it, "the unpredictable is constantly turning into the irreversible" (2012: 25). For Graeber, this is "what it means that humans live in history" (ibid.). Indeed, it is the future as a space in which the impossible is also possible that, we suggest, creates its radical immanence.

The Weirdness of the Future

An old Turkish proverb says that Man is better sitting than standing, lying down than sitting, dead than lying down. That is the true spirit of Fatalism, which, wittingly or otherwise, is the invariable leaven of all Turkish biography.

Shore 1903: 382

As with Hume's suggestion of things' "secret nature," there is something strange about these lines, which seem at first paradoxical. In them, the author suggests that what *should* happen is always less than what *might* happen, or that the appropriate stance to life is a maximalization of passivity. The "true spirit of Fatalism" is one in which not only is passivity preferable to activity, but even death is preferable to life as the ultimate maximalization of non-activity. Fatalism is not simply submitting; in this rendering, it is actively striving to submit more.

By the time these lines were written, "Oriental fatalism" was a long-standing trope in Western Europe, so widely known and used that such phrasing could introduce, without explanation, this review of a play called *Kismet*. An Arabic-derived Turkish word, *kısmet* means fate but is most often used as an ex post facto explanation for something that has not gone the way one would have wished. Its root comes from the Arabic *qism*, in Turkish *kısım*, which means a part, lot, or share. Turkish exclamations of "*Kısmettir!*", "It's fate," are most often accompanied by a sigh and shrug of the shoulders.

Despite this trope, however, so-called Oriental or Ottoman fatalism was shot through with the same contradictions that many anthropologists have observed exist in other societies known for elaborate traditions that try to predict the future: India's astrological charts (Guenzi 2012); China and Taiwan's practices of fortune-telling and divination (e.g., Harrell 1987; Sangren 2012; Stafford 2012); or, closer to our own example, both acceptance of destiny and struggle to shape it in Morocco (Elliot 2016; Menin 2015). In all these cases, ethnographers have noticed that beliefs in an irrevocable fate or destiny can go hand in hand with a striving to alter or shape it. Or, as Graeber puts it in his discussion of the "fate" of the markets, "Often, we find that the very people who most consistently evoke the notions of fate or destiny have the most elaborate technologies designed to alter them" (2012: 36).

In the Ottoman Empire, as well, there appears to have been lively discussion about the meaning of predestination and free will – indeed, to such an extent that Lady Mary Wortley Montagu, wife of the British consul to Istanbul in the early eighteenth century and one of the best-known European chroniclers, observed that many learned Ottomans of the period were deists more interested in politics than religion

(Menchinger 2016: 445). One of the only studies of ideas of predestination in the Ottoman Empire observes that there appears to have been a variety of opinion on the matter (ibid.). An Ottoman Armenian author writing in French, for example, claimed that predestination concerned only one's spiritual state, and it had no bearing on free will in relation to moral, civil, or political action. On the other hand, "Nearly everyone cleaves to the principle of an immutable destiny fixed by the decrees of heaven, and admits the exercise and effects of free will with extreme reluctance. . . . Hence that lethargic insensibility in which Muslims live, and that perfect acquiescence with which they endure, without inquiry, destructive events, private accidents, and public misfortunes" (D'Ohsson 1788–1824, I: 168–169, quoted in ibid., 451–452).

Contextualizing the period in which this was written, however, Menchinger remarks on this seeming contradiction, "If anything, Europeans may have distorted 'fatalism' by reading it as quintessentially or timelessly Muslim rather than as part of a specific intellectual discourse" (ibid., 450). That discourse was one that, starting in at least the eighteenth century, was framed by much public hand-wringing over the seeming inevitability of Ottoman decline.

This well-known historical example of "fatalism" provides us with an entry point for thinking about the ways in which causal fetishism has infected our concepts of fate or destiny. The problem of causation is of course central to the history of anthropology, whose earliest writings were concerned with magic, witchcraft, the supernatural, and in general the "mind of primitive man." The question about that mind was, of course, whether or not it could reason the way that "we" do. For instance, Evans-Pritchard, in typical pragmatic form, explained the commonplaceness of witchcraft in the Azande region as a response to unfortunate events. Rhetorically, he poses the common question about this form of belief: "But is not Zande belief in witchcraft a belief in mystical causation of phenomena and events to the complete exclusion of all natural causes?" (Evans-Pritchard 1937: 65). His answer is ready.

Giving the example of a master carver who attributes broken bowls to witchcraft, Evans-Pritchard continues:

Likewise a potter will attribute the cracking of his pots during firing to witchcraft. An experienced potter need have no fear that his pots will crack as a result of error. He selects the proper clay, kneads it thoroughly till he has extracted all grit and pebbles, and builds it up slowly and carefully. On the night before digging out his clay he abstains from sexual intercourse. So he should have nothing to fear. Yet pots sometimes break, even when they are the handiwork of expert potters, and this can only be accounted for by witchcraft. "It is broken – there is witchcraft," says the potter simply.

(ibid., 67)

As a response to unfortunate events, witchcraft had a social function, in other words could still be assimilated to the instrumentalism of efficient cause.

What seems clear from this example, however, is that explanations for what we call bad luck, good luck, chance, accident, or (mis)fortune may all address other sorts of causes than the efficient one. In Evans-Pritchard's example, for instance, we may say that carvers and potters are trying to find an explanation for why, in Aristotle's terms, a pot or carving that they had executed in a way that should have put wood or clay into a particular form, nevertheless failed to take that form. As Heidegger noted, "For a long time we have been accustomed to representing cause as that which brings something about" – to such an extent, in fact, that "we no longer even count the *causa finalis*, telic finality, as causality" (1977: 7).

The "final cause" to which Heidegger refers is, of course, Aristotle's, and it seems clear that any anthropology of the future needs to grapple with Aristotle's concept of *aitia* and the history of its influence and decline in Western European thought. This is so not only because Aristotle is a particularly interesting philosopher for anthropologists to think with, because much of his philosophy appears to be based on the analysis of common understandings of and practices in the world, but also because of his later influence on Islamic and Judaic philosophy, and through it on Christian theology. If the Enlightenment was an explicit rejection of Aristotle and embrace of Plato's Idealism, any post-Enlightenment project seems bound to return to Aristotle to find what was being rejected there. Indeed, recognition of causal fetishism and the reduction of all causes to the efficient within Enlightenment thought has in recent years led to the rise in philosophy of what is sometimes called "neo-Aristotelianism" (Gross and Greco 2013), an intellectual sibling of speculative materialism or speculative realism (e.g., Bryant *et al.* 2011; Coole and Frost 2010; Harman 2010).

Heidegger also remarks, as have many other commentators, that our understanding of "cause" does not fully translate the word *aitia*, which meant and still means in Greek "responsibility." However, Heidegger also remarks, "What we call cause [*Ursache*] and the Romans call *causa* is called *aition* by the Greeks, that to which something else is indebted" (1977: 3). Heidegger calls attention, then, to the evolution of a concept that was originally associated not with mechanistic laws but with responsibility and debt. It is this notion of indebtedness that we understand here as cause being created from effect, being indebted to effect, or causation being created out of the future.

Our metahistorical observation, then, follows simply from our previous reflections: that the causal fetishism produced by the doctrine of efficient causation has occluded other forms of causation and allowed the efficient to cannibalize others. In the example with which we opened the chapter, we might say that treating Ottoman ideas of fate or destiny as fatalistic is to view destiny as an efficient rather than as a final cause.

Of course, there are good reasons for viewing Ottoman ideas of fate this way, in that descriptions of fate or destiny in the region tend to view it as something that comes from the outside. Like the carpenter hammering wood into a table, fate or destiny depends on being made by, and our lives directed by, forces outside ourselves. One sees this idea in many languages: our own word "fate" derives from the Latin *fari*, or "to speak," and has the sense of a "thing spoken." *Fari*, in turn, comes from the Proto-Indo-European root *bha-*, which also means to speak or say. Fate as something spoken, or later written, would make its way into numerous languages, including the Sanskrit *bhagya*, the Arabic *maktub* (something written), and the Turkish *yazgı*. In both Arabic and Turkish there is also the idea of fate being "written on one's forehead" (in Turkish, *alın yazısı*), suggesting something that is always present but can only be seen by others, not by the person whose fate it is. In the Calvinist Protestant version of this, free will is itself a ruse guiding us to fulfill God's will through the hand of Providence.

While not denying the possibility that people who believe in destiny may orient themselves fatalistically toward the future, i.e., accept or await their fate, we would return to the example of Rachel, who had a reasonably strong sense of destiny but little idea of how she would get there. In narrative terms, Kermode has argued that *peripeteia*, or the wandering, the twists and turns, that lead to an ending, "depends on our confidence of an end." He remarks that "the interest of having our expectations falsified is obviously related to our wish to reach the discovery or recognition by an unexpected and instructive route" (2000: 17).

In terms of the peripeteia of a life, we see that although Rachel's sense of destiny was highly secular, it bore striking resemblance to what Nieswand (2010) calls "enacted destiny," "an idea of divine empower-ment, which enables believers to deal with risk and contingency" (p. 51). This is a destiny that can only be fully understood in retrospect but that depends on "belief in the accessibility and immanence of God" (p. 38). While "classic" Protestantism drew an "ontological cleavage that sepa-rates humankind and God" (p. 39), the temporal and corruptible world from the timelessness of the eternal, this was a historically and culturally specific understanding of what it means for one's fate to be "written," albeit one that – if Talal Asad (1993) is correct – had an overweening influence on the way that anthropology as a discipline understands the concept of religion.

Even in the case of Rachel, however, we see that destiny as an orientation in practice is considerably different from Weberian ideal-typical constructions of how one would orient oneself to the future given a belief in a future that is already "written." We suggest that the view in anthropology that destiny is a problem for agency is to confuse final with efficient causes. It is to think that because God, Allah, or the universe has a plan for us, this plan can be realized only as a carpenter makes a table. It is to take off that table the idea of peripeteia, which leaves open the possibility of contingency, of things turning out other than we expect.

Instead, we find again and again, in examples that are often presented as counterintuitive, that people "take their destiny into their own hands," as the saying goes. Whether it is young women searching for their "destined" partner in Morocco (Elliot 2016; Menin 2015); destiny viewed as a "malleable resource" for investment during middle-class astrological counselling in India (Guenzi 2012); or striving for luck amongst gamblers in Greece (Malaby 2012), we find presents that are indebted to a future that can only reveal itself at the horizon. As Paolo Gaibazzi, studying "questing for luck" amongst West African hustlers, puts it, "[A]n unpredictable and ineluctable destiny is far from merely depicting people as being victims of forces they do not control; on the contrary, it constructs human existence as being filled with possibility" (Gaibazzi 2015: 233).

The problem, then, is how anthropology has grappled – or rather, failed to grapple – with contingency, with the "secret nature" of things that may always do something other than we expect. "[T]he centrality of contingency as a facet of human experience and its possible implications for the questions we ask as anthropologists have been continually obscured," Thomas Malaby notes, in a discussion of the agency involved in seeking luck (Malaby 2012: 106).

We may now circle back to our discussion of fatalism and to our reference in the introduction to this chapter to Nietzsche's *amor fati*, or love of fate, an embracing of what comes as that which makes us. Nietzsche specifically contrasted this to the fatalism of "the Orient": "The fatalism of the Turk has this fundamental defect, that it contrasts man and fate as two distinct things. Man, says this doctrine, may struggle against fate and try to baffle it, but in the end fate will always gain the victory. Hence the most rational course is to resign oneself or to live as one pleases" (Nietzsche 1880: S61).

Of course, Nietzsche's was a Romantic stoicism that advocated suffering as a road to profundity. However, his desire "to see as beautiful what is necessary in things" (Nietzsche 1974: 276) points us again to the role of causality in Nietzsche's thought: unlike "the Turk," who attributed causality to unknown ends, *amor fati* is an embrace of the apparently contingent as the necessary.

"Contingency," Meillassoux notes, "designates the possibility whereby something can either persist or perish, without either option contravening the invariants that govern the world" (2008: 53). Nietzsche specifically resists the idea that contingency would rule our lives, returning time and again to the necessity of things being the way they are. He resists the idea of fate as Other, a vision that "contrasts man and fate as two distinct things." He saw this, however, as an overcoming of a doctrine that also had a long history in Christianity, in which free will itself appeared a ruse for predestination.

We wish to suggest, however, that this view of fate that occludes contingency and folds the future into the always becoming present makes it difficult for us to grapple with what we called earlier the uncanniness of contingency and the *weirdness* of the future's uncertainty. It fails to take account of what it means for the future to come from elsewhere, for the future to be Other (cf. Mittermaier 2012). In Chapter 3, we have already discussed speculative realist philosophers' use of the world "weird" in describing an ontology of the withdrawal of objects. A flattened ontology that sees objects as equally impenetrable and equally strange to each other presents what Harman (2012) calls a "weird realism" and Timothy Morton (2015) a "weird essentialism." "Reality itself is weird," remarks Harman, "because reality itself is incommensurable with any attempt to represent or measure it" (2012: 51).

For our purposes, it is particularly felicitous that the word "weird" evolved from an old English and Nordic noun for fate, fortune, or a power or agency that determines the course of human life. From this, it evolved into an adjective indicating someone or something with supernatural powers to control fate or destiny. For instance, Shakespeare's Weird Sisters in *Macbeth* at times appear as witches attempting to shape destiny, at times as the Fates themselves. What is important for our purposes is not only the slippage between the two, but also the way in which the word "weird," which originally meant fate or destiny, has come to mean the strange, unusual, and uncanny.

Building on speculative realism's elucidation of an ontology of immanence, we call this weirdness of the future the *immanence of the untimely*, or the way that what is beyond the horizon, beyond a time that we can know now or may ever know, is nevertheless what shapes the course that our lives are "supposed" to take. Using Catherine Malabou's observation that the future contains both "teleological necessity and surprise" (2005: 13), we develop a way of thinking about the orientation of destiny that accounts for the weirdness of becoming what "we are supposed to be."

On Aleatory Certainty

At the end of a long and difficult period of fieldwork in Cyprus, when the checkpoints dividing the island had recently opened and there was much speculation about the future, Bryant went one last time to drink coffee with a Turkish Cypriot neighbor in the village where she was then living, in the island's north. The neighbor had been displaced from her own village in the island's south and had lived by that time for thirty years in a small house on the same street as her husband's coffee shop. The neighbor that day had visitors, a young niece and her husband, and as everyone chatted, they finished their coffee and turned over their cups in the saucer to allow the coffee grounds that remained at the bottom to trickle down the sides. As the thick grounds slowly slid to the bottom, they created shapes that the neighbor, Sevgül, was going to read in order to tell the future.

Reading coffee grounds is a popular activity amongst women, who associate the shapes that the grounds make on the sides of the demitasse cups with various aspects and proximities of the future. In some cases, the trip, marriage, or money that is predicted is said to come in time expressed as a number – three, or seven, say. "You will take a trip in three – it could be three weeks, three months, or three years," the woman reading the cup will say. Often, women read the cups rapidly, much practice having given them a ready toolbox of shapes and their associations.

That day, Sevgül said that she would begin with her nephew-in-law's cup, and she took it up, turning it into the light. She began quickly reciting, using the practiced formulas of someone for whom reading coffee cups is like a memorized incantation. In the middle of her reading, she turned the cup and cocked her head, as though listening for something. "There's a map of Cyprus," she said quite matter-of-factly. "That means that you have an unsolved problem, but it will be solved."

Bryant and the niece laughed in surprise at the interpretation, while Sevgül, in turn, did not understand the source of their amusement. "We read the shapes," she said, again matter-of-factly. The association of the divided island with an unsolved problem, and the island's unsolved division with a personal or professional problem in the young man's life, was already a significant scalar leap. But in addition to that leap, Sevgül made a further jump: that, contrary to all evidence at the time, the Cyprus Problem, and by analogy the young man's problem, would be solved. For someone like Sevgül, a village woman with minimal education, someone who was hardly a "peacenik" and had in fact expressed quite harsh views about her former Greek neighbors, the resolution of the island's division was so easily assumed that it could serve as a formula for reading coffee cups.

The practice of reading cups is common amongst women throughout the Eastern Mediterranean and Middle East, and while most women do it for amusement, as a pastime, there are always women who are known for their divinatory abilities. One can never read one's own cup, it seems for the same reason that the expression *alın yazısı*, or writing on the forehead, to mean one's fate implies something that only others are able to see. Because it is primarily a pastime, something that one does when taking a break from other work, it is taken less than half seriously. Most women seem to reserve the possibility of predictions coming true in a probabilistic way that falls far short of belief. The assumption appears to be the impossibility of knowing or reading the future, along with the knowledge that, in probabilistic terms, the impossible could always happen.

In this sense, then, it relies on what Vernes called aleatory reason – the sort of probabilistic reason that we might, in fact, attribute to most forms of what we call efficient causation, in which causation is attributed to the "before" through expectation but realized only after the fact through what we understand as causal necessity. Or as Roy Wagner so wittily phrases it, "[A]ny definition of the chance of happening is confined (confided) internally by the happening of chance to it – like a lucky draw drawing its own luck" (2012: 172). Reading cups is obviously a "fortune-telling" of this type, one that does not seek to know fate, destiny, or final causes but rather gives us a shorter view of the long view. This type of fortune-telling addresses what da Col and Humphrey call the "happenstances" or "quasi-events" of everyday life: "A quasi-event is not an ordinary fact but a unique fact of the everyday, *one that forces a shift in attention toward what will happen next ... or toward what might have happened* – a mishap, an omen, a winning, a sign of hope" (Da Col and Humphrey 2012: 2; emphasis in original).

An even better reading might be one that Wagner makes elsewhere (2010), when he refers to the unspoken, unheard, or unknown occurrences of everyday life as "anti-twins." Wagner's invocation of "anti-twins" seems to coincide with what we have discussed earlier as the virtuality immanent in actuality – the way that potentiality may be concrete without being actual. In our coffee cup case, the "anti-twin" would be the uncovering of a problem, a future "happenstance," that had been unspoken or had not yet manifest itself but that shifts one's attention to the future as a quasi-event, a type of ripple in time. "Where an event," da Col and Humphrey remark, "would mark major subjective transitions, such as radical ontological shifts from humanity to divinity ... a quasi-event allows only an ephemeral assemblage of subjectivity" (2012: 2).

What is particularly interesting to us about the coffee cup example, however, is that it uses a form of analogous reasoning to determine the end of such a quasi-event. And the analogous reasoning that it uses is one that moves from a form – the shape of the island in a coffee cup – to a "final cause," the yet-unrealized potential solution of the Cyprus Problem as future actualization. This future actualization is of course virtual in the sense discussed in Chapter 3, as "the capacity of a thing to become differently" (Fraser 2006: 130). In these terms, what makes the shape of Cyprus in a coffee cup into a sign for solving a problem is that it is something that could work out otherwise but *is bound to* work out in this way. As Deleuze's predecessor Alfred North Whitehead expressed it, "*[H]ow* an actual entity *becomes* constitutes *what* that actual entity *is*" (Whitehead 1978: 23, quoted in ibid.). In the teleological terms derived from Aristotle and revived in the early Enlightenment, this was Cyprus's *entelechy*, the movement toward realization of its potentiality that we have said is something *bound to* happen.

To say that it is *bound to* happen is to say that it is part of the virtual-actual that is the future realization of potentiality in the present. In English we speak of something as "bound to" in the sense of necessity, certainty, or fate. It is also a construction used with the infinitive, a verb form that Deleuze saw as particularly important in describing the event. On the one hand, the infinitive describes something that is virtual or potential, while on the other hand "it indicates a substantive relation to a state of affairs" (Fraser 2006: 130). It is in this sense that the virtual becoming of the Cyprus Problem's solution – something that was *bound to* happen – could serve as a predictive sign for a problem that *would be* solved.

In this case, then, we have a potential quasi-event – a matter of fortune – analogized to an actual-virtual event that takes the form of fate. If counter-actualization, for Deleuze, is the part of the event that goes beyond its actualization, always offering the possibility for repetition to be actualized differently, we might say that viewing the Cyprus Problem as one that is *bound to be* solved is a counter-virtualization, the capacity of a thing *not* to become differently, or for it always to work out the same. This is surely what it would mean for fate to tame contingency through necessity.

However, the "bound to be" is a modal form that carries with it all the ambiguities of supposition – a form of logical association that Hume had viewed as less than necessity. Modal verbs are to be found in most languages, and cross-cultural linguistic study shows that, as in English, modality is "subjective, expressing attitudes like hypothesis (probability, possibility, uncertainty), permission, desirability, volition – in fact, exploring the range of possible replies between a blunt Yes or No" (Hussey 2013: 60). Unlike "It will happen," then, "It is bound to happen" is the type of construction that expresses something that is more than a wish or hope but less than a necessity, in other words a teleology that also accounts for contingency.

Obviously, Sevgül did not verbally express all of this when she found a map of Cyprus in the young man's coffee cup. However, in Turkish people commonly say that a solution to the Cyprus Problem "must happen" (*olması gerekiyor*) or is "bound to happen" (*mutlaka olacaktır*), in both cases implying outside forces and constraints for whom it is important that it happen. One might see the expression "bound to" as a variation on "supposed to" that emphasizes its necessity. Indeed, one important quality of modal verbs that entail supposition is their ability to elide "should" and "will," or necessity and probability. One linguistic blogger, in answering a question about the slippery use of "supposed to be," remarked, "[T]here is a tendency in many languages for words to shift in meaning between *probability* and *desirability*. This tendency is apparently strongest in certain verbs that are used without specifying who the judge is."[2]

So, while one sense of *supposed to* is the promise of a requirement ("I'm supposed to be there at 11 a.m."), it is a requirement imposed by others (e.g., one's boss, the conference schedule, etc.). In similar but slightly different form, *bound to* takes the shape of an obligation or natural consequence ("Given the way the economy is going, the dollar is bound to fall"), but also one that maintains a certain amount of uncertainty, or takes into account contingency ("I'm bound to be there at 3 p.m.").

The slippage between *supposed to be* and *bound to be* implies a particular type of aleatory reason, one that takes into account both teleology and the contingencies of everyday life. This is what Malabou discusses as the French *voir venir*, "to see (what is) coming":

"*Voir venir*" in French means to wait, while, as is prudent, observing how events are developing. But it also suggests that there are intentions and plans of other people which must be probed and guessed at. It is an

---

[2] https://english.stackexchange.com/questions/21706/why-do-we-say-was-supposed-to-for-should-have

expression that can thus refer at one and the same time to the state of "being sure of what is coming" and of "not knowing what is coming."

(2005: 13)

Malabou's description is, of course, quite close to our own explication of expectation, which emphasized the uncertainty built into that orientation to the future. For our purposes here, however, it points to the simultaneous necessity and contingency built into what is *supposed to* happen, as well as the way that the *supposed* implies someone else doing the supposing.

However, we suggest that it is not enough to say that the future comes from elsewhere, or that our orientations to the future simultaneously account for both necessity and contingency. If we return to the earlier quote from Whitehead – a sentence that could easily describe Aristotle's concept of entelechy – to say that an entity is constituted through its becoming does not preclude the idea that we could also become something else. Indeed, our becoming at any moment is framed by the limits of what could still be. It is this unknowability of the future, the future that seems to come from elsewhere, from beyond the horizon, that we refer to as the untimeliness that temporalizes through the "supposed to be."

We may say, then, that destiny is the "after" that makes the "before" what it "was supposed to be." The next section explores what this might mean in communal terms. We see how Rachel's ideas of her own destiny were shaped by her cultural milieu, in which a white, middle-class American girl could view the pursuit of her destiny as the definition of freedom. Because "freedom" is the ideology that replaces ethnic nationalism in the USA to create a bond amongst its citizens, it also becomes the source of communal action, as well as the hinge upon which critique turns. After a few examples of communal destiny, we turn to the idea of tricking fate, which understands the openness of the future to mean that the inevitable or inescapable might, in fact, not occur.

Destiny's Fatal Exceptions

As we enforce the just demands of the world, we will also honor the deepest commitments of our country. Unlike Saddam Hussein, we believe the Iraqi people are deserving and capable of human liberty. And when the dictator has departed, they can set an example to all the Middle East of a vital and peaceful and self-governing nation.

The United States, with other countries, will work to advance liberty and peace in that region. Our goal will not be achieved overnight, but it can come over time. The power and appeal of human liberty is felt in every life and every land. And the greatest power of freedom is to overcome hatred and violence, and turn the creative gifts of men and women to the pursuits of peace.

George W. Bush, 2003

Speaking immediately before the launch of Operation Enduring Freedom in 2003, George W. Bush attempted to rally a skeptical public with the claims of advancing liberty, the goal of bringing freedom to an unfree regime. As many commentators have noted, such claims are linked directly to the idea, strongest amongst Christians in the USA, that their country is directed by the Hand of Providence and that it has a special mission to bring freedom to the world. This is the exceptionalism of the "City on the Hill," a phrase from the Sermon on the Mount that refers metaphorically to a light that cannot be hidden and that is used by US politicians to refer to their obligation to guide the world. This is an exceptionalism that has also been framed by questions such as "Why is there no fascism in America?" – or, more critically, "Why is there no socialism in America?" (Torpey 2017). It is an exceptionalism that, for around two decades, has been subject to predictions of impending decline,[3] and that with the election of Donald Trump has been publicly shaken (Koch 2017; Kupchan 2018).[4]

---

[3] There is an extensive "decline" literature in international relations, especially that dealing with transatlantic relations. For skeptical overviews, see Quinn 2011; Russett 1985; Strange 1987, 1988; Zanchetta 2016. For arguments against American decline, see Cox 2001; Lieber 2009; Nau 2001; and Singh 2008.

[4] For more discussion of American exceptionalism, see Agnew 2003; Cattelino 2010; De Genova 2007; Löfflmann 2015; and Tomes 2014.

Of course, American exceptionalism is no exception. Although the belief that America has a unique role to play in world history has spawned all sorts of other "exceptionalisms" (e.g., refusal to join climate treaties on equal terms with other countries, or even the use of the continental term "America" to apply to a nation-state), this is not unlike the exceptionalisms of a range of other countries. Russian exceptionalism as neither Western nor Eastern (Oskanian 2018); Singaporean economic exceptionalism amongst its immediate neighbors (Barr 2016); the exceptionalism of the Chinese "rise" (Woon 2018); and Nordic or Scandinavian exceptionalism as countries that have successfully implemented social democratic models (e.g., Elgström and Delputte 2016; Reiter *et al.* 2017) are only a few of seemingly infinite examples. We could add to this list instances of geopolitical exceptionalism ("rogue states" such as Iran, North Korea, and any number of unrecognized states) or ones of historical exceptionalism, such as Greece (Gallant 1997). One of the best-known examples is Israeli exceptionalism, itself a mixture of exceptionalist claims regarding the Jewish people, Judaism, and the nation-state founded on their behalf (Alam 2009).

These exceptionalisms are invariably framed as historical narratives of a people's destiny. These are also narratives that are outside history, that suggest the possibility of going beyond history. Exceptionalism is exceptional to the historical rules, including the inevitability of decline. Graeber, in his discussion of risk and markets, argues that profit in the twentieth century has been based on opening oneself to history, which Graeber characterizes as "absolute uncertainty." "Profit," he notes, "was the capitalists' reward for having the courage to enter history" (Graeber 2012: 34).

While the history that Graeber describes would be a fair characterization of Koselleck's *neue Zeit* – the time that makes us, even as we make history – it of course falls far short of anything resembling a historiographical description of history. What Graeber's description does point to, however, is the tension that emerges again between the untimeliness of a history based on time – i.e., a history that is open to the future cannot be fully historicized – and a history based on the past. It is within this tension that a people's destiny emerges as the exceptionalism of *entelechy* – of a becoming that cannot countenance its own end.

One might also describe this as the idea that destiny, or one's own exceptional becoming, can overcome the fate of inevitable decline. We have hitherto avoided distinguishing fate and destiny, as in many languages there is no clear distinction. However, it is worth noting that many Indo-European languages draw a distinction between fate, which "implies finitude; the knowledge that life, whether of the individual or of the species, has natural limits" (Gamble 2000: 9), and destiny in its original sense, related to "destination." This is the corresponding and often conflicting idea that "we are predestined in very particular ways; not just because every life must end, but because every life has a predetermined pattern and content" (ibid.). The tension that we have described before, then, emerges in narratives of exceptionalism as one in which destiny makes fate unthinkable. American exceptionalism, for instance, is one in which the decline of the USA – for some, signaled by Trump's election – would also mean the end of the world as we know it. Recent years have also seen discussions of European exceptionalism, particularly in the form of EU exceptionalism, where the EU "projects its identity and its underlying normative understandings onto the global level" (Nolte and Aust 2013: 408). In this narrative, a decline of the EU would also signal a loss of what many view as universally applicable norms.

Returning to our earlier discussions of vernacular timespaces, we note that this sense of communal destiny as exceptionalism creates a particular teleology whose *telos* is indefinite and unclear. What would it mean for the USA to lead the world to freedom? What would it mean for the world to become more "European"? It is noteworthy, in fact, that such ideas of exceptionalism are invariably framed in relation to a "world order" (Hagen 2005: 55) that is in some way tied to that exceptionalism's continuation and whose end would signal the end of "the world as we know it." The shining "city on a hill" must continue to guide the world in order for it to go on.

Ironically, it is Ottoman exceptionalism, or the belief that "the empire and its rulers were uniquely just, favored by God, and would endure until the end of time" (Menchinger 2016: 456), that enables us to return to causation and draw together the various strands of our argument. Ottoman exceptionalism was based on the "dynastic myth" that Ottoman rulers were brought to earth to protect God's creatures and keep them in their appropriate places (Şahin 2013). However, this sense of predestination was also a source of consternation for Islamic philosophy, which was greatly concerned with reconciling destiny and free will. The Ashʿarī school of theology, which is at the heart of Sunni Islam's doctrines, attempted as early as the eleventh century to resolve the seeming contradiction of agency and predestination by arguing that because God was "the causer of causes," he "created the link between cause and effect anew at any given moment" (Hagen and Menchinger 2014: 101). The prominent sage of this school, the philosopher al-Ghazālī, aligned this form of necessary contingency with Aristotle's metaphysics through what he called "divine habit," "which restored the predictability of the effect of any known cause" (ibid.).

It was Kâtib Çelebi, the famous seventeenth-century Ottoman historian and geographer, who saw an impending Ottoman decline even then and pleaded for reform of the empire and its administration. He did so in the form of an advice treatise that combines Aristotelian thought with insights from Islamic theology:

And, His majesty be exalted, He made this world the world of causes and revealed all events of providence in the "world of generation and corruption" by way of a cause. Therefore, all events that occur are in essence traces of the power of God, free agent and almighty, showing power from behind an invisible curtain, through providence. Out of His pure goodness and benevolence, He granted His servants particular volition. *He enabled everyone to use their particular volition in some respect and realized His custom to create the effects (of this volition).* In order to teach that one who has a wish should concern himself with the (secondary) causes (leading to its realization), and make an effort at the means, and care about them, God gave orders in several instances in the noble scripture, absolute commands regarding definite causes, and mandatory commands regarding assumed causes.

(Kâtib Çelebi, Tuḥfetü l-kibâr, quoted in Hagen
and Menchinger 2014: 102; emphasis added)

Only eight decades later, the Scottish philosopher would echo the Ottoman historian in divorcing cause from effect, as well as in reducing causality to custom. In this instance, however, custom is what al-Ghazālī had called "divine habit," allowing us to believe in the relationship between cause and effect, while attributing to God's hand what Hume would call the "constant conjunction" that emerges from custom and habit.

God's servants should concern themselves with "secondary causes," the historian says, thereby invoking the idea that God had created material and corporeal beings in consonance with the universe and had allowed them to evolve of their own accord. In al-Ghazālī, however, secondary causes might better be described as "the semblance of causes," since God, as the Primary Cause, is "the one who makes causes function as causes" (Menchinger 2016: 447). This appears to be what Kâtib Çelebi means when he remarks, *"By concerning himself with the causes the servant has fulfilled his duty; to let the effect happen remains up to Him who makes causes take effect. If He wills he creates (the effect) and makes it happen; if He wills it not He does not. To obtain (the effect) is not the duty of the servant"* (Hagen and Menchinger 2014: 102; emphasis added). It is up to God's servant, then, to act in the world, and up to God to decide whether or not to allow a cause to have effect. Menchinger remarks, regarding these sources, that their frequent qualification of causes as "visible," "virtual," or "customary" "signals a suppositious rather than an actual relationship between cause and effect" (Menchinger 2016: 448, n. 7).

We have now come full circle and have returned to the primacy of supposition in thinking about destiny. We mentioned earlier that "supposition" comes from *supponere*, one meaning of which is "to act as a subject." Other meanings, however, include "to subject to" and "to falsify." On the one hand, one may suppose that something will happen as a matter of probabilistic certainty. On the other hand, one may be "supposed to" do something as a requirement or necessity. But contradicting both of these, we may also suppose in the manner of fantasy: if we say, "Suppose the world ends today," we are asking you to imagine a reality different from the one we currently know. We suggest that all of these are present in Malabou's *voir venir*, in Meillassoux's necessary contingency, as well as in Ottoman or American predictions of decline that go hand in hand with strong belief that it is not supposed to happen, that its realization would end the world as we know it.

Given these tales of hand-wringing over decline and hopes that one may still trick fate – given the primacy, in temporalizing temporality, of suppositional causation over efficient – it seems that we can return to our opening epigraph and paraphrase Meillassoux. It appears that if we still cannot think the unthinkable, we may respond by extending the thinkable into the indefinite future. If we can imagine that the impossible may still be possible, we can also imagine that the thinkable may vanquish the unthinkable.

Conclusion

Having wound our way through Humean skepticism, Cypriot prognostication, and Ottoman and American "declinism," we may conclude with a second metahistorical observation. Our second observation returns us to Koselleck's well-known argument that history in modernity is inextricable from a modern understanding of time as succession, something that makes us rather than we making it. If we have, throughout this book, bracketed discussions of the metaphysics of time, it is because there is a thread running through those discussions in the modern era that, as Carol Greenhouse (1996) pointed out, assumes that time is "natural" or "real," and that cultures only interpret its reality. Kevin Birth's extended critique of "clock time," or the idea of time as something within which we exist, shows why, as he claims, "Temporal relativism is a more common theoretical principle in time metrology and physics than it is in anthropology" (Birth 2017: 6).

If our reflections on destiny as the untimely that temporalizes have implications for anthropology, it is in questioning our own puzzlement over the ability to act while still believing in predestination. While Birth argues that horological time has parasitically colonized other forms of temporality and impeded anthropologists' ability to understand other temporalities, we suggest that a similar argument may be made for anthropology's approaches to the future. It is surely no accident that a causal fetishism occluding the indebtedness of cause to effect emerged at the same historical moment that the future itself was being occluded in the study of time.

The common assumption – what Heidegger called the "vulgar under-standing" of temporality – is that we live in a present dependent on the past, a succession of moments that follow one from another. In this, in order to understand how things are caused, we have to look at the effect of the past on the present. Heidegger had described this common understanding of time as a "succession of nows" that "pass by and arrive at the same moment" (Malabou 2005: xix). Derrida, in turn, refers to it as a "figure of succession" when he asks,

Why has this interpretation of time become generally accepted, dominant, hegemonic, self-evident, and even legitimate, accredited as such and at face value? And most of all, why has it come to deny and even erase or forbid all thought of a future? Well because, by passing through its passage, the "course" of time would only *follow* the series of present moments, the very essence of the present, all of the nows here present.

(2005: xix; emphasis in original)

What is lost, it seems, is the recognition that causation is always already the future looking back on the present.

A belief in efficient causality magically turns fate into progress, into the inevitable "march of history." Our second metahistorical observation, then, may be seen as a hypothesis, and one that would have to be tested by reading back into the history of anthropology and cognate disciplines. The hypothesis is that because causal fetishism occludes the indebtedness of cause to effect, the future itself has been occluded in the study of temporality. If we are made by history rather than making history, it is because we are no longer indebted to the future.

Conclusion
The Future as Method

In this book we have asked what an attention to the future can contribute to anthropology's engagement with time. We have put the future at center stage of anthropological inquiry, arguing that the future awakens the present though a plethora of orientations with indeterminate teleologies. Focusing on orientations to the future in everyday life adds invaluable detail to our ethnographic quest to better understand the quotidian. We are constantly anticipating, expecting, hoping for, and speculating about – and thus living – the future in everyday life. These orientations to the future should, we suggest, be better incorporated into our methodological and analytical toolkit.

Understanding temporality has been fundamental to discussions over anthropology's methods and scope from the beginning of the discipline. While the Saussurean-inspired question of whether anthropology should examine social and cultural phenomena *in* time – synchronously – or *through* time – diachronically – has influenced discussions of the relationship between anthropology and history, as well as anthropology and other social sciences, the question nevertheless acknowledged the essential temporal relationship to be that of the past to the present. In synchrony, past and present coexist, while in diachrony the past shapes the present.

If we take anthropology's relationship to the present, and hence to temporality, to be fundamental to the history and development of the discipline, a new attention to the future surely spells a new sort of anthropology. It appears to entail a reorientation of the discipline from being to becoming, from structure to agency, and from social institutions to the hope, planning, practices, and action that project those into the yet-to-come. Rather than taking for granted that such institutions will or should last, this new anthropology asks about the fragile and tentative ways in which the present is projected into the future, and the future drawn toward the present and past.

Anthropological studies of temporality have recently regained prominence in the discipline in a wave of publications: time in relation to fieldwork methods (Dalsgaard and Nielsen 2015), or to modernity and capitalism (Bear 2014), as well as interventionist approaches to anthropological study of the future (Salazar et al. 2017), for instance. What we have offered in this book is ethnographic and philosophical reflection on how people orientate themselves to the future in everyday life, building on a moment in our discipline where ethnographers have begun to acknowledge the uncertain, fragile, and often terrifying ways in which the future is emerging as integral to the lives of people we study. We have made heuristic distinctions between orientations that, at an experiential level, may be difficult to distinguish or define. Where, for instance, does hope spill into speculation, or when does expectation become anticipation? We believe, however, that our heuristic distinctions allow for more fine-grained analysis of the ways and means by which temporal orientations shape action.

The orientations discussed in this book – and many more besides – lend texture to our experience of the "now" and how we prepare the groundwork for the future in the present. They provide a sense of thickness or porosity to the threshold between present and future, holding the future at an indeterminate distance – sometimes seemingly within reach and with tangible form in the present, at other times little more than a hazy, partially formed dream set in a far-off land. Providing "temporal textures of experience" (Pandian 2012: 548), orientations make the future appear malleable, open to manipulation, or set in stone, implacable. Orientations capture the flux of experience, the rollercoaster of aspirations and fears that inhabits every one of us.

Vernacular Timespaces

We have built on the arguments of philosopher Theodore Schatzki to suggest that the practices of everyday life are structured by timespaces that may overlap or be entangled but that are each characterized by sets of teleoaffects. A timespace includes all the orders of people and objects that share a teleoaffective structure and focus on specific goals. Within a timespace there are networks that can be activated, as well as connections that lie dormant or unappreciated, as we have seen in the case of unrealized potential. We have argued that the realm of the "otherwise-than-actual" is also part and parcel of the timespace and is equally important in driving futural momentum.

At the communal level, we have suggested, such timespaces and their teleoaffects are often described in the vernacular in epochal terms – a Time of War, a Time of Prosperity, a Time of Brexit. There is a collective sense of living in an era that has a particular temporality with a set of ways to express experiences of that period. The Time of Brexit may evoke nausea, panic, apocalyptic speculation for the Remainer. A Time of Peace in the Middle East may be eaten into by the anticipation of imminent displacement and violence. Moreover, such epochal thinking – what we call vernacular timespaces – may be shared beyond boundaries of cities and nations, as in the collective sense that the Trump administration beckoned in a new era of politics with global consequences and a new set of catchwords and imaginaries, or the shared hope expressed by people across austerity-ravished Europe when the radical left came to power in Greece in 2015.

We frequently move between timespaces as we go about daily lives, while different forms of activity open different timespaces. Timespaces are also multi-scalar. Just as we may exist in the timespace of academic life and that of family life, so we may live in a Time of War and a Time of Trump. Vernacular timespaces produce their own teleoaffects – hope, resignation, anticipation – scaling the individual and collective. For anthropology, we believe that it is important to be able to make distinctions between the affective time produced by, for instance, expecting a gift from one's spouse, and expectation as part of what it means to live in a Time of Peace. The present may feel particularly elongated, even inescapable, at a Time of Crisis where there is no sense of emergence or possibility for change, while the future may be already breaking into the present when anticipating meeting a loved one at the airport this evening.

We have stressed the importance that the concept of timespace is open and not preordained, and orientations have indeterminate teleologies. The understanding of teleology as linear, we argue, is associated with modernity and does not necessarily have to be accepted. Instead, we have proposed that teleology is about ends, but is open and indeterminate. We have also made a case for activity in the timespace to have teleoaffective structure, what Schatzki defines as the "ends, projects, actions, and combinations thereof that participants should or acceptably pursue" (2010: loc. 1363). The teleoaffective structure guides futural orientation in providing a set of endorsed, acceptable ends for which people can aim. In some instances, such as during election campaigns, the teleoaffective structure could also be channeled through political rhetoric or "technologies of imagination." On other occasions our orientations can be "tricked," as when we place our confidence in false causes, in pathways where, when compared to our expectations, the future is doomed to failure.

Depending on the nature of the vernacular timespace, the teleoaffective structure presents people with projects, recommended paths, and futures to aspire to, drawing the future into the present and giving it a vibrant essence as something that not only should be sought after, but is also ultimately achievable. In extreme cases, this makes the future a foregone conclusion but usually, we argue, the teleoaffective structure guides practice within the timespace without forgoing novelty. In the cases of Rachel and David, being born into timespaces with very powerful teleoaffective structures did not prevent them from eventually following pathways with distinctively different sets of aspirations, ambitions, and investments. Further, what is desired or pursued, when actualized, will only ever be a resemblance of its otherwise-than-actual state. The future need not be prescribed at birth, or for that matter, as in pre-economic crisis Greece, be deemed a birthright. Innumerable potentialities, both positive and negative, may be actualized within the timespace, and there is always room for novelty, for particular forms and arrangements of life and substance, to flourish (see Kirksey 2015; Pandian and Howe 2016).

When discussing such large assemblages as timespaces which can encompass numerous epochs and capture audiences across continents, it is equally important to acknowledge the significance of the infinitesimally small moments where much future-oriented action takes place. The interval where the threshold between present and future is transcended, even temporarily, is precisely the moment where the most fertile ground for future-making is located. Of course, this moment constantly moves with us as we press into the temporal horizon, but it is here, at the threshold, that wondering, uncertainty, and imagination reside. We have talked a lot about orientations existing in gaps, intervals, delays – between potential and actual, movement and rest, known and unknown, reality and perception, presence and absence. Like Kermode's moment of novelty between tick and tock, for us the gap or interval is a realm of conjecture, fantasy, and imagination that can be filled with any one or more of our orientations, such as deceptive expectation or speculative hope. The momentary pause as we cross the threshold is where we congregate the perception of the present, memory of the past, prospects of the future and all the affects that comprise life.

Indeed, our experience of orientations to the future is at once on the unimaginably small and the unfathomably large. The moment we feel hope or identify anticipation, the time our heart flutters, a wave of "something" passes across us, we go light-headed, we wonder how we should act to best fulfil our goals, we pause to take stock, we daydream. The excitement, the feeling of our stomach giving way, the dagger to the heart. These are moments that come and pass rapidly. Further, at their passing, we cannot comprehend at once all the networks of relations required to help bring these orientations to fruition (or, indeed, what is required to avoid the undesirable). But these fleeting moments in quotidian life are when temporality is laid bare: we briefly become acutely aware of a futural trajectory through momentary thoughts and bodily reactions. This is one aspect, one scale if you like, of everyday orientations to the future that we insist requires further anthropological study.

On the other hand, our planning for the yet-to-come can incorporate projections months, years, decades into the future and include abstract notions of future relations on other continents and in other timespaces. When we sit in our offices contemplating our professorial futures – as we so regularly do – we travel years into the future and implicate actions and sets of relations which are currently unknown, abstract, and global in their scale. The books we will write, the power breakfasts we will partake in, the relocation of our future families to another country, what the UK/US academies will "look like" as a workplace "then," "one day." These musings are sites of speculation, hope, perhaps even destiny, on a different scale but which are equally important to our endorsement of foregrounding the future as method in anthropological study of the quotidian.

So-called "life plans" may be strategically implemented in the desire to get from "A" the orientation to "B" the goal. In maintaining the indeterminate teleology of our future-oriented activity, we turn back to Levi Bryant (2011), who suggests that novelty in the outcome of action is maintained due to the distinction between potential and actuality. The multiple unpredictable complications that must be overcome to get from A to B mean that the end goal is only a resemblance of the original orientation. Desire and reality may be comparable but are never precise copies. We maintain that both scales of orientation to the future – the fleeting affective moments that capture body and mind, and more structured projections or plans that are expressed in epochal terms – are equally important as examples of the transcendence of a threshold and the future awakening the present.

Thresholds and Frontiers

To paraphrase Anand Pandian (2012: 548), who advocates the search for newness in the temporal textures of everyday experience, anthropology should pay more attention to the ways in which the future arises in what informants already do. Orientations reside in the everyday; in every action and interaction the future is present. The future is encountered in novelty and repetition, but also in aspiration and inertia. In every muttering of hope expressed, in the formation of each new relationship, in every glance out the window toward passers-by, in each knock at the door, in all the scribbled notes on the calendar, in hitting the brake to let children cross at every red light, in the choice to stay in and read a good book rather than party the night away, a seed of the future is planted.

Anticipation, expectation, speculation, potentiality, hope, destiny intermingle to inform the decision-making (or non-decision) moment (see Knight and Stewart 2016: 11). At moments of (non-)decision and (in-)action, a projection or imagining of the future bubbles into the present and influences what we do; time opens up beyond ourselves, providing "an atmosphere within which alone life can germinate and with the destruction of which it must vanish" (Nietzsche 1997: 68). This is to say that shifting horizons of the ever-changing "now" mean that orientations always remain in flux; much like Cooper's micro-utopias, they are "tasters" of potential futures penetrating the present, only to dissipate and return to the "otherwise" to be replaced by the next episode of "normal life," with its own temporal rhythms and textures. The threshold is the liminal space at the frontier where we press forward into the future, potentially briefly crossing into it. The atmosphere, to borrow from Nietzsche, on the threshold provides a ripe environment for positive orientations toward the future, orientations of hope and innovation, things we can associate with movement and momentum. But the threshold can also be filled with exhaustion, hopelessness, and resignation, orientations we might associate with stasis and inertia.

The threshold is neither the point at which the past perpetually reiterates itself as its own future, nor the space in which we usually reach toward a future already determined, but instead it is a point where the flux of experience can take either well-planned and expected, or perhaps unanticipated and unknown, forms (Pandian 2012: 558). It is where our actions in time creatively materialize, where the present is temporarily placed in suspension and the "magic of the future" happens (Battaglia 2017).

Orientations to the future are directed toward the other side of the frontier, however thick, thin, near, or far that might be. They take place within, but also help shape new timespaces. Scholars such as Anna Tsing (2004) and Debbora Battaglia (2017) argue that a distinctive feature of a frontier is its magical vision that allows people to see something that doesn't yet exist, even if what is to be found on the other side is something "already here, already known, clearly warranted, and naturalized to human designs on the cosmos" (Battaglia 2017: 277). Imaginaries of the future that tangibly exist in the present – such as in Battaglia's examples of The Genesis Machine in *Star Trek* or Disney's Epcot Center Future World – allow people to step into the elsewhere and elsewhen and nurture orientations that might otherwise be disregarded. In a similar vein to how Rachel or David were influenced to change direction in life as they moved through alternative timespaces comprised of different actors and environs, so the impact of seemingly fantastical instalments in providing imaginaries of the future that change people's trajectory should not be underestimated. In the context of media rhetoric at election time promoting futures of hope or in speculation about the abundance of oil in Saõ Tomé and Príncipe, words and images that form teleoaffective structures of the present inform how people envisage materializing their "deeply internalized dreams of fairytale living" (Battaglia 2017: 272) or their apocalyptic anticipation of social breakdown (Schneider-Mayerson 2015).

The magical vision of the future on the other side of the threshold can also be actively promoted through technologies of imagination, such as in Bear's (2015a) case of Indian bureaucratic propaganda during structural economic change, or the ability of rhetoric produced by central banks to noticeably influence financial markets and consumer activity (Holmes 2013). There is immense power in the fantastical realms of television, cinema, and popular culture to shape orientations to the future. Technologies first released into public imagination during 1960s science-fiction television programs pulled the future into the present while inspiring a whole generation of scientists and inventors to attempt to make science fiction into science fact by materializing those futures as part of their reality (e.g., Battaglia 2005b). Lifeworks have been dedicated to conquering the technological challenges first floated in the original *Star Trek* series, for instance. In this case the future has a sense of self-fulfilling prophecy since inactive make-believe television-show props have been actualized.

This again emphasizes the indeterminate nature of orientations to the future and the disparate sources of inspiration for the future enlivening activities in the present. Action can take the form of inaction, apathy, or inertia. To stay put is to pass comment on the future as much as migration (Dzenovska 2018a). Suicide, we might argue, is the ultimate critique of the future. We also reiterate the interconnected characteristic of timespaces comprised of human and nonhuman actors, from the power of words designed to influence action, emergent technologies, and global social and ecological crises, to interpersonal relationships, families, and coincidence.

The End/*Τέλος*/*Fin*

The study of the quotidian – the time of the everyday – is enriched by attention to varying depths of future time. In Heideggerian tradition, we advocate that the future awakens the present. Future-orientedness is part of who we are and how we experience everyday life. We are pulled in the direction of the future in numerous affective ways – by hope and great expectations, through anticipation or fantastical speculation, or by acts of faith or believing in fate. We constantly prepare the groundwork for the future through thoughts and desires as we push toward actualizing potentiality. The affective dimension of time appears to pause or jump-start, forestall or postpone, the future and thus temporality.

Our intention in this book was to orient anthropology toward orientations and to help anthropologists to think about the indeterminate and open-ended teleologies of everyday life across scales of future imaginings. Repositioning teleology to center-stage of anthropological analysis is the only way to make further sense of the role of the future in orienting quotidian action, introducing a more rounded, detailed, and nuanced understanding of the quotidian into anthropology's quest to disentangle the everyday.

References

Abram, S. 2014 "The Time It Takes: Temporalities of Planning." *Journal of the Royal Anthropological Institute* 20(S1): 129–147.

2017 "Contemporary Obsessions with Time and the Promise of the Future." In *Anthropologies and Futures: Researching Emerging and Uncertain Worlds*. Salazar, J. F., S. Pink, A. Irving and J. Sjöberg, eds. London: Bloomsbury, pp. 61–82.

Agamben, G. 1999 *Potentialities: Collected Essays in Philosophy*. D. Heller-Roazen, ed. Stanford, CA: Stanford University Press.

Agnew, J. 2003 *Hegemony: The New Shape of Global Power*. Philadelphia, PA: Temple University Press.

Alam, M. S. 2009 *Israeli Exceptionalism: The Destabilizing Logic of Zionism*. New York, NY: Routledge.

Althusser, L. 1970 "The Errors of Classical Economics: Outline of a Concept of Historical Time." In *Reading Capital*. L. Althusser and E. Balibar, translated by B. Brewster. London: New Left Books, pp. 91–144.

Anderson, B. 1983 *Imagined Communities: Reflections on the Origin and Spread of Nationalism*. London: Verso.

Appadurai, A. 2011 "The Ghost in the Financial Machine." *Public Culture* 23: 517–539.

2013 *The Future as Cultural Fact: Essays on the Global Condition*. London: Verso.

Argenti, N. 2017 "The Presence of the Past in the Era of the Nation-State." *Social Analysis* 61(1): 1–25.

Argenti, N. and D. M. Knight 2015 "Sun, Wind, and the Rebirth of Extractive Economies: Renewable Energy Investment and Metanarratives of Crisis in Greece." *Journal of the Royal Anthropological Institute* 21(4): 781–802.

Aristotle 1943 *Aristotle, On Man in the Universe: Metaphysics/Parts of Animals/ Ethics/Politics/Poetics*. Edited by L. R. Loomis. New York, NY: Walter J. Black.

1989 *Metaphysics Books I–IX*. Cambridge, MA: Harvard University Press.

Asad, T. 1993 *Genealogies of Religion: Discipline and Reasons of Power in Christianity and Islam*. Baltimore, MD: Johns Hopkins University Press.

Augustine. 1998 *Confessions*. Translated by Henry Chadwick. Oxford: Oxford Paperbacks.

Austen, J. 1992 *Sense and Sensibility*. London: Wordsworth Classics.

Auyero, J. 2012 *Patients of the State: The Politics of Waiting in Argentina*. Durham, NC: Duke University Press.

Baca, G., A. Khan, and S. Palmié (eds.) 2009 *Empirical Futures: Anthropologists and Historians Engage the Work of Sidney W. Mintz*. Chapel Hill, NC: University of North Carolina Press.

Bachelard, G. 2016 *The Dialectic of Duration*. Translated by Mary McAllester Jones. Lanham, MD: Rowman & Littlefield.

Bakhtin, M. 1984 (1968). *Rabelais and His World*. Transl. Helene Iswolsky. Bloomington: Indiana University Press.

Barr, M. D. 2016 "Ordinary Singapore: The Decline of Singapore Exceptionalism." *Journal of Contemporary Asia* 46(1): 1–17.

Battaglia, D. (ed.) 2005a *E.T. Culture: Anthropology in Outerspaces*. Durham, NC: Duke University Press.

2005b "Insiders' Voices in Outerspace." In *E.T. Culture: Anthropology in Outerspaces*. D. Battaglia, ed. Durham, NC: Duke University Press, pp. 1–37.

2005c "For Those Who Are Not Afraid of the Future: Raëlian Clonehood in the Public Sphere." In *E.T. Culture: Anthropology in Outerspaces*. D. Battaglia, ed. Durham, NC: Duke University Press, pp. 149–179.

2014 "Diary of a Space Zucchini: Ventriloquizing the Future in Outer Space." Platypus, July 7, 2014. http://blog.castac.org/2014/07/diary-of-a-space-zucchini-ventriloquizing-the-future-in-outer-space (accessed October 29, 2018).

2017 "Aeroponic Gardens and Their Magic: Plants/Persons/Ethics in Suspension." *History and Anthropology* 28(3): 263–292.

Battaglia, D., D. Valentine, and V. Olson (eds.) 2012 "Extreme: Humans at Home in the Cosmos." Special edition, *Anthropological Quarterly* 85(4).

Baumgarten, A. I. (ed.) 2000 *Apocalyptic Time*. Leiden: Brill.

Bear, L. 2014 "Doubt, Conflict, Mediation: The Anthropology of Modern Time." *Journal of the Royal Anthropological Institute* 20(4): 3–30.

2015a "Capitalist Divination: Popularist Speculators and Technologies of Imagination on the Hooghly River." *Comparative Studies of South Asia, Africa and the Middle East* 35(3): 408–423.

2015b *Navigating Austerity: Currents of Debt on a South Asian River*. Stanford, CA: Stanford University Press.

References

Bear, L., R. Birla, and S. S. Puri 2015 "Speculation: Futures and Capitalism in India." *Comparative Studies of South Asia, Africa and the Middle East* 35(3): 387–391.

Benson, P. and S. Kirsch 2010 "Capitalism and the Politics of Resignation." *Current Anthropology* 51(4) : 459–486.

Bentham, J. and J. S. Mill 1961 *The Utilitarians*. Garden City, NY: Dolphin Books.

Berdahl, D. 1999 *Where the World Ended: Reunification and Identity in the German Borderland*. Berkeley, CA: University of California Press.

Bergson, H. 1994 *Matter and Memory*. Translated by N. M. Paul and W. S . Palmer. New York, NY: Zone Books.

Berlant, L. 2011 *Cruel Optimism*. Durham, NC: Duke University Press.

Birth, K. 2012 *Objects of Time: How Things Shape Temporality*. New York, NY: Palgrave Macmillan.

　2017 *Time Blind: Problems in Perceiving Other Temporalities*. New York, NY: Palgrave Macmillan.

Blanchot, M. 1995 *The Writing of the Disaster*. Translated by Ann Smock. Lincoln, NE and London: University of Nebraska Press.

Blattner, W. 2005 "Temporality." In *A Companion to Heidegger*. H. L. Dreyfus and M. A. Wrathall, eds. Oxford: Blackwell Publishing, pp. 311–324.

Bloch, E. 1986. *The Principle of Hope*. London: Blackwell.

Bloch, E. and T. Adorno 1988 "Something's Missing: A Discussion between Ernst Bloch and Theodor Adorno on the Contradictions of Utopian Longing (1964)." In *The Utopian Function of Art and Literature: Selected Essays*. J. Zipes and F. Mecklenburg, eds. Cambridge, MA: The MIT Press, pp. 1–17.

Boas, F. 1920 "The Methods of Ethnology." *American Anthropologist* 22(4): 311–321.

Bock, J. J. 2016 "Approaching Utopia Pragmatically: Artistic Spaces and Community-Making in Post-Earthquake L'Aquila." *Cadernos de Arte e Antropologia* 5(1): 97–115.

Bou Akar, H. 2012 "Contesting Beirut's Frontiers." *City & Society* 24(2): 150–172.

Bromley, D. G. 1997 "Constructing Apocalypticism: Social and Cultural Elements of Radical Organization." In *Millennium, Messiahs, and Mayhem: Contemporary Apocalyptic Movements*. T. Robbins and S. J. Palmer, eds. London: Routledge, pp. 31–46.

Brough, J. B. and W. Blattner 2006 "Temporality." In *A Companion to Phenomenology and Existentialism*. H. L. Dreyfus and M. A. Wrathall, eds. New York, NY: Blackwell Publishing, pp. 127–134.

Brown, K. and D. Theodossopoulos 2003 "Rearranging Solidarity: Conspiracy and the World Order in Greek and Macedonian Commentaries of Kosovo." *Journal of Southern Europe and the Balkans* 5(3): 315–335.

Bryant, L. 2011 "Potentiality and Onticology." blog post May 26, 2011. https://larvalsub jects.wordpress.com/2011/05/26/potentiality-and-onticology (accessed October 29, 2018).

2018 *The Democracy of Objects*. Ann Arbor, MI: University of Michigan Press. [Kindle edition].

Bryant, L., N. Srnicek, and G. Harman (eds.) 2011 *The Speculative Turn: Continental Materialism and Realism*. Melbourne: Anamnesis.

Bryant, R. 2010 *The Past in Pieces: Belonging in the New Cyprus*. Philadelphia, PA: University of Pennsylvania Press.

2012 "Partitions of Memory: Institutions and Witnessing in Cyprus." *Comparative Studies in Society and History* 54(2): 332–360.

2014 "History's Remainders: On Time and Objects after Conflict in Cyprus." *American Ethnologist* 41(4): 681–697.

2016 "On Critical Times: Return, Repetition, and the Uncanny Present." *History and Anthropology* 27(1): 19–31.

2017. "Remembering Loss, Forgetting Gain? Security, Minorities, and the Refugee Experience." Keynote address, Migration, Forced Displacement and Loss: Rethinking Turkey in Times of Crisis Conference, Istanbul Bilgi University, June 20–23.

Bryant, R. and M. Hatay 2019 *De Facto Dreams: Building the So-Called State*. Philadelphia, PA: University of Pennsylvania Press.

Butler, J. 1993 *Bodies That Matter: On the Discursive Limits of "Sex."* New York, NY: Routledge.

Cattelino, J. 2010 "Anthropologies of the United States." *Annual Review of Anthropology* 39: 275–292.

Cavell, S. 1988 "The Uncanniness of the Ordinary." *In Question of the Ordinary: Lines of Scepticism and Romanticism*. Chicago, IL: University of Chicago Press, pp. 153–180.

Choi, V. Y. 2015 "Anticipatory States: Tsunami, War, and Insecurity in Sri Lanka." *Cultural Anthropology* 30(2): 286–309.

Chu, J. Y. 2010 *Cosmologies of Credit: Transnational Mobility and the Politics of Destination in China*. Durham, NC: Duke University Press.

Collins, J. 2008 "Dromocratic Palestine." *Middle East Report* 248: 8–13.

Collins, S. G. 2008 *All Tomorrow's Cultures: Anthropological Engagements with the Future*. Oxford: Berghahn.

Comaroff, J. and J. L. Comaroff 2000 "Millennial Capitalism: First Thoughts on a Second Coming." *Public Culture* 12(2): 291–343.

Connerton, P. 1989 *How Societies Remember*. Cambridge: Cambridge University Press.

References

Coole, D. H. and S. Frost (eds.) 2010 *New Materialisms: Ontology, Agency and Politics*. Charlotte, NC: Duke University Press.

Cooper, D. 2014 *Everyday Utopias: The Conceptual Life of Promising Spaces*. Durham, NC: Duke University Press.

Cottingham, J. 2016 "Hope and the Virtues." In *Hope*. Claremont Studies in Philosophy of Religion. U. Ingolf and M. A. Block, eds. Tübingen: Mohr Siebeck, pp. 13–31.

Cox, M. 2001 "Whatever Happened to American Decline? International Relations and the New United States Hegemony." *New Political Economy* 6(3): 311–340.

Crapanzano, V. 1986 *Waiting: The Whites of South Africa*. New York, NY: Vintage.
2003 "Reflections on Hope as a Category of Social and Psychological Analysis." *Cultural Anthropology* 18(1): 3–32.

Da Col, G. and C. Humphrey 2012 "Introduction: Subjects of Luck—Contingency, Morality, and the Anticipation of Everyday Life." *Social Analysis* 56(2): 1–18.

Dalsgaard, S. and M. Nielsen (eds.) 2015 *Time and the Field*. New York, NY: Berghahn Books.

Das, V. 1997 *Critical Events: An Anthropological Perspective on Contemporary India*. Delhi: Oxford University Press India.
2006 *Life and Words: Violence and the Descent into the Ordinary*. Berkeley, CA: University of California Press.

De Genova, N. 2007 "The Stakes of an Anthropology of the United States." *CR: The New Centennial Review* 7(2): 231–277.

Deleuze, G. 1991 *Bergsonism*. New York, NY: Zone.
1993 *The Fold: Leibniz and the Baroque*. Minneapolis, MN: University of Minnesota Press.
1994 *Difference and Repetition*. New York, NY: Columbia University Press.

Deleuze, G. and F. Guattari. 1987 *A Thousand Plateaus*. Translated by B. Massumi. Minneapolis, MN: University of Minnesota Press.
1994 *What Is Philosophy?* London: Verso.

Derrida, J. 1997 "Perhaps or Maybe: Jacques Derrida in Conversation with Alexander García Düttmann." *Warwick Journal of Philosophy* 6 (Responsibilities of Deconstruction): 1–18.
2005 "Preface: A Time for Farewells: Heidegger (Read by) Hegel (Read by) Malabou." Translated by J. D. Cohen. In *The Future of Hegel: Plasticity, Temporality and Dialectic*. C. Malabou. London and New York, NY: Routledge, pp. vii–xlvii.

Devji, F. 2013 *Muslim Zion: Pakistan as a Political Idea*. Cambridge, MA: Harvard University Press.

Dickens, C. 2007 [1860]. *Great Expectations*. Ware: Wordsworth Classics.

Doyle, R. 2005 "Close Encounters of the Nth Kind: Becoming Sampled and the Mullis-ship Connection." In *E.T. Culture: Anthropology in Outerspaces*. D. Battaglia, ed. Durham, NC: Duke University Press, pp. 200–217.

Dzenovska, D. 2018a "Emptiness and Its Futures: Staying and Leaving as Tactics of Life in Latvia." *Focaal: Journal of Global and Historical Anthropology* 80: 16–29.

2018b *School of Europeanness: Tolerance and Other Lessons in Political Liberalism in Latvia*. Ithaca, NY: Cornell University Press.

Dzenovska, D. and N. De Genova 2018 "Introduction: Desire for the Political in the Aftermath of the Cold War." *Focaal: Journal of Global and Historical Anthropology* 80: 1–15.

Edgar, I. and D. Henig 2010 "*Istikhara*: The Guidance and Practice of Islamic Dream Incubation Through Ethnographic Comparison." *History and Anthropology* 21 (3): 251–262.

Edwards, J. 2009 "Skipping a Generation and Assisting Conception." In *Kinship and Beyond: The Genealogical Model Reconsidered*. S. Bamford and J. Leach, eds. London: Berghahn, pp. 138–157.

Elgström, O. and S. Delputte 2016 "An End to Nordic Exceptionalism? Europeanisation and Nordic Development Policies." *European Politics and Society* 17(1): 28–41.

Elliot, A. 2016 "The Makeup of Destiny: Predestination and the Labor of Hope in a Moroccan Emigrant Town." *American Ethnologist* 43(3): 488–499.

Evans-Pritchard, E. E. 1937 *Witchcraft, Oracles and Magic among the Azande*. Oxford: Oxford University Press.

Eyerman, R. 1991 "Modernity and Social Movements." In *Social Change and Modernity*. H. Haferkamp and N. J. Smelser, eds. Berkeley, CA: University of California Press, pp. 37–55.

Fabian, J. 1983 *Time and the Other*. New York, NY: Columbia University Press.

Fehérváry, K. 2002 "American Kitchens, Luxury Bathrooms, and the Search for a 'Normal' Life in Postsocialist Hungary." *Ethnos* 67(3): 369–400.

Ferguson, J. 1999 *Expectations of Modernity: Myths and Meanings of Urban Life on the Zambian Copperbelt*. Berkeley, CA: University of California Press.

Ferme, M. 2001 *The Underneath of Things: Violence, History, and the Everyday in Sierra Leone*. Berkeley, CA: University of California Press.

Fortun, M. 2008 *Promising Genomics: Iceland and deCODE Genetics in a World of Speculation*. Berkeley, CA: University of California Press.

Fraser, M. 2006 "Event." *Theory, Culture & Society* 23(2–3): 129–132.

References

Gaibazzi, P. 2015 "The Quest for Luck: Fate, Fortune, Work and the Unexpected among Gambian Soninke Hustlers." *Critical African Studies* 7(3): 227–242.

Gallant, T. W. 1997 "Greek Exceptionalism and Contemporary Historiography: New Pitfalls and Old Debates." *Journal of Modern Greek Studies* 15(2): 209–216.

Gamble, A. 2000 *Politics and Fate*. Cambridge: Polity Press.

Gell, A. 1992 *The Anthropology of Time: Cultural Constructions of Temporal Maps and Images*. Oxford: Berg.

Giddens, A. 1990 *The Consequences of Modernity*. Stanford, CA: Stanford University Press.

Gilbert, A., J. Greenberg, E. Helms, and S. Jansen 2008 "Reconsidering Postsocialism from the Margins of Europe: Hope, Time and Normalcy in Post-Yugoslav Societies." *Anthropology News* 49(8): 10–11.

Gillis, J. (ed.) 1994 *Commemorations: The Politics of National Identity*. Princeton, NJ: Princeton University Press.

Gökaçtı, M. A. 2003. *Nüfus Mübadelesi: Kayıp bir Kuşağın Hikayesi*. Istanbul: İletişim Yayınları.

Gosden, C. 1994 *Social Being and Time*. Oxford: Blackwell.

Graeber, D. 2012 "The Sword, the Sponge, and the Paradox of Performativity: Some Observations on Fate, Luck, Financial Chicanery, and the Limits of Human Knowledge." *Social Analysis* 56(1): 25–42.

Greenberg, J. 2011 "On the Road to Normal: Negotiating Agency and State Sovereignty in Postsocialist Serbia." *American Anthropologist* 113(1): 88–100.

Greenhouse, C. 1989 "Just in Time: Temporality and the Cultural Legitimation of Law." *Yale Law Journal* 98(8): 1631–1651.

1996 *A Moment's Notice: Time Politics across Cultures*. Ithaca, NY: Cornell University Press.

Gross, R. and J. Greco (eds.) 2013 *Powers and Capacities in Philosophy: The New Aristotelianism*. New York, NY: Routledge.

Guenzi, C. 2012 "The Allotted Share: Managing Fortune in Astrological Counseling in Contemporary India." *Social Analysis* 56(2): 39–55.

Guyer, J. 2007 "Prophecy and the Near Future: Thoughts on Macroeconomic, Evangelical, and Punctuated Time." *American Ethnologist* 34(3): 409–421.

Halbwachs, M. 1992 *On Collective Memory*. Chicago, IL: University of Chicago Press.

Hage, G. 2003 *Against Paranoid Nationalism: Searching for Hope in a Shrinking Society*. Annandale: Pluto/Merlin.

2009 "Waiting out the Crisis: On Stuckedness and Governmentality." In *Waiting.* G. Hage, ed. Melbourne: Melbourne University Press, pp. 97–106.

Hagen, G. 2005 "Legitimacy and World Order." In *Legitimizing the Order: The Ottoman Rhetoric of State Power.* H. T. Karateke and M. Reinkowski, eds. Leiden: Brill, pp. 55–84.

Hagen, G. and E. L. Menchinger 2014 "Ottoman Historical Thought." In *A Companion to Global Historical Thought.* P. Duara, V. Murthy, and A. Santori, eds. Maiden, MA: John Wiley & Sons, pp. 92–106.

Haraway, D. 1988 "Situated Knowledges: The Science Question in Feminism and the Privilege of Partial Perspectives." *Feminist Studies* 14: 575–599.

1991 *Simians, Cyborgs and Women: The Reinvention of Nature.* New York, NY: Routledge.

Harman, G. 2005 *Guerrilla Metaphysics: Phenomenology and the Carpentry of Things.* Chicago, IL: Open Court.

2009 *Prince of Networks: Bruno Latour and Metaphysics.* Melbourne: Re. Press.

2010 *Towards Speculative Realism: Essays and Lectures.* Ropley: Zero Books.

2012 *Weird Realism: Lovecraft and Philosophy.* Alresford: Zero Books.

2018 *Object-Oriented Ontology: A New Theory of Everything.* London: Pelican Books.

Harrell, S. 1987 "The Concept of Fate in Chinese Folk Ideology." *Modern China* 13(1): 90–109.

Harris, R. 2009 "Freedom of Speech and Philosophy of Education." *British Journal of Educational Studies* 57(2): 111–126.

Harvey, P. 2005 "The Materiality of State-Effects: An Ethnography of a Road in the Peruvian Andes." In *State Formation: Anthropological Perspectives.* C. Krohn-Hansen and K. G. Nustad, eds. London: Pluto, pp. 123–141.

Harvey, P. and H. Knox 2012 "The Enchantments of Infrastructure." *Mobilities* 7(4): 521–536.

Haugerud, A. 2013 *No Billionaire Left Behind: Satirical Activism in America.* Stanford, CA: Stanford University Press.

Hegel, G. W. F. 1971 *Philosophy of Mind [Spirit]. Part 3 of the Encyclopaedia of the Philosophical Sciences* (1830). Translated by W. Wallace, together with the *Zusätze* in Boulmann's text (1845), translated by A. V. Miller, with foreword by J. N. Findlay. Oxford: Clarendon Press.

Heidegger, M. 1962 *Being and Time.* Translated by J. Macquarrie and E. Robinson. New York, NY: Harper Collins.

1977 *The Question Concerning Technology.* Translated and with an Introduction by W. Lovitt. New York, NY: Harper Torchbooks.

1996 *Being and Time.* Oxford: Wiley-Blackwell.

References

Henkle, R. B. 1980 *Comedy and Culture: England, 1820–1900.* Princeton, NJ: Princeton University Press.

Hermez, S. 2012 "'The War Is Going to Ignite': On the Anticipation of Violence in Lebanon." *PoLAR: Political and Legal Anthropology Review* 35(2): 327–344.

Hirsch, E. and C. Stewart 2005 "Introduction: Ethnographies of Historicity." *History and Anthropology* 16(3): 261–274.

Hobbes, T. 1962 *Leviathan, or the Matter, Forme, and Power of a Commonwealth Ecclesiasticall and Civil.* Edited by Michael Oakeshott. New York, NY: Collier Books.

Hodges, M. 2008 "Rethinking Time's Arrow: Bergson, Deleuze and the Anthropology of Time." *Anthropological Theory* 8(4): 399–429.

—— 2010 "The Time of the Interval: Historicity, Modernity and Epoch in Rural France." *American Ethnologist* 37(1): 115–131.

—— 2014 "Immanent Anthropology: A Comparative Study of Process in Contemporary France." *Journal of the Royal Anthropological Institute* 20(S1): 33–51.

Holmes, D. 2013 *Economy of Words: Communicative Imperatives in Central Banks.* Chicago, IL: University of Chicago Press.

Hume, D. 1949 *A Treatise of Human Nature.* Oxford: Clarendon Press.

—— 2000 *An Enquiry Concerning Human Understanding: A Critical Edition.* T. L. Beauchamp, ed. Oxford: Clarendon Press.

Huron, D. 2006 *Sweet Anticipation: Music and the Psychology of Expectation.* Cambridge, MA: Massachusetts Institute of Technology.

Husserl, E. 1964 *The Phenomenology of Internal Time-Consciousness.* Bloomington, IN: Indiana University Press.

—— 1991 *On the Phenomenology of the Consciousness of Internal Time (1893–1917).* Translated by J. B. Brough. Collected Works, vol. 4. Dordrecht: Kluwer.

Hussey, S. 2013 *The English Language: Structure and Development.* New York, NY: Routledge.

Jaffe, A. 2016 "From Aristotle to Marx: A Critical Philosophical Anthropology." *Science & Society* 80(1): 56–77.

Janeja, M. K. and A. Bandak (eds.) 2018 *Ethnographies of Waiting: Doubt, Hope and Uncertainty.* London: Bloomsbury.

Jansen, S. 2014 "On Not Moving Well Enough: Temporal Reasoning in Sarajevo Yearnings for 'Normal Lives'." *Current Anthropology* 55(S9): s74–s84.

—— 2015 *Yearnings in the Meantime: "Normal Lives" and the State in a Sarajevo Apartment Complex.* Oxford: Berghahn Books.

2016 "For a Relational, Historical Ethnography of Hope: Indeterminacy and Determination in the Bosnian and Herzegovinian Meantime." *History and Anthropology* 27(4): 447–464.

Jeffs, R. 2012 "The Future of the Future: Koyré, Kojève, and Malabou Speculate on Hegelian Time." *Parrhesia: A Journal of Critical Philosophy* 15: 35–53.

Jeganathan, P. 2000 "On the Anticipation of Violence: Modernity and Identity in Southern Sri Lanka." In *Anthropology, Development and Modernities: Exploring Discourses, Counter-Tendencies and Violence*. A. Arce and N. Long, eds. New York, NY: Routledge, pp. 111–126.

2003 "Checkpoint: Anthropology, Identity and the State." In *Anthropology in the Margins of the State*. V. Das and D. Poole, eds. Santa Fe, NM: School of American Research Advanced Seminar Series, pp. 67–80.

Junker, K. W. 2000 "Words: 'Expectation'." *Futures* 32: 695–702.

Kelly, A. 2008 "Living Loss: An Exploration of the Internal Space of Liminality." *Mortality* 13(4): 335–350.

Kelly, T. 2008 "The Attractions of Accountancy: Living an Ordinary Life During the Second Palestinian *Intifada*." *Ethnography* 9(3): 351–376.

Kermode, F. 2000 *The Sense of an Ending: Studies in the Theory of Fiction*. Oxford: Oxford University Press.

Kirksey, E. 2015 *Emergent Ecologies*. Durham, NC: Duke University Press.

Kleist, N. and S. Jansen 2016 "Introduction: Hope over Time: Crisis, Immobility and Future-Making." *History and Anthropology* 27(4): 373–392.

Knight, D. M. 2012 "Cultural Proximity: Crisis, Time and Social Memory in Central Greece." *History and Anthropology* 23(3): 349–374.

2013 "The Greek Economic Crisis as Trope." *Focaal: Journal of Global and Historical Anthropology* 65: 147–159.

2015a *History, Time, and Economic Crisis in Central Greece*. New York, NY: Palgrave Macmillan.

2015b Wit and Greece's Economic Crisis: Ironic Slogans, Food, and Anti-Austerity Sentiments. *American Ethnologist* 42(2): 230–246.

2016 "Temporal Vertigo and Time Vortices on Greece's Central Plain." *Cambridge Journal of Anthropology* 34(1): 32–44.

2017a "Anxiety and Cosmopolitan Futures: Brexit and Scotland." *American Ethnologist* 44(2): 237–242.

2017b "Energy Talk, Temporality, and Belonging in Austerity Greece." *Anthropological Quarterly* 90(1): 167–192.

2017c "The Green Economy as Sustainable Alternative?" *Anthropology Today* 33 (5): 28–31.

References

2018 "The Desire for Disinheritance in Austerity Greece." *Focaal: Journal of Global and Historical Anthropology* 80: 30–42.

Knight, D. M. and C. Stewart 2016 "Ethnographies of Austerity: Temporality, Crisis and Affect in Southern Europe." *History and Anthropology* 27(1): 1–18.

Koch, N. 2017 "Orientalizing Authoritarianism: Narrating US Exceptionalism in Popular Reactions to the Trump Election and Presidency." *Political Geography* 58: 145–147.

Kompridis, N. 2006 *Critique and Disclosure: Critical Theory between Past and Future.* Cambridge, MA and London: Massachusetts Institute of Technology Press.

Konrad, M. 2005 *Nameless Relations: Anonymity, Melanesia and Reproductive Gift Exchange between British Ova Donors and Recipients.* Oxford: Berghahn Books.

Koselleck, R. 1985 *Futures Past: On the Semantics of Historical Time.* Translated by K. Tribe. Cambridge, MA: Massachusetts Institute of Technology Press.

2000 *Critique and Crisis: Enlightenment and the Pathogenesis of Modern Society.* Cambridge, MA: MIT Press.

2006 "Crisis." Translated by M. W. Richter. *Journal of the History of Ideas* 67(2): 357–400.

Kravel-Tovi, M. and Y. Bilu 2008 "The Work of the Present: Constructing Messianic Temporality in the Wake of Failed Prophecy among Chabad Hasidim." *American Ethnologist* 35(1): 64–80.

Kroeger, K. 2003 "AIDS Rumors, Imaginary Enemies, and the Body Politic in Indonesia." *American Ethnologist* 30(2): 243–257.

Kubler, G. 1962 *The Shape of Time.* New Haven, CT: Yale University Press.

Kupchan, C. A. 2018 "The Clash of Exceptionalisms: A New Fight over an Old Idea." *Foreign Affairs* March/April, pp. 139–148.

Leach, M. 2012 "The Dark Side of the Green Economy: 'Green Grabbing'." *Al Jazeera*, June 20th, 2012. www.aljazeera.com/indepth/opinion/2012/06/201261885431273708.html (accessed January 1, 2017).

Lepselter, S. 2005 "The License: Poetics, Power, and the Uncanny." In *E.T. Culture: Anthropology in Outerspaces.* D. Battaglia, ed. Durham, NC: Duke University Press, pp. 130–149.

2016 *The Resonance of Unseen Things: Poetics, Power, Captivity, and UFOs in the American Uncanny.* Ann Arbor, MI: University of Michigan Press.

Lieber, R. J. 2009 "Persistent Primacy and the Future of the American Era." *International Politics* 46(2): 119–139.

Lipovetsky, M. 2011 *Charms of the Cynical Reason: The Trickster's Transformation in Soviet and Post-Soviet Culture.* Boston, MA: Academic Studies Press.

Löfflmann, G. 2015 "Leading from Behind – American Exceptionalism and President Obama's Post- American Vision of Hegemony." *Geopolitics* 20(2): 308–332.

Lollar, K. 2010 "The Liminal Experience: Loss of Extended Self after the Fire." *Qualitative Inquiry* 16(4): 262–270.

Malabou, C. 2005 *The Future of Hegel: Plasticity, Temporality and Dialectic.* Translated by Lisabeth During. London and New York, NY: Routledge.

Malaby, T. M. 2003 *Gambling Life. Dealing in Contingency in a Greek City.* Champaign, IL: University of Illinois Press.

2012 "Our Present Misfortune: Games and the Post-Bureaucratic Colonization of Contingency." *Social Analysis* 56(2): 103–116.

Malinowski, B. 1922 *Argonauts of the Western Pacific.* London: Routledge and Kegan Paul.

1946 *The Dynamics of Culture Change: An Inquiry into Race Relations in Africa.* P. M. Kaberry, ed. New Haven, CT: Yale University Press.

Mar, P. 2005 "Unsettling Potentialities: Topographies of Hope in Transnational Migration." *Journal of Intercultural Studies* 26(4): 361–378.

Marx, K. 1978 "Theses on Feuerbach." In *The Marx-Engels Reader.* Second edition. New York, NY: W. W. Norton.

1978 *Theory of History: A Defence.* Oxford: Oxford University Press.

Massumi, B. 2002 *Parables for the Virtual: Movement, Affect, Sensation.* Durham, NC: Duke University Press.

Mauss, M. 2001 [1925] *The Gift: Forms and Functions of Exchange in Archaic Societies.* London: Routledge.

McAllister, K. and J. Ruggill 2010 "Is He 'Avin a Laugh?: The Importance of Fun to Virtual Play Studies." In *Utopic Dreams and Apocalyptic Fantasies: Critical Approaches to Researching Video Game Play.* J. Talmadge Wright, D. G. Embrick, and András Lukács, eds. Lanham, MD: Lexington, pp. 43–58.

McManus, S. 2015 "The Privatization of Hope: Ernst Bloch and the Future of Utopia" [Review]. *Contemporary Political Theory* 14(4): e18–e21.

Meillassoux, Q. 2008 *After Finitude: An Essay on the Necessity of Contingency.* Translated by R. Bassier, with a preface by Alain Badiou. London: Bloomsbury.

Menchinger, E. L. 2016 "Free Will, Predestination, and the Fate of the Ottoman Empire." *Journal of the History of Ideas* 77(3): 445–466.

Meneley, A. 2008 "Time in a Bottle: The Uneasy Circulation of Palestinian Olive Oil." *Middle East Report* 248: 18–23.

Menin, L. 2015 "The Impasse of Modernity: Personal Agency, Divine Destiny, and the Unpredictability of Intimate Relationships in Morocco." *Journal of the Royal Anthropological Institute* 21: 892–910.

References

Merleau-Ponty, M. 2012 *The Phenomenology of Perception*. Translated by D. A. Landes. London: Routledge.

Messeri, L. 2016 *Placing Outer Space: An Earthly Ethnography of Other Worlds*. Durham, NC: Duke University Press.

2017 "Resonant Worlds: Cultivating Proximal Encounters in Planetary Science." *American Ethnologist* 44(1): 131–142.

Meyer, L. B. 1956 *Emotion and Meaning in Music*. Chicago, IL: University of Chicago Press.

Middleton, T. 2013 "Anxious Belongings: Anxiety and the Politics of Belonging in Subnationalist Darjeeling." *American Anthropologist* 115(4): 608–621.

Mittermaier, A. 2012 "Dreams from Elsewhere: Muslim Subjectivities beyond the Trope of Self-cultivation." *Journal of the Royal Anthropological Institute* 18: 247–265.

Miyazaki, H. 2004 *The Method of Hope: Anthropology, Philosophy and Fijian Knowledge*. Stanford, CA: Stanford University Press.

2006 "Economy of Dreams: Hope in Global Capitalism and Its Critiques." *Cultural Anthropology* 21(2): 147–172.

Miyazaki, H. and R. Swedberg (eds.) 2017 *The Economy of Hope*. Philadelphia, PA: University of Pennsylvania Press.

Morgan, L. 2013 "The Potentiality Principle from Aristotle to Abortion." *Current Anthropology* 54(S7): S15–S25.

Moroşanu, R. and F. Ringel 2016 "Time-Tricking: A General Introduction." *Cambridge Journal of Anthropology* 34(1): 17–21.

Morton, T. 2010. *The Ecological Thought*. Cambridge, MA: Harvard University Press.

2015 "This Biosphere Which Is Not One: Towards Weird Essentialism." *Journal of the British Society for Phenomenology* 46(2): 141–155.

Muehlebach, A. 2012 *The Moral Neoliberal: Welfare and Citizenship in Italy*. Chicago, IL: University of Chicago Press.

Muehlebach, A. and N. Shoshan 2012 "Introduction to Special Collection on Post-Fordist Affect." *Anthropological Quarterly* 85(2): 317–343.

Munn, N. 1992 "The Cultural Anthropology of Time: A Critical Essay." *Annual Review of Anthropology* 21: 93–123.

Muñoz, J. E. 2009 *Cruising Utopia: The Then and There of Queer Futurity*. New York, NY: New York University Press.

Narotzky, S. and N. Besnier 2014 "Crisis, Value, and Hope: Rethinking the Economy." *Current Anthropology* 55(S9): S4–S16.

Nau, H. 2001 "Why 'The Rise and Fall of the Great Powers' Was Wrong." *Review of International Studies* 27(4): 579–592.

Nicolini, D. 2017 "Practice Theory as a Package of Theory, Method and Vocabulary: Affordances and Limitations." In *Methodological Reflections on Practice Oriented Theories*. M. Jonas, B. Littig, and A. Wroblewski, eds. Cham, Switzerland: Springer International, pp. 19–34.

Nielsen, M. 2011 "Futures Within: Reversible Time and House-Building in Maputo, Mozambique." *Anthropological Theory* 11(4): 397–423.

2014 "A Wedge of Time: Futures in the Present and Presents without Futures in Maputo, Mozambique." *Journal of the Royal Anthropological Institute* 20(S1): 166–182.

Nieswand, B. 2010 "Enacted Destiny: West African Charismatic Christians in Berlin and the Immanence of God." *Journal of Religion in Africa* 40(1): 33–59.

Nietzsche, F. 1880 *The Wanderer and His Shadow*. London: Alexander Harvey.

1974 *The Gay Science: With a Prelude in Rhymes and an Appendix of Songs*. New York, NY: Vintage.

1989 "Ecce Homo." Translated by W. Kaufmann. In *On the Genealogy of Morals/ Ecce Homo*. W. Kaufmann, ed. New York, NY: Vintage Books.

1994 [1878] *Human, All Too Human: A Book for Free Spirits*. London: Penguin.

1997 *Untimely Meditations*. Cambridge: Cambridge University Press.

Nolte, G. and H. Aust 2013 "European Exceptionalism?" *Global Constitutionalism* 2 (3): 407–436.

Nora, P. 1989 "Between Memory and History: *Les lieux de memoire*." *Representations* 26, 7–25.

Nordstrom, C. 2004 *Shadows of War: Violence, Power, and International Profiteering in the Twenty-First Century*. Berkeley, CA: University of California Press.

Oskanian, K. K. 2018 "A Very Ambiguous Empire: Russia's Hybrid Exceptionalism." *Europe-Asia Studies* 70(1): 26–52.

Ouroussoff, A. 2010 *Wall Street at War: The Secret Struggle for the Global Economy*. Cambridge: Polity.

Painter, J. 2006 "Prosaic Geographies of Stateness." *Political Geography* 25: 752–774.

Palmié, S. and C. Stewart 2016 "Introduction: For an Anthropology of History." *HAU: Journal of Ethnographic Theory* 6(1): 207–236.

Pandian, A. 2012 "The Time of Anthropology: Notes from a Field of Contemporary Experience." *Cultural Anthropology* 27(4): 547–571.

Pandian, A. and C. Howe 2016 "Lexicon for an Anthropocene yet Unseen." Cultural Anthropology. https://culanth.org/fieldsights/803-lexicon-for-an-anthropocene-yet-unseen (accessed October 29, 2018).

Pedersen, M. A. 2012 "A Day in the Cadillac: The Work of Hope in Urban Mongolia." *Social Analysis* 56(2): 136–151.

References

Pels, P. 2015 "Modern Times: Seven Steps toward an Anthropology of the Future." *Current Anthropology* 56(6): 779–796.

Peteet, J. 2017 *Space and Mobility in Palestine*. Bloomington, IN: Indiana University Press.

2018 "Closure's Temporality: The Cultural Politics of Time and Waiting." *South Atlantic Quarterly* 117(1): 43–64.

Pettit, M. 2013 *The Science of Deception: Psychology and Commerce in America*. Chicago, IL: University of Chicago Press.

Pierson, G. W. 1962 "The M-Factor in American History." *American Quarterly* 14/2, pt. 2: supplement (Summer): 275–289.

Pink, S., Y. Akama, and A. Fergusson 2017 "Researching Future as an Alterity of the Present." In *Anthropologies and Futures: Researching Emerging and Uncertain Worlds*. J. F. Salazar, S. Pink, and J. Sjöberg, eds. London: Bloomsbury, pp. 133–150.

Pipyrou, S. 2014 "Altruism and Sacrifice: Mafia Free Gift Giving in South Italy." *Anthropological Forum* 24(4): 412–426.

2018 "Rumor Has It: Leisure, Gossip and Distortion at Funerals in Central Greece." In *Leisure and Death*. A. Kaul and J. Skinner, eds. Boulder, CO: University of Colorado Press, pp. 244–258.

Potamianou, A. 1996 *Hope: A Shield in the Economy of Borderline States*. London: Routledge.

Puri, S. S. 2015 "Betting on Performed Futures: Predictive Procedures at Delhi Racecourse." *Comparative Studies of South Asia, Africa and the Middle East* 35(3): 466–480.

Quinn, A. 2011 "The Art of Declining Politely: Obama's Prudent Presidency and the Waning of American Power." *International Affairs* 87(4): 803–824.

Rakopoulos, T. 2018 "Show Me the Money: Conspiracy Theories and Distant Wealth." *History and Anthropology* 29(3): 376–391.

Ranciere, J. 2010 *Dissensus: On Politics and Aesthetics*. S. Corcoran, ed. and trans. London and New York, NY: Continuum Books [Kindle edition].

Rapport, N. 1998 "Gossip." In *Encyclopaedia of Social and Cultural Anthropology*. A. Barnard and J. Spencer, eds. London: Routledge, pp. 266–267.

Reed, A. 2011 "Hope on Remand." *Journal of the Royal Anthropological Institute* 17 (3): 527–544.

Reiter, K., L. Sexton, and J. Sumner 2017 "Theoretical and Empirical Limits of Scandinavian Exceptionalism: Isolation and Normalization in Danish Prisons." *Punishment & Society* 20(1): 92–112.

Ricoeur, P. 1988 *Time and Narrative, vol. 3*. Translated by K. Blamey and D. Pellauer. Chicago, IL: University of Chicago Press.

2004 *Memory, History, Forgetting*. Translated by K. Blamey and D. Pellauer. Chicago, IL: University of Chicago Press.

Ringel, F. 2014 "Post-Industrial Times and the Unexpected: Endurance and Sustainability in Germany's Fastest-Shrinking City." *Journal of the Royal Anthropological Institute* 20(S1): 52–70.

2016 "Can Time Be Tricked? A Theoretical Introduction." *Cambridge Journal of Anthropology* 34(1): 22–31.

2018 *Back to the Postindustrial Future: An Ethnography of Germany's Fastest Shrinking City*. Oxford: Berghahn.

Robbins, J. 2007 "Continuity Thinking and the Problem of Christian Culture: Belief, Time, and the Anthropology of Christianity." *Current Anthropology* 48(1): 5–38.

Robbins, T. and S. J. Palmer 1997 "Introduction: Patterns of Contemporary Apocalypticism." In *Millennium, Messiahs, and Mayhem*. T. Robbins and S. J. Palmer, eds. London: Routledge, pp. 1–30.

Roitman, J. N. D. 2011 "Crisis." Political Concepts: A Critical Lexicon. www.politicalconcepts.org/issue1/crisis (accessed January 4, 2015).

2014 *Anti-Crisis*. Durham, NC and London: Duke University Press.

Rosenberg, D. and S. Harding (eds.) 2005 *Histories of the Future*. Durham, NC: Duke University Press.

Roth, C. F. 2005 "Ufology as Anthropology: Race, Extraterrestrials, and the Occult." In *E.T. Culture: Anthropology in Outerspaces*. D. Battaglia, ed. Durham, NC: Duke University Press, pp. 38–93.

Russett, B. 1985 "The Mysterious Case of Vanishing Hegemony; or, Is Mark Twain Really Dead?" *International Organization* 39(2): 207–231.

Rutherford, D. 2016 "Affect Theory and the Empirical." *Annual Review of Anthropology* 45: 285–300.

Şahin, K. 2013 *Empire and Power in the Reign of Süleyman: Narrating the Sixteenth-Century Ottoman World*. Cambridge: Cambridge University Press.

Sakwa, R. 2009 "Liminality and Postcommunism: The Twenty-First Century as the Subject of History." *International Political Anthropology* 2(1): 110–126.

Salazar, J. F., S. Pink, A. Irving, and J. Sjöberg (eds.) 2017 *Anthropologies and Futures: Researching Emerging and Uncertain Worlds*. London: Bloomsbury.

Samuels, D. 2005 "Alien Tongues." In *E.T. Culture: Anthropology in Outerspaces*. D. Battaglia, ed. Durham, NC: Duke University Press, pp. 94–129.

Sangren, P. S. 2012 "Fate, Agency, and the Economy of Desire in Chinese Ritual and Society." *Social Analysis* 56(2): 117–135.

Schatzki, T. R. 2002 *The Site of the Social: A Philosophical Account of the Constitution of Social Life and Change*. University Park, PA: The Pennsylvania State University Press.

References

2010 *The Timespace of Human Activity: On Performance, Society, and History as Indeterminate Teleological Events.* Lanham, MD: Lexington Books [Kindle edition].

Schmaltz, T. M. (ed.) 2014 *Efficient Causality: A History.* Oxford: University of Oxford Press.

Schneider-Mayerson, M. 2015 *Peak Oil: Apocalyptic Environmentalism and Libertarian Political Culture.* Chicago, IL: University of Chicago Press.

Schutz, A. 1997 *The Phenomenology of the Social World.* Evanston, IL: Northwestern University Press.

Serres, M. 1995 *Genesis.* Ann Arbor, MI: University of Michigan Press.

Serres, M. and B. Latour 1995 *Conversations on Science, Culture, and Time.* Ann Arbor, MI: University of Michigan Press.

Seybold, M. 2018 "Confidence Tricks." Aeon. https://aeon.co/essays/the-financial-world-and-the-magical-elixir-of-confidence (accessed October 29, 2018).

Shomaker, D. 1989 "Age Disorientation, Liminality and Reality: The Case of the Alzheimer's Patient." *Medical Anthropology* 12(1): 91–101.

Shore, W. T. 1903 "Kismet." *The Academy and Literature, 1902–1905,* issue 1640, October 10, 1903, 382–383.

Shryock, D. and D. L. Smail 2011 *Deep History: The Architecture of Past and Present.* Berkeley, CA: University of California Press.

Siebers, J. 1998 *The Method of Speculative Philosophy: An Essay on the Foundation of Whitehead's Metaphysics.* Kassel: Kassel University Press.

Simmel, G. 1971 [1908] "The Stranger." In *On Individuality and Social Form.* D. N. Levine, ed. Chicago, IL: University of Chicago Press, pp. 143–149.

Simpson, B. 2013 "Managing Potential in Assisted Reproductive Technologies: Reflections on Gifts, Kinship, and the Process of Vernacularization." *Current Anthropology* 54(S7): s87–s96.

Singh, R. S. 2008 "The Exceptional Empire: Why the United States Will Not Decline – Again." *International Politics* 45(5): 571–593.

Sluka, J. A. 2009 "In the Shadow of the Gun: 'Not-War-Not-Peace' and the Future of Conflict in Northern Ireland." *Critique of Anthropology* 29(3): 279–299.

Sneath, D., M. Holbraad, and M. A. Pedersen 2009 "Technologies of the Imagination: An Introduction." *Ethnos* 74(1): 5–30.

Ssorin-Chaikov, N. 2006 "On Heterochrony: Birthday Gifts to Stalin, 1949." *Journal of the Royal Anthropological Institute* 12(2): 355–375.

2017 *Two Lenins: A Brief Anthropology of Time.* Chicago, IL: HAU Books.

Stäheli, U. 2013 *Spectacular Speculation: Thrills, the Economy, and Popular Discourse.* Stanford, CA: Stanford University Press.

Stafford, C. 2012 "Misfortune and What Can Be Done about It: A Taiwanese Case Study." *Social Analysis* 56(2): 90–102.

Starn, R. 1971 "Historians and 'Crisis'." *Past and Present* 52: 3–22.

Stein Frankle, R. L. and P. L. Stein 2005 *Anthropology of Religion: Magic and Witchcraft*. Boston, MA: Longman.

Stewart, C. 2012 *Dreaming and Historical Consciousness in Island Greece*. Cambridge, MA: Harvard University Press.

2016 "Historicity and Anthropology." *Annual Review of Anthropology* 45: 79–94.

Strange, S. 1987 "The Persistent Myth of Lost Hegemony." *International Organization* 41(4): 551–574.

1988 "The Future of the American Empire." *Journal of International Affairs* 42(1): 1–17.

Strathern, M. 1996 "Potential Property: Intellectual Rights and Property in Persons." *Social Anthropology* 4(1): 17–32.

2005 *Kinship, Law and the Unexpected: Relatives Are Always a Surprise*. Cambridge: Cambridge University Press.

2012 "Gifts Money Cannot Buy." *Social Anthropology* 20(4): 397–410.

Taillefer, J. 2017 Just-Is: Contingency, Desire and Temporality. An Inquiry on the Relation between Law and Justice. Ph.D. Thesis, Department of Psychosocial Studies, Birkbeck College, London.

Taussig, K.-S., K. Hoeyer, and S. Helmreich 2013 "The Anthropology of Potentiality in Biomedicine: An Introduction to Supplement 7." *Current Anthropology* 54 (S7): S3–S14.

Thompson, P. 2013 "Introduction." In *The Privatization of Hope: Ernst Bloch and the Future of Utopia SIC 8*. Thompson, P. and S. Žižek, eds. Durham, NC: Duke University Press, pp. 1–20.

Thompson, P. and S. Žižek (eds.) 2013 *The Privatization of Hope: Ernst Bloch and the Future of Utopia SIC 8*. Durham, NC: Duke University Press.

Tomes, R. R. 2014 "American Exceptionalism in the Twenty-First Century." *Survival* 56(1): 27–50.

Torpey, J. 2017. "The End of the World as We Know It? American Exceptionalism in an Age of Disruption." *Sociological Forum* 32(4): 701–725.

Trigg, D. 2006 *The Aesthetics of Decay: Nothingness, Nostalgia, and the Absence of Reason*. New York, NY and Frankfurt am Main: Peter Lang.

2012 *The Memory of Place: A Phenomenology of the Uncanny*. Athens, OH: University of Ohio Press.

Tsing, A. 2004 *Friction: An Ethnography of Global Connection*. Princeton, NJ: Princeton University Press.

Turner, V. W. 1969. *The Ritual Process*. New York: Penguin.

References

Valentine, D. 2012 "Exit Strategy: Profit, Cosmology, and the Future of Humans in Space." *Anthropological Quarterly* 85(4): 1045–1067.

2016 "Atmosphere: Context, Detachment, and the Modern Subject in Outer Space." *American Ethnologist* 43(3): 511–524.

2017a "Gravity Fixes: Habituating to the Human on Mars and Island Three." *HAU: Journal of Ethnographic Theory* 7(3): 185–209.

2017b "For the Machine." *History and Anthropology* 28(3): 302–307.

2018 "Futurities: Ethnography in the Register of Surprise." Ladislav Holy Memorial Lecture, delivered at the University of St Andrews, March 15th, 2018.

Valentine, D., V. Olson, and D. Battaglia 2012 "Extreme: Limits and Horizons in the Once and Future Cosmos." *Anthropological Quarterly* 85(4): 1007–1026.

Van Gennep, A. 1909. *Les rites de passage*. Paris: Émile Nourry.

Veatch, H. B. 1974 *Aristotle: A Contemporary Appreciation*. Midland Books, vol. 174. Bloomington, IN: Indiana University Press.

Vernes, J.-R. 2000 *The Existence of the External World: The Pascal-Hume Principle*. Translated by Mary Baker. Ottawa: University of Ottawa Press.

Vigh, H. 2011 "Vigilance: On Conflict, Social Invisibility, and Negative Potentiality." *Social Analysis* 55(3): 93–114.

Virno, P. 2015 *Déjà Vu and the End of History*. London: Verso [Kindle edition].

Wagner, R. 2010 *Coyote Anthropology*. Lincoln, NE: University of Nebraska Press.

2012 "Afterword: The Lottery of Babylon, or, the Logic of Happenstance in Melanesia and Beyond." *Social Analysis* 56(1): 165–175.

Wallman, S. (ed.) 1992 *Contemporary Futures: Perspectives from Social Anthropology*. London: Routledge.

Weszkalnys, G. 2015 "Geology, Potentiality, Speculation: On the Indeterminacy of 'First Oil'." *Cultural Anthropology* 30(4): 611–639.

White, R. 2003 "Information, Markets, and Corruption: Transcontinental Railroads in the Gilded Age." *Journal of American History* 90(1): 19–43.

Whitehead, A. N. 1978 [1929] *Process and Reality*. Corrected edition. D. R. Griffin and D. W. Sherburne, eds. New York, NY: The Free Press.

Wieseltier, L. 1986 "Under the Spell." *The New York Times*, November 23, 1986. www.nytimes.com/1986/11/23/books/under-the-spell.html (accessed March 23, 2018).

Withy, K. 2009. *Heidegger on Being Uncanny*. Cambridge, MA: Harvard University Press.

Woon, C. Y. 2018 "China's Contingencies: Critical Geopolitics, Chinese Exceptionalism and the Uses of History." *Geopolitics* 23(1): 67–95.

Wydra, H. 2001 *Continuities in Poland's Permanent Transition*. New York, NY: Palgrave Macmillan.

Wyllie, B. 2016 "Shape-Shifters, Charlatans, and Frauds: Vladimir Nabokov's Confidence Men." *Cambridge Quarterly* 45(1): 1–19.

Zanchetta, B. 2016 "Deconstructing Declinism: The 1970s and the Reassertion of American International Power." *International Politics* 52(3): 269–287.

Zee, J. C. 2017 "Holding Patterns: Sand and Political Time at China's Desert Shores." *Cultural Anthropology* 32(2): 215–241.

Zeitlyn, D. 2015 "Looking Forward, Looking Back." *History and Anthropology* 26(4): 381–407.

Žižek, S. 2014 *Event: Philosophy in Transit*. London: Penguin.

Index

Index

Index